781.10709

W9-AKE-169

TOM DOOLEY
The Story Behind the Ballad

Karen Wheeling Reynolds

LITTLE CREEK BOOKS

A division of Mountain Girl Press
Bristol, VA

LITTLE CREEK BOOKS

A division of Mountain Girl Press
Bristol, VA

TOM DOOLEY *The Story Behind the Ballad*
Karen Wheeling Reynolds

Published May 2011 by Little Creek Books.
Originally published by Thursday Printing, Inc.,
North Wilkesboro, NC in 2002.

This is a work of creative nonfiction based on local legend.

You may contact the publisher at:
Little Creek Books
c/o Mountain Girl Press
2195 Euclid Avenue, Suite 7
Bristol, VA 24201-3655
Email: publisher@littlecreekbooks.com

Cover Design by Jessica Barlow, CPP
Jessica Barlow Photography
Custom Children's Portraiture
Studio, Location, & Commercial Photography
NC Photographer of the Year 2010
http://jessicabarlowphotography.com

Foreword

I wasn't sure what to expect when I first sat down to read *Tom Dooley, The Story Behind the Ballad,* but it only took a few seconds to realize how well-written the book is and how captivating the story.

This is great historical fiction, and although it reads like a novel, it is very factual. Written by Karen Wheeling Reynolds, who grew up where the story took place, it delves very comprehensively into the lives of Tom Dooley, Laura Foster, Anne Melton and all the circumstances which led up to that fateful murder (Tom Dooley always maintained his innocence.)

This book paints a complete picture, and in reading it, I got to know the characters of the story better than just the legend tells.

A great read for anyone interested in a true telling of the lives and events of the legend of Tom Dooley.

> —**Bob Shane**, member of The Kingston Trio
> Recipient of a 2010 Lifetime Achievement Grammy Award
> www.kingstontrio.com

Author's Note

Several books were helpful to me in developing the historical background for both the play and the novel:

The Ballad of Tom Dula—*John Foster West* (1977 Second Printing)

Tom Dooley—*Rufus Gardner* (1960)

The Complete Idiot's Guide to the Civil War—*Alen Axelrod* (1998)

The Land of Wilkes—*Johnson J. Hayes* (1962)

Tom Dooley—*Thomas W. Ferguson* (1958)

Songs quoted:

Are You Washed in the Blood—*Elisha A. Hoffman*—(1830)

Amazing Grace—*John Newton*—(1725)

Tom Dooley—*Frank Profitt* and *Adeline Pardue version*—(1939)

In the pines and fog on the banks of old Elk Creek,
They run,
Laughing and dancing under the stars, amidst the lightning bugs . . .
Moonbeam children with their faces aglow,
Bursting with energy and light,
The water knows their secrets.
The truth is there in the whisper of the water as it flows gently over
the rocks,
It is said that if you open yourself to the sounds of the creek
Long and hard enough,
You will see the three

. . . And the water will tell you what you've come to hear.

—Karen Wheeling Reynolds

*To my husband, David, my best friend and supporter,
and to my children, Ben and Maggie. I love you all.
Keep telling the tale so that Roslin and Ethan can pass it on!*

*Also dedicated to the memory of William Moffett:
my teacher, friend, and mentor*

PROLOGUE

Murderer! Baby killer!

The damning voices were back again.

Lotty Foster tried to push them from her mind as she struggled to free the new life inside her. If she lost this one she feared her accusers would return; but no matter how hard she tried to block them, the voices became louder and would not go away. Tormented by their vicious and cruel accusations, she thrashed in the tangled sheets on the old tick mattress.

Murderer! Baby killer!

It was late and her labor had been long. As the pains grew closer together they became stronger, and her head rolled from side to side with each moan and scream. Yet the old midwife paid her no mind. Sure of herself and capable, the old woman acted as if this was the most natural thing in the world. She ignored Lotty's commotion and kept to her work. Hours slowly passed until finally the exhausted young girl began to drift in and out of consciousness and finally back . . . *to the first one . . .*

Although the baby was tinier than most and a few weeks early, the little girl had seemed healthy enough. She was perfectly shaped from head to toe. The daintiness of the baby's little fingers captivated the new mama. Lotty's own mama had been alive then and had come to help. When the baby was born, her mama had handed it to her immediately to suckle. The tiny infant was quick to latch on, and all seemed well. After the baby fed, the new grandma took the little one and cleaned her up. She placed the baby in the small cradle beside her daughter's bed.

"She's gonna be a beauty, Carlotta, just look at her!"

Lotty took a long look at her mama's face. She was a handsome woman with graying hair and wrinkles that crinkled around her eyes and mouth when she smiled. Lotty remembered how beautiful her mama had been growing up and how much she'd always loved her. But now, on the day of her own daughter's birth, she realized that she loved her mama more than she ever thought possible.

1

"I'm sorry for all the trouble I've caused ya," Lotty told her.

Tears sprang to her mother's eyes as she sat by Lotty's bed, gently rubbing her hair back from her forehead.

"I love you, girl. You gotta put your wildness behind you now. This baby's gonna need a good mama, and I believe you can be just that. In my heart I know this little girl's gonna set you straight. Yes ma'am, God has sent her to you, and she's gonna save your life."

Lotty's mama stood up and leaned over the swaddled baby in the cradle. She put her finger beneath its tiny palm, and intuitively the little girl held on. The two women smiled at each other.

"I'm gonna start a fire in the wood stove so I can fix you somethin' to eat. You're gonna need plenty if you're gonna feed that child."

Lotty drifted off to sleep feeling warm and safe for the first time in a long while. She had been a wild one, and it had come with a hefty price. But that was all behind her now. Lotty believed her mother's words. She had been given a second chance, and that night she drifted off to sleep feeling peaceful and full of hope.

A few days later, her mama left to go back home, and Lotty was left all alone with her new daughter. The old abandoned cabin had belonged to her grandma who'd passed in the early spring. Lotty was sent there after her death—the day her daddy turned her out. Her mama took her there and helped her get set up. She told her it would be warm enough and big enough for the two of them to make it through the winter.

The boy who fathered the baby denied that it was his as soon as Lotty told him she was with child. Hopes that he might come back after the baby was born vanished the minute Lotty saw that it was a girl. If it had been a boy—maybe—just maybe he would have tried to love her. Deep down she was convinced a boy would have made all the difference. Her own daddy had always favored her brothers over her.

The new mother had no real friends to speak of. She tried to turn to the church, but quickly found out that the church was no place for sinners. An outcast with a child out of wedlock, Lotty found herself depressed and tired all the time. She walked about the tiny cabin in a daze, talking to herself and rocking the baby day in and day out.

The only company she had was when Nancy Montgomery and Delila Barnett came to visit. They were her closest neighbors and visited regularly in those few weeks after the baby was born. They were nice to Lotty, bringing little presents for the baby—a quilted blanket and a hand painted gourd rattle. One day, they brought a jar of molasses for her biscuits. Nancy said the iron in the molasses would help her get back on her feet.

Nothing worked, though. After a couple of weeks, people began to notice how thin Lotty was getting. Her clothes began to hang on her slight frame. She became nervous and easily agitated. The only thing she wanted to do was sleep. Nancy came by a couple of times during those weeks and rocked the baby while Lotty napped. She always remarked at what a good little girl she was. The infant never cried. In fact, she slept most of the time.

"You've had your last baby first," Nancy told her. "First babies aren't supposed to be this easy. Lord, how I walked the floors with my first one! Course after two, I wasn't so nervous anymore. So when my youngest came along, he learned to be patient real fast. I had two others runnin' around to look after—so he had to be."

Sometimes Delila came with Nancy.

One afternoon while Lotty tried to rest, she overhead Nancy and Delila talking.

"All Lotty needs is some sleep," Nancy said.

"Well then, it looks like her mama would let her come stay with her for a few months," Delila snapped. "A new mama shouldn't be actin' like this. Miz Foster should know that!"

"Sssshh! She'll hear you," Nancy chided. "You know good and well that her mama would, if Lotty's daddy would let her! I heard he told Miz Foster that he was not gonna make his cabin a home for bastard children. That's exactly what I heard he said."

"Well can anyone really blame him?" Delila asked.

"Thou shalt not judge," Nancy quoted to her friend.

Lotty remembered the day that she had finally mustered up the courage to tell her daddy the truth. He'd grabbed her clothes and thrown them into the yard—yelling and cursing at her—saying that she was dead to him.

Betrayed by her daddy and betrayed by her lover, when Lotty left to begin a life on her own in her grandma's cabin, she was fourteen years old. There would be a warm place in hell for both of them someday, she thought. Angry and hurt, hot salty tears ran down her cheeks as she listened to the women talk. She turned her face to her pillow and muffled her sobs so they wouldn't hear.

Several more weeks passed and Lotty still had not given the baby a name. For some reason, she just didn't have the heart to. Fact was, she didn't have the heart to do anything.

One morning, about a month after the baby was born, Lotty woke up to the sound of a barking dog. When the familiar sound registered, she started to close her eyes again, but something made her stop. She suddenly realized that the room was unusually quiet, and the baby had not waked her in the middle of the night to be fed.

Straining to hear the sound of her daughter's tiny breaths, Lotty heard nothing. The deafening sound of silence rang in her ears announcing a horror she could not and would not accept. The young mother burrowed herself under the quilts on her bed and tried to convince herself that nothing was wrong. Her fierce will to deny the truth kept her from going to the cradle.

Hours passed. Finally, reluctantly, she accepted the fact that she needed to check on the baby. Pushing back the covers, Lotty turned towards the cradle. Slowly she sat up and rose to her feet. When she reached the tiny bed, she gazed down and saw her baby girl lying motionless, like a tiny doll, with her eyes wide open and set. The child's delicate fingers lay splayed open as if she were reaching for something, and her lips were bright blue against the gray color of her skin.

Lotty reached down and gently picked the tiny baby up, cradling it in her arms. Carrying the baby back to her bed she laid back down and covering them both with quilts, tried to warm her child.

Later that afternoon, Delila and Nancy came by. When no one answered the door they became worried and let themselves in to look around. They found Lotty lying on the bed, clutching the baby to her breast. When they tried to question her she couldn't tell them how long she'd been there or what had happened. No words would come. Delila ran for the doctor, leaving Nancy to watch over Lotty. It was the slam of the front door that finally got her attention. She grabbed the baby and sat straight up. Nancy urged her to lay back down and rest, encouraging her the whole time to speak. She snapped her fingers and clapped her hands, but nothing worked. When Delila returned with the doctor, the only thing Lotty could remember was seeing her walk over and point an accusing finger.

"Murderer!" Delila said. "Baby killer!"

The doctor pried the baby from her arms and it was only then that Lotty realized her baby was dead. That's when she started to scream. She screamed and screamed and screamed until the doctor gave her something to make her sleep. Plied with laudanum, Lotty drifted off into nothingness and was grateful for it.

When she finally woke up, three days had passed. News of the baby's death had spread like wildfire in and around Elkville.

Delila's accusations led to her arrest a few days later. Nancy had defended her in court, and so had the doctor that was called in to examine her and the baby. Yet *even after she was acquitted in a court of law, the doubt that was cast had stayed with folks in the community.*

Murderer! Baby killer! Murderer! Baby killer! Murderer! Baby . . .

A splash of cold water brought Lotty back to the present. She gasped and opened her eyes. Panicked, she tried to sit up but the midwife put the palm of her hand to Lotty's forehead and pushed her back down.

"Dis baby's breach," the old woman told her. "Now I'se gonna have ta pull it out as bes' I kin, and I don't have no time to be fightin' wif you. You undahstan me?"

Lotty knew she would have to stay calm and do what the old woman asked. She nodded, knowing she couldn't do this alone.

The midwife began to chant. The pungent odor of herbs and spices mingled with the wood smoke in the room. The strange smell wafted over Lotty, and she let it fill her lungs. Strangely enough, it seemed to soothe and calm her.

"What are you doin'?" she asked.

"Some things be beyond our powah," the old woman answered.

The midwife handed Lotty a charm. It was wrapped in burlap. The young mother began to understand. She nodded to the old woman. *Whatever it takes*, she thought. As long as her baby lived nothing else mattered.

"Do what you have to do," she told her.

As the charm took hold, things that were real became unreal. Lotty was aware of the pain; but it was distant; and she was removed from it. Floating somewhere in a mist above, out of harm's way, she looked down on the room and saw herself lying on the bed. The midwife was working patiently between her legs. As Lotty watched, a tiny glow came to light beside her. The light was so full of love and warmth and joy that she wept with relief. All the horrible fears and pain melted away, replaced by comfort and calm.

When the baby let out its first cry, it seemed distant. Lotty floated with uncertainty between the world she knew and a world she wanted to know with the tiny glow surrounding her.

"Go to her," it whispered. "Go to her."

But Lotty was not sure that she wanted to return. The light was so full and she was so empty. If she could just stay there for a little while longer Lotty knew she would be whole again. Drawing back further into its warmth she wanted to forget everything and pleaded to stay, but the glow engulfed her and she began to swirl. Spinning around and down, she found herself crashing back to the world below.

"Go to her," the soft whisper told her; "go to your child."

Drenched in sweat, Lotty was aware of the damp bed sheets that stuck to her skin. Looking down over her now flattened belly, she could see blood on her thighs and bedsheets. The old midwife bent down and placed the baby in her arms.

"You back," she laughed, looking down at Lotty and the baby. "We wuz 'bout to think you done lef' us. I couldn't get you to he'p me, so's I had to pull her out wif my hands. You got yourself a baby girl, Missy . . . and she be strong."

The old woman shook her head and sat on the edge of the bed, taking Lotty's hand.

"You take care of her now. She be special like you. I seen one of her eyes is jus' a tiny bit smallah than the othah. That mean she gonna see bof sides. She gonna walk 'tween two worlds. You take care of 'dis chile."

The old woman cleaned up the blood with the wet rags she had used to birth the baby. She put the afterbirth in a bucket at the foot of the bed to carry outside and put in the garden. It was full of good things and would make the ground fertile. Then she gently wiped away the thick curd-like coating on the baby's head and skin. With tight cloths, she bound the baby's middle to make the bellybutton turn in. The old woman didn't stop until the room, the baby and the mother were all clean. Once she was satisfied that everything was in order, she turned to Lotty and shook a bony finger at her.

"You remember 'dis Miss Lotty. Jus' 'cause you is different don't make you wrong. People be scared of different, das all. No mattah what people try to make 'a you, you be what you wuz born to be."

She looked at the baby in Lotty's arms.

"She look like a angel to me. My mama lef' me with my granny when I wuz born. Said no slave man would have her if she kept a white man's chile. Granny didn't pay her no never mind. Said my mama was no count and didn't know what a blessin' I wuz. Granny always said she wuz lucky to have a lil' angel like me. Granny give me my name. Angeline. Yes'm, said I looked like a lil' angel to her."

Lotty nodded and smiled at the old woman.

"Now I gonna try and sleep in dis rocker for a time. In the morning I gonna fix you a good breakfast and cook a big pot of beans for ya. Then I gotta go home for awhile. But I be back in the evening and check on ya. You be needin' to know some thangs and I'se happy to teach ya."

Angeline was good to her word. The old woman taught Lotty much. She taught her things not practiced in any church—but just as real and just as powerful.

The next morning when breakfast was done and the beans were cooked, Lotty found herself alone in the little cabin with her new baby. The young mother took a look at the little girl in her arms. All ten fingers and all ten toes were where they should be. Her hair was black and curly. And when she cried out, the child sounded like she had something to say. Her eyes were bright and alive. Greedily she suckled from her mama's breast and her tiny fingers latched on to Lotty's finger with a vengeance.

Before any harm will come to this child, it will come to me or to someone else, Lotty thought to herself.

"You will live," she declared aloud inside that little cabin, "and I will kill anything or anyone to protect you."

And so it was, that in the foothills of the Blue Ridge Mountains, Angeline Foster Melton came to be. Little Anne answered her mama with a fierce cry that filled the room. It was loud and strong—and the most beautiful thing Lotty Foster had ever heard in all her life.

CHAPTER ONE

Anne slowly set her left foot down on the cabin floor. Carefully, she rolled it from sole to toe until her full foot was firmly planted. Likewise, she placed her right foot down. Sitting on the bed, the young girl surveyed the room around her.

It was late and the fire was almost out. The chilly room was lit only by moonlit windows and a few fading embers in the fireplace. Anne waited and listened. Grateful there was no sound coming from the body slumped in the rocker by the window, she slowly stood up, grabbing her quilt from the bed. It was only a few steps to the front door. The danger would be in trying to pass her sleeping mama.

Anne Foster made her way stealthily to the front door, taking great pains with every step. As she reached for the latch, sounds from the rocker stopped her cold. Searching for the right words to say, she turned to explain but stopped, relieved. Anne gazed upon her mother, Lotty Foster, in all her drunken splendor and sighed. Lotty murmured jumbled words as she slept, still holding a jug of 'shine in her lap. Anne was grateful for the corn liquor. It would keep her mama asleep for a long while.

The daughter gazed down at her mother, loving and hating her all at the same time. A moonlit halo of tousled red hair surrounded Lotty's head. The golden glow of the fireplace embers masked the harshness of her once beautiful face. 'Shine and sleep silenced her cruel mouth. Night could hide many truths visible by day. Anne smiled. Her mother looked strangely peaceful—but the girl was not fooled. Too many times Lotty's daughter had suffered the back of her mama's hand. Too many times she'd been taken in by her mother's lies and her cruel words when she was drinking. Shaking her head, the young beauty pulled the latch on the door and stepped defiantly outside.

Tom Dooley stood in the shadow of the trees and waited. Closing his eyes, he could hear the sound of the crickets chirping softly in the forest. The water gurgled and whispered its lazy lullaby as it flowed over the rocks nearby.

It was the kind of night that he and his girl enjoyed most, and yet tonight would be different. Tonight he would tell her. Chill bumps covered his arms. Tom could not be sure if it was the cool night air of early spring or the dread of telling Anne what he was about to do that caused them. He opened his eyes and rubbed his icy fingers together.

It was then he saw her coming through the trees. She was a swirl of shawl, muslin and quilt with raven black hair falling down around her shoulders. To the handsome young man with tousled black curls and dusky dark eyes, this was the most beautiful girl he'd ever seen. Stepping out of the shadows, he ran to meet her.

To be seventeen and in love is a powerful thing. Tom Dooley and Anne Foster knew much about life and hardship in the spring of 1862, but the young lovers did not yet know the pain of a broken heart. They loved each other completely, knowing no other way.

The two collided. Tom kissed Anne's hair, her face, her mouth, as he clumsily fumbled with the buttons of his pants. Anne unbuttoned Tom's shirt and hungrily put her lips to his chest. He shuddered as they brushed his skin. Anne pushed Tom away and stepped back, dropping her gown from her shoulders and letting it fall to the ground. Tom liked what he saw and although the sight of her was beautiful, he greedily pulled her back to him. A flurry of arms and legs tangled together as they fell to the ground. Before they made love, Tom stopped and looked into Anne's eyes.

"I love you," Tom whispered. "I love you and I always will."

The handsome young man tenderly made love to his sweetheart. The rhythm of the water flowing over the rocks matched the rythym of the young lovers as they writhed on the ground. Tom Dooley and Anne Foster made love under the stars of a southern sky, in a world that was all their own.

Afterwards, Anne sat on a quilt leaning up against a tree. She cradled Tom's head in her lap watching Tom's breath as it mingled with the cool night air. Perspiration sparkled on his forehead in the moonlight. Neither said a word — they didn't have to. Sometimes just being together was enough for them. Anne reached down and fingered Tom's dark curls. Lovingly, she trailed the line of his nose with her finger and bent over to kiss a dark eyebrow. As Anne leaned down, she could smell the spices he always kept in his pocket just for her. She loved the lusty intoxicating smell of the ginger and ginseng.

Sitting up to stretch, Anne noticed Tom's expression. It was dark and serious. He had been quiet all night and it worried her.

"Somethin's on your mind, I know it. What's wrong, Tom?"

Tom had been waiting for the right time to tell her, but deep down he knew there would never be a right time for Anne. He knew he had to let her know what he planned to do. Abruptly he blurted out his news.

"Anne, I'm leavin' for the war tomorrow mornin'."

The words were blunt and bold. Anne tried to speak, but he stopped her.

"Now just listen, before you go gettin' all mad. This is somethin' I've been thinkin' about for a long time. You know that. It's somethin' I have to do. I love my home and I love you, but it's time I stood up for what I believe in."

Anne sat motionless, waiting for him to continue.

Looking around the woods and up to the star-filled sky, Tom declared in a solemn tone, "I can't afford to sit by any longer, Anne. This war is getting closer to us every day. I can't wait until it's in our backyard. I've got to help put a stop to this. William and John need me. What kind of brother would I be if I didn't stand and fight alongside them?"

Tom waited for Anne to answer but she did not. He expected her to cry or get angry. She did neither. Finally, Anne stood up and walked to the edge of the creek. Oddly enough, she'd half expected this to happen. After Tom's brothers left for war, he became restless. He wanted to be with them and had told Anne so many times. Still, now that the time had finally come, she was not prepared for the pain it caused her. Fighting back tears she struggled for the right thing to say.

Closing her eyes, she listened to the gentle trickling waters of the creek. She had always depended on its whispers when she needed answers. On this night, there was not a word she could decipher. Anne was on her own.

Tom stood behind Anne, watching. In her haste to move away from him, she had dropped her quilt. The delicate lines of her body were revealed in silhouette under her thin muslin gown. Lithe and smooth she stood there with reflections from the water dancing in her raven black hair. The sight of her was so beautiful to Tom that it pained him to look.

Tom followed Anne to the water. He put his arms around her and held her close. Anne looked up at him.

"Tom, I have a bad feelin' about this."

"Anne, don't start," he answered, shaking his head.

She ignored him.

"No, now it's time for you to listen to me. Sometimes I see things and you know it. I wish I didn't, but I do."

Anne looked hard at him.

"Tom, if you leave, nothin' is ever gonna be the same. I have a strong feeling about this. You've got to believe me. I have the gift, like Mama."

Tom tried to laugh off her words. Her warnings always made him nervous. What frightened him most was that more often than not, she was right.

"Yeah, every man in Elkville knows what kind of gift your mama has," he teased.

Anne flashed an angry look at him. Still smiling, Tom reached out and tenderly held her by the shoulders.

"Anne, this is somethin' I have to do. William and John have done gone to war, and my daddy's gone to God. I need to be with other men folk. I've been in a house full of women too long."

Anne studied Tom's face. Although his square jaw was set and determined, his eyes pleaded to her for understanding. However wrong he might be, she knew he was sincere. She had been with him through the painful loss of his father and knew how much he missed his brothers. He had not been at peace since they left, and it was sad to witness at times. Yet, to let him go would tear her whole world apart. Anne not only loved Tom — he was her only friend.

"What will I do without you?" she asked.

"Anne, you're the prettiest girl in Elkville and you're tough. You can take care of yourself while I'm gone."

He lifted her face to his, and looked into her dark eyes. They were large and soulful — the eyes of his one true love and the person he trusted most in the world. A part of him wanted to stay with her. It would surely be the easiest thing to do, but he would find no peace within himself if he stayed. Tom had convinced himself that he could come back and pick up right where he left off. Young and foolish, he was confident that things would remain the same. He bent down and put his lips to hers. They were warm and full.

"When I come back, I'll be a man that you can be proud of. Besides, I'm lookin' forward to comin' home and seein' the woman I love, waitin' for me. When I come back, I aim to take you away from your mama and make you my wife."

"If you really mean that, then marry me now, Tom," Anne pleaded. "Don't let time pass between us and change what we have. Stay here and marry me now."

"I have to do this," Tom insisted. "It will be all right, you'll see."

He tried to make light of it, smiling at her and kissing her forehead, but Anne wouldn't allow it.

"I want you the way you are now. This Tom is the Tom that I love. You think bein' a man will change everything for the best. Well just what if you're wrong? What if you are at your best right now? What if we both are?"

Anne hugged Tom tighter than she had ever hugged him before.

"All I know is, if you leave, nothin' is ever gonna be the same."

It was Tom's turn to be surprised.

"How can you say that, Anne? How many times have we sworn to each other that nothin' will ever come between us?"

Anne loved Tom Dooley with all her heart and knew him well enough to know he meant what he was saying. But she also knew from more experience than she cared to admit, that men and women did not think alike. Tom had convinced himself that he could go off and fight for as long as it took. He did not ponder the future enough to think about what might happen along the way. That was what separated them sometimes. Anne fretted over what would happen over time. She thought in more detail than Tom and always had. Despite her young years, she knew that there were moments that could change the course of a life forever. Anne was convinced that Tom would live to regret what he was about to do and sadly enough, she feared she would, too.

Anne sat with Tom and they talked until almost daybreak. Nothing Anne said could sway Tom from leaving. Sometimes they argued. Sometimes they wept. Finally, when there was nothing more to say, they made love on the creek bank once more. Anne and Tom managed to block out the rest of the world one last time with their youth and innocence.

Just before the sun came up, they parted. Tom walked with her from the creek to the edge of the woods near her cabin. The little valley looked beautiful in the early dawn. The trees were just starting to bud. Morning fog lay on the ground and the sky had a pink tinge to it. *Red sky at morning, shepherd take warning.* The pink sky told Tom bad weather was coming. He would need to go soon if he wanted to say goodbye to his family. Colonel Hendrix and the men would be leaving from Calvin Cowles' store by mid-morning and he didn't aim to go without his fiddle and the sack his mama had packed for him.

When Anne turned to say goodbye, she was different. There was an edge to her that he had seen many times before. Her guard was up. What bothered him was that until now, he had only seen it with other people. He understood, though. Anne was protecting herself. When he kissed her goodbye, her lips were cold and the eyes that had looked so lovingly upon him down by the creek were now distant. Still, he optimistically told himself that everything would be all right. He convinced himself that she would come to know that he had only done what he had to do.

As Anne started walking towards the cabin, he called after her, "Will you come to the store to see me off?"

Anne did not look back. She kept on walking through the fog.

"You wait for me! You hear me?" Tom yelled.

Anne stopped and turned to him. "I'll be there," she answered.

Anne turned and began walking to the cabin. The thick morning mist lay close to the ground, covering her feet. Tom's last vision of his childhood sweetheart was watching her appear to float across the field.

Tom turned and disappeared into the woods headed towards home.

Anne ran to the cabin. The sun was coming up and she needed to be in her bed when her mama woke up. She stepped on to the porch and made her way to the window. Peering inside, she could see the outline of her mama, still sleeping. Relieved, she opened the cabin door and passed by the rocker on the way to her bed. As Anne passed, Lotty reached out and grabbed her daughter's arm, digging her nails into Anne's flesh.

"Mama, I just went out for some air. I was feelin' sick and I needed some air!" Anne pleaded, wincing in pain. She watched a small drop of her own blood drip from her wrist.

"Don't lie to me, girl." Lotty screamed. "I been looking out that window for a long time. I saw ya with him. I know where ya been."

There was no reason to lie anymore. Beating or no beating Anne decided to tell her mama the truth. One way or another she was going to see Tom off with the others.

"He's leavin', Mama. Tom joined up and he's leavin' this mornin' with Lieutenant Hendrix. They're meetin' at Calvin Cowles' store."

Anne bowed her head, ready for whatever came next.

Lotty grinned and clapped her hands.

"Well that's the best news I've heard in a long time."

"I'm goin' to tell him goodbye. I just came home to get dressed and then I'm goin' to the store to see him off. There's nothin' you can do to stop me."

Lotty eyed Anne for a long moment.

"Well, I suppose it can't hurt. Go on then! Say your goodbyes. After this mornin' I won't have to worry about him comin' 'round here no more."

Anne nodded to her mama and turned to her bed. She intended to get cleaned up and head for the store.

She went directly to her chest at the foot of her bed. The men would leave soon and time was short. She would wear her best skirt and blouse this morning. Just as she kneeled to open the chest, Lotty called to her.

"Anne, the fire's out and I'm chilled to the bone. Go over to the pantry and pull out a quilt for me, would ya, girl?"

Anne took the quilt from her shoulders and started to hand it to Lotty but Lotty motioned it away.

"I don't want creek mud all over my nightgown, thank ya. I want a clean quilt from the shelf."

Anne turned up the wick on the oil lantern by her bed and carried it across the room to the pantry. She opened its heavy cedar door and went inside. The little room smelled of cedar and herbs. Shelves lined the inside with canned goods, lanterns, quilts—most anything that needed to be stored was kept there. Anne looked around until she found the quilts. They were on a high shelf in the back. Stepping over buckets and brooms, and dodging hanging candles and animal traps, she walked to the shelf and reached for the quilt above her head. A loud click interrupted her. Anne heard something behind her. It was the sound of something sliding across the floor. Then she heard a loud thud against the door With horror, Anne knew immediately what had happened. Her mother had shut her in.

Anne ran to the door and tried to open it but it would not budge. Frantically, she pounded her fists and pleaded with her mother.

"Mama, please don't do this! Let me out! Please!" Anne begged.

Lotty didn't answer. She walked away from the door and sat back down in her rocker. Picking up the jug of 'shine from the floor, she took a long swig.

"It's for your own good, Anne. I'm doing this for your own good."

Lotty listened to her daughter's pleads and sobs as she drank from her jug of shine. A tinge of guilt swept over her—but she knew as hard as this was for Anne, it was the right thing to do. Lotty convinced herself that Anne would thank her for it one day

Once Tom was gone Anne would find someone else. Her girl was beautiful and she could do better than Tom Dooley. Lotty knew if her daughter ended up with the likes of that boy, she wouldn't have a pot to pee in or a window to throw it out of!

Lotty Foster drank away her daughter's pleas and sank into a troubled sleep.

CHAPTER TWO

The rifle kicked back against Tom's shoulder as it discharged and the Yank dropped to the ground through a thick fog of smoky haze. The blast was loud and hurt Tom's ears but he was thankful for it. The deafening sound drowned out the soldier's final words making him less human. Tom had found that the less human the enemy was to him, the easier it was to kill them.

Beside the fallen Yank a young man mumbled incoherently, searching the ground, looking for his spectacles. When the two Union soldiers stumbled across the campfire and overtook them, one of them had punched the little man, knocking them off.

Two dead Yanks lay sprawled on the ground. Tom quickly stamped out the campfire that had drawn attention to them, knowing it could easily do the same again. Once the fire was out, he made his way to the dead soldiers and systematically began pillaging through their belongings. Having done this now many times, he knew to look for the most important things that would be easiest to carry. He took a pistol and an ammunition belt from the first one—and from the other he discovered a little tobacco, some sowbelly; and most important, he took the man's shoes, figuring them to be about his size. He tried them on and they felt good on his tired feet. The sowbelly strips would be a welcome change from the hardtack he had eaten for days. The crackers had been out of the barrel and in his pocket long enough to be stale. He looked forward to the salty meat. Tom was hungry. Hell, everywhere he went people were starving. It was a time when even dogs and cats were scarce. Hastily, he stuffed his spoils into the pocket of his shoddy jacket.

Tom left the man to his search with the two dead Yanks on the ground and turned his attention to the wounded one. Tom squatted down beside him and pushed his shirt up to examine his belly. In Tom's opinion, it was a mortal wound. The bullet had entered the boy's gut; but examining the man as best he could, he saw no exit wound. Instant death from a clean shot, straight through, would have been merciful. But this—the bullet would work its way around inside the boy until it did enough damage to kill him.

The little man on the ground stopped his mumbling and held his spectacles up to the light of the late afternoon sun to examine the damage. The glass lens was cracked on one side, and the wire rims were bent. Still, with much relief, he put them on and made his way to Tom and his wounded friend.

Tom studied the man's face as he approached. Pale, wearing crooked spectacles and covered in dust he stood there, eyes wide with fear. He reminded Tom of a deer frozen in the light of a lantern. Tom stifled a laugh. The stress of the situation and the absurd look of the little man caught him off guard. Tom sobered himself and turned back to the wounded man. Blood oozed from under his shirt. He placed his hands on the wounded man's belly, over the ooze, and applied pressure. *This is useless*, he thought. Still, he held the wound tight and tried not to think about the death that would come. Instead he pondered the last few months of his life.

It was late October and chilly in Richmond, Virginia. *Cold enough to kill hogs*, Tom thought. After almost six months of war, Tom's idea of manhood had changed. Tom was a real soldier now in a real war. The picture Lieutenant Hendrix had painted when he came down from Happy Valley to recruit them had been very different. There was no glory here, and there were no heroes. Things happen to a man who is given the right to kill. Some can handle it—many cannot. The men who were revered as heroes back home were in actuality no more than cold-blooded killers. Others were simply cowards who deserted when things got rough. Many of the true heroes had been silenced on the battlefields, their stories never to be told.

The young soldier from Elkville spent his first few months after enlisting, inquiring about his brothers. By the time he left Salisbury, North Carolina, he had gathered enough information to know that both John and William were dead. He had been a fool allowing himself to be ordered around by women. Tom knew now that he should have left long before he did. He was convinced things would have been different had he done so. After he learned the fate of his brothers, he allowed guilt and failure to define him. Now, many men called him brave; but he knew what he really was. The guilt of being alive was unbearable for Tom at times. When he couldn't shake those feelings, rage took over. Rage became his courage. Tom fought to avenge the lives of his brothers and to make his father proud. It was during the heat of battle that he felt their presence and in some odd way their approval. Being alive was only luck. He had taken many foolish risks in battle; and why he was still standing, when many of his comrades were not, he did not know.

Tom wondered often if his ma knew about his brothers. Had she received word? He prayed she had. If not, he knew she would still be walking the floors, waiting for his brothers to come home.

Tom took out his Bowie knife and cut away some of the man's shirt. He would use the cloth to pack the wound and try to slow the bleeding. While he held on to the doomed boy, he studied his knife and allowed his thoughts to drift to his father. Each of his sons had been given a Bowie knife on their fourteenth birthday. Their father told them it was part of being a man and was careful to teach them the responsibilities that came with it. They learned to clean and sharpen it and handle it safely. Most of all, they were taught that it was not a weapon, but a tool. Their daddy also made it clear that should they decide to ignore his lessons they would lose their privilege. None of the Dooley boys lost their knives. It ended up being the last gift he would give Tom. Not long after Tom's fourteenth birthday he lost his father to consumption. He still missed him terribly.

The memory of his father's death saddened him and he struggled to think of happier times, remembering his father's voice, the sound of his laughter and the stories he used to tell. He smiled to himself as he remembered wrestling with his father and brothers outside in their yard. For years the boys were no match for him, but in the last few years of his life it became harder and harder for their father to pin them down. There would come a time, he told his sons, when he wouldn't be able to pin them anymore; and that's when the wrestling would stop. After that, they deliberately let their daddy win so their special time with him would not end.

Tom's father was a muscular man with dark hair and eyes and a booming voice. He was hardworking and strong. Although he was rough with his boys, with his wife and daughters he was always gentle and soft-spoken. Tom never heard his father raise his voice to his ma or sisters. Women were to be loved and protected, he once told Tom; and a virtuous woman was to be cherished above all others. Tom had always tried to show the women in his family respect. The Dooley women were virtuous; and he was proud of that; but as he grew up, he couldn't help but notice the ones who weren't. Tom was always crossing paths with those women it seemed, and they liked him a lot. He confided this to his daddy once, and the older man laughed out loud.

"I'll let you in on a little secret," his father told him. "There are two kinds of women, boy—the marrying kind, and the ones you don't bring home to meet your mama."

Tom realized very fast that he had more than a passing interest in the latter of the two. Tom had not planned to fall in love with Anne Foster—but everything his father had told him flew out the window the day he met her. Anne made things far from black and white. She broke every rule and made nothing ever feel the same again.

After his father died and his brothers left for war, no matter how much he loved them, Tom started resenting the women in his house. Deep down he knew it wasn't their fault; and he showed them no disrespect; but he did not want to be there. He wanted to be with his brothers. His ma had made him wait because she said he was too young. He'd been angry with her for it. Now, he was riddled with guilt. Tom was genuinely sorry for arguing with her; but even more—he regretted not joining the war sooner. *If he ever got home . . .*

No, he corrected himself. <u>*When*</u> *he got home, not* <u>*if*</u>.

He remembered hearing Colonel Isbell say once that it was the men who believed they would come home that did. Tom knew he was right, too. He saw so many of the new soldiers arrive to the camps with fear in their eyes, and time and time again he noticed that those men were the first to die. He worked hard on keeping his mind where it should be and when he wasn't on the battlefield he kept his thoughts set on going home.

Short gasps from the man on the ground brought Tom back to the present and he found himself once again surrounded by death and dying. Elkville seemed farther away than ever. Tom looked into the worried face of the man with the broken spectacles. What he saw there was familiar to him. The man stared back at Tom in shame and was clearly full of guilt.

When he finally spoke, Tom was surprised to hear an irish brogue. "He's gonna die, isn't he?"

Tom gave the only answer he thought was fair. "Probably."

"It's all my fault. Samuel and I write for a local paper in Connecticut. My ambition to be recognized brought me here. I felt it was something I had to do—convinced I was destined to write something meaningful."

Tom smiled and shook his head. "I'm not sure I would call any of this meaningful," Tom quipped, "but I do believe it needs to be told."

The reporter continued, "Samuel wanted to come with me, but he was scared. Like a fool, I convinced him everything would be all right. I told him the stories we could write about this war would make us famous. We just wanted to write about the war, that's all."

The small man bowed his head in shame. "He was afraid of the risk, but I kept telling him we'd be fine. Tell me, how am I gonna live with this?"

This hit a nerve with Tom. Sometimes it was easier to give advice than try to follow it yourself, and so he did.

"You listen to me. People make their own choices, and people die when it's their time. Live with that. Don't waste precious time on something that's already happened. You can't change it. The only thing you can do is keep on walking and let life take you where it wants you to go."

The young man seemed grateful for Tom's words. Whether he would take heed to them was another story, but he seemed to find comfort in the advice just the same. He managed a smile and offered his hand.

"My name's Michael O'Hara."

Tom offered his hand, "Tom Dooley," he answered.

"We wanted to tell the true story—both sides. I thought if we were careful and kept ourselves in the middle, we could do that. It worked for awhile. Most folks seemed glad to talk to us. Then today those two fellas came along. We told 'em what we were doing, but they wouldn't listen. They wanted to make sure the stories we wrote supported the Union. They were bound and determined that we choose sides—Union or Confederate. Samuel didn't think they were serious at first. He just laughed and told them he wasn't a soldier—just a journalist. He couldn't bring himself to believe a man could die for something as simple as that. That's when they shot him. I tried to go to him; but they knocked me to the ground; and that's when you came along."

The look of fear and amazement on the young man's face told it all. Michael O'Hara had just lost his innocence. Nothing would ever be the same for him again.

"If you hadn't come along when you did, they would have shot me, too." Again, the young writer shook his head in disbelief. "You just aimed your gun and fired. You didn't say a word. Until today, I've never seen anybody killed before, at least not up close."

The reporter pointed to Tom's left eye. "Your eye is bleeding."

Tom wiped his eye and realized the skin was broken just above the eyelid. The second Yank had luckily been out of lead shot, so he'd hit him with the butt of his rifle when Tom shot his buddy. Dazed for a moment, Tom found presence of mind to grab his knife. After a long struggle the Yank stopped moving, and Tom cut his throat to finish him off.

Rubbing his own blood between his fingers, he looked at the reporter and shook his head in amazement.

"What did you expect to see when you came here? This is what war's all about."

"All I know right now is that I'm lucky you showed up today."

Michael O'Hara turned to his friend Samuel and watched him take his last breath. The young writer slumped to the ground, put his head in his hands and wept. Tom gave him a minute to collect himself and then handed him one of the two Union jackets he'd packed in his sack.

"We need to skedaddle," Tom told him. "The only way to get by the Yanks and find my regiment is to disguise ourselves and fool them into thinking we're Union, too. Now put this on if you want to live to write your story."

O'Hara nodded and did as he was told.

"I want to write for the *New York Herald* someday," he said.

Tom laughed, "A man with a dream! That's all the more reason to get you out of here. This is no place for dreams. When you get home, you tell the real story. Not just one side, but both sides, like you said."

O'Hara nodded, "Just get me and Samuel out of here."

"We have to leave your friend, I'm sorry. We'd never get out of here if we tried."

O'Hara knodded. Deep down he knew, but it was hard to comprehend walking away from his dead friend.

"But, I do need a favor from you."

"If I can do it, I will," O'Hara replied.

"I haven't heard from my girl since I left home. She was supposed to see me off, but she never showed. I've sent several letters, but never heard back. This ain't like her. Something's wrong. I need to write a letter to my girl back home, and I need you to see that she gets it. I need to let her know I'm still standing and to wait for me."

"It's done," the reporter said with relief.

As they started to stand, they heard the click of a pistol. The two turned to see three Union soldiers behind them. Their pistols and rifles were pointed straight at them.

"Rise up real slow and easy, boys."

Tom sized up the soldier giving orders. He was surprised to see that it was a boy. *Couldn't be more than fourteen*, he thought.

Tom and O'Hara did as they were told. As they rose to their feet, one of the soldiers noticed the Confederate gray sticking out from under the Union jacket Michael O'Hara was wearing. He ripped the jacket from him and put a pistol to his head. Another threw Tom to his knees and put a rifle to his back.

The child soldier leaned over to Tom and asked, "Now tell us, boy, what side are you on?"

It's funny what one's mind will do when it's pushed too far or thinks it's close to death. Tom could hear the battle sounds clearly and distinctly in the distance. He could smell the sharp odor of gunpowder, and somewhere in the trees he heard the crunch of dry, brittle leaves. The ground felt hard and cold, and small rocks dug into his knees. In his mind, he saw his father and John and William. He heard his ma's voice and the laughter of his sisters. Tom remembered his last night with Anne by the creek. At that moment he knew exactly who he was and what he believed in. Without shame or guilt driving him, he took a deep breath, remembering all the things dearest to him and told them the only thing he knew to tell them—the truth.

"I'm a Confederate soldier."

With that, he heard laughter ring out among the men. They unbuttoned their Union coats to reveal their red shirts.

Michael O'Hara shouted to the top of his lungs, "Bushwhackers! Saints above, they're Bushwhackers!

O'Hara had learned all about the infamous Bushwhackers. They were tired of the certain death that came from traditional battlelines. These men fought for the same Confederacey as the Rebs, but ingnored the rules of war using their cunning instead. Their battlefield could be anywhere at anytime. Sometimes they would disguise themselves as the enemy or lie in wait for a surprise attack. No Yank was safe when they were in the bushes. They fought without the trappings of tradition and answered to no one but themselves. Many a Union soldier had been tricked or whacked by these men, but only a very few ever lived to tell about it.

Tom turned to see for himself. A knowing smile broke out on his anxious face when he realized what the writer had joyously announced was true. With great relief he shook hands all around.

"You boys are a long way from home, ain't ya?" Tom asked.

"Maybe," answered the one holding the rifle to Tom's head. He lowered his weapon. "We've come to scout things out. Folks in Minnesota and Kentucky think this war would be over a lot sooner if we didn't have Mr. Lincoln around. We can't stand much more. When we're not fightin' the Union — we're fighting the Sioux. They're hungry and they're mad, and they don't want any more talk. They want food."

Another Bushwhacker shook his head in agreement.

"I had an uncle that ran a store up in New Ulm. When the Indians complained that they weren't gettin' the rations and supplies they were promised by the government, my uncle got mad and said as far as he was concerned, if they were hungry, they could eat grass. Chief Little Crow heard about it, and those Redskins attacked my uncle's store and shot him dead. After they scalped him, they stuck grass in his mouth. That's how my aunt and her young'uns found him. Those heathens took all the supplies my uncle Andy had and burnt the store to the ground. I'm tellin' you boys, somethin's gotta be done. I'm happy to help you Rebs anyways I can. We need to end this. We're not just fightin' the Yanks, boys — we're fightin' the Redskins, too."

Turning to the innocent young man with the dusty tear-streaked face, Tom said, "You see, O'Hara, it does help to know which side you're on."

With that, Tom led his new friend into the woods flanked by the Bushwhackers. Leaving Samuel behind, Michael O'Hara reluctantly left with the motley band of Rebels and disappeared into the smoke and the pines.

CHAPTER THREE

Tom opened his eyes and looked around. Through blurred vision he could see sunlight streaming through a window. Reaching around he felt rough cotton sheets and breathed in the smells of alcohol and ammonia. The smell was so strong it burned his eyes and nose. Peering from side to side he saw rows of beds lining a long hall. Ladies in dark skirts and blouses tended to the men in their beds, bandaging, sponging and feeding them. Moaning and wailing sounds of pain and suffering filled his ears. How long had he been in a hospital, he wondered. He didn't remember coming and tried to recount the events that brought him there.

It was while on outpost duty in the Blackwater section of Virginia that Tom believed he first contracted typhoid fever. The conditions there were bad for the soldiers. Although the officers had warned them, many of the men still drank, bathed and threw away waste in the same water.

By November of 1862, Tom came down with a high fever, and he was taken to the Confederate States Hospital in Petersburg. He lay there for days—his entire body shaking with chills as his fever continued to climb. Nurses worked in shifts, sponging him with cool water. They placed raw slices of onion on the bottoms of his feet and covered them with his socks to draw the fever out. Each morning they would replace the cooked onions with fresh ones.

It took days for Tom's fever to finally break completely. It happened right before his regiment left for Williamsburg. Not wanting to be separated from his company, he left with them, despite his bad health. The trip took its toll on Tom; and by the time they reached Williamsburg, he was admitted to the Episcopal Church Hospital. That had been on December 2nd.

Despite the pain in his head, Tom managed to sit up. He was thirsty. A nurse noticed that he was awake and made her way to his bed.

"Welcome back," she said.

"What month is this?" Tom asked. "How long have I been here?"

"A couple of weeks," she answered. "It's December 14th".

Tom nodded his head and tried to smile. The smile stretched his lips and they cracked. Licking them, he tasted blood. His mouth was so dry he was almost grateful for the liquid.

"Let me get you some water," the nurse said. "Your headache was so bad when you first came here, that we gave you laudanum to help you rest. Laudanum and high fever can make you parched. I'll be back in a minute."

Tom dropped back on his pillow with a thud and closed his eyes. He was exhausted.

"You'll rest better tonight if you can stay awake some today," the nurse told him before she left.

Knowing she was right, Tom forced himself to open his eyes and propped up with his elbows. Looking around, he noticed a man in the bed beside him. He looked to be about Tom's age. Both of his eyes were bandaged.

"Thought you were going out again! I heard your head hit the pillow," the bandaged man explained. "My name's Joseph—Joseph Blevins." Awkwardly, he held his hand out in Tom's direction.

"Pleased to meet ya," Tom answered, taking his hand and shaking it. "I'm Tom Dooley."

"You been out for days," Blevins continued. "I wasn't sure if you were coming back."

"Got typhoid fever," Tom answered. That was the one thing he did know. He studied Joseph Blevins with curiosity. "What happened to you?"

Joseph Blevins shook his head and laughed. It was an odd kind of laugh. There was a lot of bitterness in it, Tom thought.

"I was a sapper. A few weeks ago I went on ahead of my regiment—just as I always had—clearing out the underbrush and saplings. Turned out to be my day! The Yanks had taken to the high ground, so they saw me coming. One of 'em threw Greek Fire, and it hit the ground right in front of me and exploded. Doc says I'll never see again." Joseph was quiet for a moment. Then he laughed again. "Doc says I'm lucky. A couple of inches more and I wouldn't be here at all. But I'm not so sure about that."

Tom wasn't sure how to answer that, so he said nothing. He knew all about Greek Fire. It was used by both the Rebs and the Yanks. A mason jar with just the right amount of sulphur, charcoal, saltpeter and quicklime could change a man's life forever—even end it. Joseph Blevin's life would never be the same. Tom shuddered at the thought of losing his sight.

"I'm sorry," Tom said. It was all he knew to say.

Joseph Blevins didn't laugh this time. "Me, too," he answered. "Doc says I'll be going home in a couple of weeks. I used to spend most of my days dreaming about that, but now, I'm not sure I want to."

Tom understood. Looking around the room he saw men missing limbs, wearing eye patches, a few talking out of their heads. How would any of them feel about going home?

The nurse returned with a pitcher of water and a glass. She poured a glass of water for Tom and handed it to him. She placed the pitcher on the small table between Tom's and Joseph's beds.

"Take small sips at first. Too much too fast can make you sick. I'll be back in a little while with some soup and I'll let the Doctor know you're awake."

Tom sipped the glass of water. It felt good. His mouth was like cotton.

Over the next few days Joseph and Tom shared their war stories to pass the time. They became fast friends as many men do in war time.

Joseph was the first to be discharged. His family came in a wagon to pick him up, and Joseph introduced his family to Tom. They were nice enough people he thought, but Tom couldn't help noticing how uncomfortable Joseph was leaving with them. He thought his friend acted almost embarrassed for his family to see him like that. Before he left, Joseph found his way back to Tom's bed and shook his friend's hand once more.

"It's been nice knowing ya, Tom. Stay safe out there," he warned. Then he laughed his usual bitter tinged laugh. "Don't be a sap like me, ya hear?"

Tom tried to laugh with his friend. "I'll do my best, Joseph," Tom told him. You got a nice family. You'll be fine. I guarantee it."

Joseph put his head down. This time there was no bitterness or sarcastic tone to his voice. "No, Tom," he said in a somber tone, "I don't think so."

With that, Joseph Blevins turned and allowed his parents to lead him through the hall. Tom watched his defeated friend until he was out of sight, wondering what the rest of the war would bring for him when he was well enough to return to his regiment.

On Christmas Day, Tom was returned to Company K. He stayed in his quarters for most of January and February. It was a cold and lonely time for the young soldier who had always been so full of himself. Playing his fiddle was the only thing he found to do that would pass the time. Tom was getting his strength back when his regiment left for Fort Fisher in Wilmington in October of 1863. His company needed supplies and they knew that blockade runners delivered regularly to the port city. Before he left, his rank was changed from "private" to "musician" in Company K of the 42nd Regiment. Apparently, his many hours of fiddle playing had paid off.

Tom liked Wilmington. Fort Fisher was on the oceanfront, and Tom had never seen the ocean before. It fascinated him. The sounds of the waves, the salty ocean breezes — all different from the world he knew in the foothills of North Carolina.

Home seemed far away to him now. There was still no word from Anne. Day after day, month after month, he sat with the other men as letters from home were delivered. Each time, he left empty handed. He soon turned to other women for comfort, and Wilmington with its bars and taverns offered an abundant supply. Barmaids and hookers became something he looked forward to.

Tom was not particularly handsome, but he was good looking enough and charming. At parties back home in Elkville, he was always laughing and playing his fiddle, and his charm and music proved irresistible to the ladies. Confidence was something else Tom seemed to have plenty of. He knew they were drawn to him and enjoyed it. This had always been a problem for Tom and Anne. Women threw themselves at him, and he rarely refused. His romantic escapades and the fights between him and Anne were a source of juicy gossip for the folks back home.

During the war, it was no different. His music made him popular with both the soldiers and the women he met along the way. At nineteen years of age, he and his buddies in the 42nd Regiment lived day to day. It was hard to turn a pretty girl down; especially when a man was afraid for his life and homesick every day. Women helped pass the time.

Tom had known plenty of pretty young girls in his short life, but his experience with older women was limited. The night he met Elizabeth changed all of that. Although she was ten years older than Tom, she didn't look it. He first met her at one of the parties held by a colonel in Wilmington. Being a company musician, Tom was invited to come and play his fiddle; and he brought several of the company musicians with him. They played, ate and drank to their hearts' content.

The plantation was filled with officers and their pretty wives or girlfriends. Tom had never been around such wealth. He was amazed that there were people who actually lived this way. The columns on the front of the huge white house were bigger around than any tree he'd ever seen. The floors inside were marble and pine and polished to perfection. Lanterns inside and out lit the evening sky and everything around. Wisteria and Spanish moss hung in the huge oak trees outside. In the shadows of the trees, Tom thought the gray moss looked like Confederate jackets. The trees took on a ghost-like quality in the moonlight. It was easy to see why children told ghost stories about seeing dead soldiers hanging in them. With a shudder, he turned towards the torches that were placed along the inlet.

The slaves were sent out to the inlet to roast oysters in the sand. The musicians made many trips during the evening to eat with them and drink their hard cider. He loved the way the warm breezes and the salt water felt on his skin. The sound of the waves was like music to his ears. It was different than the sounds of old Elk Creek back home, but he loved it just the same. The slave women sat by the fire and cooked. They took big pieces of hog fat and dropped them in their deep cast iron pans, frying it until it sizzled and spattered. Then they would pour little lumps of corn bread batter into the hot grease. It was so hot that the batter would fry in seconds. They called the little fried corn bread lumps hush puppies, and they were delicious. The hunting dogs had been tied at the edge of the woods during the party as a courtesy to the guests. When they barked too loudly, the slave women would throw them the round fried batter and tell them to be quiet.

"Hush puppies!" the women would yell.

As the evening wore on, everyone was feeling the full effects of the hard cider. Tom enjoyed watching the beautiful southern belles twirling around in the light of the torches as he played. They were all pretty, but one stood out for Tom in particular. She was clearly enjoying the cider, too. All night she had boldly returned Tom's stares. He had noticed her right away. She stood out in the crowd. She was charming, and all the men enjoyed dancing and talking with her, much to the dislike of her officer husband. The man stood with a group of his officer friends on the outskirts of all the dancing and watched his pretty wife being whirled around by handsome young soldiers. The look of disapproval on his face told Tom that there was trouble between the two. *A man with a woman like that needed to be dancing with her*, he thought. It was obvious she needed and wanted attention. With her looks, men would not be scarce.

As she danced, Tom watched her. She was bewitching to look at, just like Anne, but in a different way. *They were alike in spirit*, he thought. It was that kind of spirit that drove Tom wild. He looked for it in a woman. He liked a good challenge, and this woman was all that and more. She had thick blonde hair and eyes that were as blue as the ocean. *Yes*, he thought watching her,

eyes like the ocean and cornsilk hair that fell down her back in waves and curls.
Anne was petite and delicate with dark features, like his mother's. This
woman was fair-haired, full bodied and taller. Once in awhile she would look
at him and smile. All eyes were on her, and her eyes were on him. Tom liked
that. It flattered him.

As the evening drew on, the woman's husband went to talk about the
war with the other officers on the porch. As soon as he was out of sight, she
found her way over to Tom. The other ladies had gone inside to freshen up.
She looked at Tom with a boldness he had not seen with any other woman
but Anne.

"I've enjoyed your music," she said politely.

Tom quickly noticed her eyes. They were talking to him and so was
the rest of her. The cut of her gown was clearly meant to tempt and tempt
him it did. The bodice was deliberately cut low to show off the fullness of
her breasts. Smiling at her, Tom could feel the heat in the air and the heat
between the two of them. The hard cider made him feel even warmer. Drops
of perspiration trickled down her neck and chest disappearing into places
Tom could only imagine. His eyes followed the droplets and lingered there.
Her laughter brought his attention back to her face, making him blush. After
a moment he realized she was laughing with him and not at him. She was
enjoying his interest and curiosity. Tom noticed her smile—full lips curled
into a devilish grin. Her laughing eyes sparkled as she gave him a knowing
nod. The woman knew he liked what he saw.

Pointing towards the river, she grinned and said, "I live just down the
road. Why don't you come by for a little visit tomorrow night? My husband
leaves tomorrow morning for Charleston. He'll be gone a few weeks."

Tom knew enough to know that supper was not the only thing on her
mind. He smiled and nodded. "I'll make a point of droppin' by."

She ran a finger lazily along the edge of his fiddle lying on the barrel
beside him. Seductively she leaned over and whispered in his ear.

"I'm countin' on it."

As she walked away, Tom called out to her, "I don't even know your name!"

She never turned around. Instead she laughed and yelled back to him.
"Elizabeth!"

Tom watched her until she was completely out of sight. He made up his
mind he would see Elizabeth again.

CHAPTER FOUR

It was well after midnight when Tom stepped out of the shadows of the large oak tree nearest Elizabeth's house. For some reason, he had not bragged to the men in his company about her. Although conquests were always a favorite topic — and she was something to brag about — he chose to keep her invitation a secret. Stepping onto the porch of the large brick home, he made his way to the front door and knocked. There was no answer. He walked to one of the large low windows on the porch and peered inside. The rooms looked dark and deserted with no Elizabeth in sight. Knocking again several times, with no response, Tom turned to leave, finding himself feeling disappointed and rejected.

"Don't run off so fast," he heard her say.

Surprised, Tom looked up to see Elizabeth leaning against one of the large white columns on the porch wearing a thin cotton gown that he could see straight through. Realizing that she must have been watching him the whole time, he felt embarrassed. She'd caught him off guard.

"I just thought that maybe . . . "

Boldly she ran to Tom and kissed him full on his mouth, pressing her body against him. Feeling the fullness of her breasts and the warmth of her skin, he quickly forgot his embarrassment. Tom buried his face into her golden lavendar scented hair and tried to push her shawl from her shoulders, but she stopped him.

"Let's go inside," she whispered.

Opening the door, Elizabeth took Tom's hand and led him in. Hastily, she fetched a hurricane lamp from a marbled table at the foot of the large staircase in the entryway. The wick was lit, but very low. She turned the wick until the flame was bright enough to light the room. In the lamp's glow, Tom realized just how wealthy Elizabeth and her husband really were. The polished heart pine floors were covered in large lush rugs with heavy tapestry draperies hanging from the large windows. Ornate lanterns graced every table. Across the hall he saw what appeared to be a drawing room with a large fireplace. Curious, he walked over and looked inside. Over the mantle was a portrait of Elizabeth's husband in uniform. Tom suddenly felt like the intruder he was and turned away from the painting. Moving back into the entryway he spied a large grandfather clock counting the hours. It looked to be mahogany, with ornate carvings and shiny brass workings that Tom saw through its long glass door. At the bottom was a picture of Elizabeth's house, painted directly on the glass. The poor boy from Elkville suddenly felt uncomfortable and out of place.

Elizabeth must have sensed that he was ill at ease. She took him by the hand and led him to the stairs.

"Come with me," she said. Elizabeth held the lamp out illuminating the steps, and Tom eagerly followed. When they reached the top Elizabeth stopped and pointed to the first door. She led him into her bedroom and shut the door behind them.

Once inside the two wasted no time. Hurriedly she unbuttoned his shirt and pulled his suspenders from his shoulders as he lifted her gown over her head and threw it to the floor. She loosened the bow that held her hair back and the two fell onto the soft goose down mattress. Their first night together was a blur of feather pillows, lamplight, warm flesh and lovemaking.

After that night, a pattern developed between them. Tom would wait for the men in his camp to settle in for the evening so that he didn't draw attention to himself. Once most were asleep he would leave to be with Elizabeth. At her request, after their lovemaking, Tom would stay until she fell asleep. He didn't mind. Her bed was soft and so was she. There was no sleep for him at Elizabeth's house.

During those two weeks he was a member of the living dead. Being with an older woman was different for Tom. She was bold and told him what she wanted in bed without the slightest bit of hesitation. At first, Tom was offended by it and told her so.

Elizabeth just laughed. "Tom, a man who truly listens to what a woman needs can have any woman he wants."

She was matter of fact with him; and once Tom relaxed a little, he realized she was not making fun at all—just being honest and open. The young man began to listen to what she told him and soon learned that there were many other positions that pleased a woman more than just the one he was used to. Tom also found that lovemaking was far more pleasurable when the woman got as much satisfaction from it as he did. He proved to be a fast learner; and, by the second week, the relationship became intense. He didn't love her, but he did enjoy the time he spent with her. Their liason was one of convenience and sexual desire, and Tom was grateful for it. With Elizabeth, Tom was open and free to explore anything that gave the two of them pleasure. Sometimes after lovemaking, when Elizabeth wasn't sleepy, they would talk until sunrise.

Elizabeth told Tom about her marriage. Her family had arranged it with her husband's — both from old money. Charles's people were in the import and export business. They deployed cargo vessels to England for Confederate supplies — blankets, weapons, ammunition — anything that would help further the Confederate cause. Elizabeth grew up on a cotton plantation. Before the war, her family had been wealthy, too. Like so many southern families, the Yanks had taken everything they could carry from their home and burned it to the ground along with the barns and out buildings. They even took the livestock, and what they didn't take — they killed. After that, her family had no choice but to live with her father's parents.

"I was never in love with Charles," Elizabeth told Tom, "but I liked him and understood him. He needed a wife, and I needed a husband with means enough to support me. I no longer had a proper dowry, and my father let me know in no uncertain terms that my options were now limited. Charles would be a good match. His parents were family friends, and they liked me enough . . . and they needed me."

Elizabeth stopped for a moment. It was the only time Tom thought she seemed vulnerable.

"You see, she continued, "there had been talk that he . . . well . . . that Charles preferred men to women. His family was anxious to put these rumors to rest."

Tom was shocked.

"Does he?" Tom blurted out.

Now it was Elizabeth's turn to seem surprised by Tom's boldness. Tom was immediately sorry for being so thoughtless. He started to apologize, but she stopped him.

"Don't worry, Tom. You can't hurt me. I stopped caring years ago."

She never actually came out and answered Tom's question, which was answer enough for Tom. He did not press her further on the subject.

Tom talked to Elizabeth about Anne. She seemed almost jealous at times. He didn't think she was particularly jealous of Anne, just jealous of the nature of their relationship—one she could not have as long as she was married to Charles.

Two weeks passed by faster than he expected. One morning in the wee hours, after a long night of lovemaking, Tom woke to the sound of a door slamming downstairs. Sitting up, he looked out the window and realized it was close to daybreak. Tom realized that he had slept much longer than he planned. He turned to see that Elizabeth had heard it, too. She sat up just in time to pull the covers around her before her husband opened the bedroom door.

As Tom's pulse quickened, time began to slow down. In slow motion, he looked up and saw the expression on Elizabeth's husband's face. Charles had been betrayed and would want satisfaction. Wasting no time, Tom jumped from the bed and pounced on the man at the bedroom door. Charles reached for his pistol. Tom saw him and grabbed his hand, trying to pry it from his grasp. The two men struggled to gain control of the gun. The husband managed to throw Tom to the floor; and he reacted by hooking his foot around Charles's leg, throwing him off balance. It gave Tom just enough time to get back to his feet and grab for the pistol, still clenched in his hand. Fingers fought for control of the trigger. Nails clawed, and bodies collided as each sought to aim the weapon in the other's direction. Tom knew that if he gave up, he would die. The two men were joined together in a fight for their lives.

A single shot rang out in the room. It was loud and clear in the quiet of the morning.

Tom's trembling fingers burned from the pressure of the exploding pistol, as he frantically searched for a wound. There was none. Through a thick fog of sulfur smoke, Tom stared into the expressionless face of Elizabeth's husband. Standing frozen, he tried to make sense of the situation. Elizabeth screamed as her husband fell to the floor with a thud. There was no need to examine the man, Tom knew he was dead. The part of his forehead that was missing told him all he needed to know.

Looking down at the body, Tom was struck by the dead man's expression. It was very much in death as it had been in his last moments when he opened the door. The expression was empty—dead. *This man was dead before the fight began*, Tom thought.

Tom turned to find Elizabeth still on the bed. Naked and screaming, she clutched the sheets to her body. Spatters of red blood splashed across the clean white cotton bed linens.

"What have you done?" she shrieked. "What have you done?"

Tom looked at the woman who had so eagerly invited him into her bed just two weeks before. For the first time, he noticed that she was clearly older than he was. The morning light washed away any illusion of youth. There was no candlelight or shadow to soften her twenty-nine years. Tom looked again to the dead man on the floor. Feelings of anger and shame washed over him. This man had tried so hard to be what he was not and done everything he could to please his family—and for what? Hands shaking, Tom put on his clothes. He picked up the pistol from the floor and slid it in the waist of his pants. As he walked to the door, he turned back to the older woman on the bed.

Elizabeth glared at Tom, hurling accusations.

"You've killed him! You've killed my husband!"

Tom looked to his older lover with contempt.

"No, Elizabeth. You killed your man before any shot was ever fired. You better think on that before you go screamin' to your neighbors."

Repulsed, he walked quietly to the front door and headed towards his camp. He could hear her screams behind him, but he never looked back. This was the first time a woman had put him in danger. He made a promise to himself to leave married women alone. It was a promise he should have kept.

CHAPTER FIVE

Tom reached camp shortly after sunrise. He was grateful that he'd kept his silence about Elizabeth. Most men just assumed he had taken up with a hooker near the camp, and he planned to let them keep on thinking that. In the days that followed, he tried to second-guess what Elizabeth would do. If she told the truth, she would be a tarnished woman and Elizabeth was a woman of position. If she lied, she condemned her soul. Tom put his money on the latter. The little coward would cover it up. Elizabeth had enough weighing on her soul already. What difference would one more lie make to her? Tom soon found out that his hunch was right; no one came to arrest him in the weeks that followed. He did hear tales of a robbery at one of the plantations down the road. A Yankee looter had murdered an officer right in front of his poor wife. Tom could only shake his head as he listened to the men in camp share the news. Elizabeth would use her husband's death to her advantage. Ironically he thought, she had just traded one lie for another. Still, the little cat had landed on her feet.

The 42nd Regiment left Wilmington, traveling through Tarboro towards Petersburg in April of 1864. They fought at the battles of Swift Creek and Bermuda Hundred along the way. At Swift Creek, his best banjo player was killed by cannon fire. At Bermuda Hundred, so many men were lost he tried not to think about it. Each time he walked away from a skirmish, Tom made a promise to himself that he would make it home. He had to believe that. He wondered often about the life Joseph Blevins had returned to and prayed that his friend could find peace with what had been taken from him. He also prayed that he would return home a whole man. Tom's company arrived in Petersburg on June 14. It was while in Petersburg that Tom felt shame as a Confederate soldier.

Three days after Tom's arrival, the Confederates received word that the Yanks were headed towards Petersburg. The messenger estimated they were a half day away at most. Word was, a lot more Yankees were coming than there were Confederate soldiers. So the Rebs spent the morning building breastworks of wood and rock to hide behind, all around the city. To scare the Yanks, the Rebs took big logs and set them up to look like cannons around the outer perimeter. These "Quaker cannons" as they were called, would make the Union think the Rebs had more artillery than they actually did.

By late afternoon, Colonel Burnside and his men arrived and surrounded the city. The Yanks had just retreated from the battle at Cold Harbor and they looked war torn and sluggish. It appeared to the Confederates there wasn't much fight left in them. After several days, the Union fell quiet. Tom's regiment and several others assumed they were waiting for reinforcements, but that was not the case. While the Confederates waited, Union soldiers were digging a tunnel under the city. They intended to set an explosion off in the tunnel and blow the Confederate camps to smithereens, taking Petersburg. Tom and the others waited for over a month.

When something finally happened, Tom was asleep in his tent. The explosion shook the entire city. Four tons of black powder exploded at the entrance to Petersburg. Running out into the light, he saw an enormous blast hole. The picket line had gone up with the blast. Tom grabbed his rifle and joined the other men. They were told to gather ammunition, line up near the hole, and wait.

Surprisingly to Tom, about an hour later, the Rebs got the chance they had been waiting for. Incredibly, Yanks started marching into the blast hole. It was clear they planned to use that route to enter Petersburg. Tom didn't understand. They were like salt fish in a barrel for him and the other soldiers. Did Burnside not care what happened to his men? *Clearly*, he thought, *this was the case*. The Yanks were sent into the hole without even one ladder to escape. Tom took aim at the trapped soldiers, feeling shame as he shot them, one by one. While the young man beside him reloaded for him, Tom took a minute to look around. Confederate soldiers were lined up around the blast hole, firing their rifles into the bloody river below. There was no pride or glory. Everyone was solemn and quiet. Someone told Tom later that the blast hole was one hundred and seventy five feet across and thirty-five feet deep. Over 4,000 Yanks died in battle that day. Tom shook his head in disgust. To him, it'd been a slaughter — just cold blooded murder.

Days after, when the Yanks retreated, Tom's regiment left Petersburg. He started having nosebleeds. Typhoid fever was not through with him yet. In August he was hospitalized once more. Just as he was getting his strength back, Fort Fisher fell on January 14, 1865. Tom's regiment left for Kinston and on March 10, Tom was captured along with 300 other Confederates and sent to a war camp up North in Point Lookout, Maryland. Weary, hungry, and in bad health, he spent four months in Maryland as a prisoner of war. His fiddle and thoughts of Anne were the only things that gave him hope during one of the bleakest times in his short life.

CHAPTER SIX

Lotty let out a sigh of relief as Anne waved goodbye and headed down the familiar path to Cowles' store. She'd worked hard to get the girl out of the house. With very little money for any kind of trading, she finally convinced her daughter that she had a hankering for fried apple pies and sent her for some dried apples. She knew full well that Anne loved her mama's pies and that made it easier to sway her.

The boys were working in the fields. At breakfast, she convinced them to follow the creek banks on the way home so they could look for branch lettuce. She would chop up a couple of boiled eggs and some early spring onions, mix them with the lettuce and pour hot oil over it to make a "salet." Lotty wished she had some bacon to fry up and crumble in it. The bacon would be the only thing missing—but hogs, like everything else, were scarce with the war going on.

This morning she needed to be alone; and if it meant cooking a big meal for her family—then so be it. James Melton had passed Lotty on the road a few days before when she was out delivering some ironing to Colonel Horton's wife. He asked her if he could come by and speak to her in private about an important matter. Curious, she asked him what it was about; but James put her off and would only say it was personal. That had been on Monday. Frustrated, Lotty asked him to come by on Wednesday around noon. She apparently had something the man was interested in, and she had not wanted to appear too eager.

James was an unusual man, Lotty thought. He was nice enough but quiet and to himself. His cabin and farm were just down the road from hers. He had a few hogs, some cows and chickens and worked as a cobbler. Everyone around took their shoes to him to be mended.

It would be to her advantage to know James Melton better, Lotty thought.

Anxiously, she ran to her room at the back of the cabin and picked up a hand mirror from her dresser. She'd taken special care with herself today.

With the war going on and so many people in Elkville hungry and sick, she hadn't thought about how she looked in a long time. With a critical eye she looked at the woman staring back at her in the glass. At thirty-five years of age, she hadn't completely lost her looks. Her auburn hair was twisted back at the nape of her neck. Little curls escaped the bow and curled around her face. She still looked nice enough, she thought. Holding the mirror away from her body, she tried to get a better look at the rest of herself. Lotty smoothed her blouse and skirt with her hands, and took notice of her figure. She used to be fuller. The war had taken that away from her. Although her skirt and blouse were loose and tattered, she was pleased to feel the womanly curves underneath. *Thank God for that*, she thought. *Maybe when the war was over she could put back on some of the weight she'd lost.* Men had always liked the fullness of her, and she knew it.

Satisfied that she looked as good as she possibly could, Lotty made her way back to the front of the cabin. She ran to the window to check the road between her house and James Melton's. All was clear. She decided it would be nice to offer James some coffee. Well, it wasn't exactly coffee. Since coffee beans were also scarce, she made it from ground chicory and okra. The taste was a little bitter, but she'd gotten used to it. People had gotten used to doing a lot of things different since the war began. She hoped James would like it. Instinct told her it was important for her to be hospitable to him. Lotty had learned to take advantage of the few chances for personal gain when they presented themselves to her. With age, they were getting fewer and farther between. Her gut told her James was just such an opportunity.

As she removed the steeping cloth bag with its special blend of okra and chicory from the water, Lotty heard the rap of James' cane on the porch. She discreetly peered out the kitchen window and saw him making his way to her door. Waiting for him to knock, she took a deep breath. When it came, she slowly made her way to the door, so as not to appear too anxious, and opened it. James stood there in a suit coat and tie. His hair was slicked down and he held a jar of pickles in his hand. He looked uncomfortable and anxious.

"Well, James, it's good to see ya. Come on in and have a seat."

James nodded to Lotty without so much as a hello, handed her the pickles and entered. Lotty motioned him to a chair at the table in the kitchen.

"Would you like some coffee, James?" she asked in her sweetest voice.

Polite as always, James accepted her offer. Lotty took two cups down from the shelf above the stove and set them on the table. As she poured the coffee she wondered if she should start the conversation. She'd never heard the man say more than a few words in all the years she had known him. James smiled at Lotty and took a sip of the brew. His face showed no sign of surprise at all. She wondered if he was wealthy enough to buy coffee beans—she wondered if the store even sold them anymore. Coffee beans or not, he was polite to her and she liked that. Most of the men she knew in Elkville were not so polite. Although James was a simple man and average to look at, he had kind blue eyes and a gentle smile. As they sipped their coffee, Lotty tried to break the ice.

"I sent Anne to the store. She won't be gone too long, so we best get down to business, James. What is it you came to say?"

Lotty waited for what she thought would be some bartering for companionship. Even someone as nice as James Melton had needs. After all, he was a man—but what he had to say stunned her.

"I know I'm an older man," James stammered, "and that may make me look like a fool to most folks, but I don't care really. I've come to ask you to speak to Anne for me."

Lotty opened her mouth to answer, but James held up his hand and continued.

"I promise you that your daughter wouldn't want for nothin' ever again and I'll make sure you're taken care of, too."

Lotty could not believe her ears, or her good fortune. She tried to conceal her excitement.

"Are you askin' to marry my daughter, James?"

He nodded nervously.

My God, she thought, he was dead serious! Her mind raced. It would be important to get the most of this situation, and she would need to choose her words carefully.

"Well, she's a beautiful woman, James. I reckon you know that she could have any man she wants," Lotty smiled. "She's only seventeen and you're . . . "

James bowed his head.

"I'm twenty-three."

Again Lotty was surprised. Only six years? She always thought he was much older.

James continued.

"Most people think I'm older because of my limp and the way I act. My father always told people when I was a young'un that I was old before my time. I know your daughter's a beautiful woman, Lotty and I've seen the way men look at her."

He stopped for a moment as if he had forgotten what he had planned to say.

Then he raised his head and looked Lotty straight in the eye.

"I expect you're right about her bein' able to have any man she wants. But, not any man in these hills can give her . . . or her mother . . . the things I can; and you know it. Most men farm the land. I do a little of that to get enough to eat, but I make my living making shoes. You know as well as I do, at some time or other, everybody in Elkville needs at least one pair . . . or they need holes patched, or new soles in the ones they got."

James reached across the kitchen table and touched Lotty's hand. Lotty could tell he was looking for an agreement and she pulled her hand away. She wasn't so sure that she could get Anne to agree.

"I'm lonely, Lotty, and I'm willing to strike a deal with you," he continued.

Lotty thought of the conversation she would have to have with Anne to make this work and laughed out loud.

"You may get more than you bargained for, James Melton."

She took James' hand in hers and squeezed it.

"I'll talk to Anne, but these things take time. Give me until next week."

Lotty couldn't help but notice that James seemed openly disappointed that the deal couldn't be closed right then. She was amazed at how naïve he was and how unconcerned he seemed about whether or not Anne would want to go along with it. Love was never mentioned. James was a hard man to figure out and she decided it was best not to try.

James stood to leave. "I'll be back next Wednesday for Anne's answer."

Again, Lotty was cautious not to appear too eager. "Then we'll see you next week," she answered. Determined to get as much from this deal as she could, she added, in her sweetest voice, "By the way, I could use a new pair of shoes." James nodded and started to leave, but she wasn't finished, "And do you still know those folks that have that ham house up past Darby?"

James nodded again.

"Well, I ain't had any bacon in a long time."

James Melton knew from the moment he left Lotty's cabin that this deal would cost him much more than a little bacon and some shoes, but he didn't care. He mind was made up. He had chosen a bride and he intended to have her no matter what the cost.

Lotty was glad that they understood each other. She waved from the porch and smiled as he walked down the path to his house—happy in the knowledge that she'd have bacon grease on her salet by the next week if she handled things just right.

Before she could get back inside, Billy Hendrix came running across the yard. The boy sometimes helped at Calvin Cowles' store, loading feed and delivering mail to folks that didn't get to the store often. As he approached the porch, he eagerly reached in his shoulder sack and handed a letter to Lotty.

"Miz Foster, Calvin Cowles told me to bring this to you. It came on the mail pony this morning. He says it's for Anne."

Lotty glared at the little intruder.

"It's from the war, Miz Foster! Calvin says it's probably from Tom Dooley. Ole Calvin says Tom Dooley's a regular war hero now. He says . . . "

Lotty raised her hand and stopped the boy in mid sentence.

"Well, thank you for your time. I'll see to it that Anne gets it. You give my best to Mr. Cowles."

Excited, the boy ignored her and continued, "Calvin says he'll read it for Anne if she wants him to."

Lotty Foster turned on the boy. "I said I'll see to it that Anne gets it. Now, thank ya for your time!," she snapped.

Lotty stepped off the porch and edged the boy across her yard. She had important things to do and Anne would be home soon. The young boy looked at the angry woman in front of him. Her face was red and her eyes were flashing fire. He'd heard the rumors about her. That's when he saw the axe sticking out of the old stump by the porch steps. There was no doubt in his mind that if he said another word, she would chop him into little bits and feed him to the hogs. He turned and ran down the road to his next delivery as fast as his legs could carry him.

Lotty made her way back to the porch and watched until the foolish boy was out of sight. She was tired of being hungry. She was tired of being worn out all the time. She was tired of sewing for people all hours of the day and tired of entertaining men she didn't like all hours of the night. Lotty was ashamed that her daughter had taken part in the entertaining over the last few years—but her youth had faded, Anne's had blossomed and men were fickle. Lotty knew that chances like this one with James were few and far between. The chance of a lifetime had just fallen into her lap and she didn't intend for her family to lose it.

"*I won't let you ruin this for us, Tom Dooley,*" she murmured to herself. "*My daughter can do better than you!*"

Lotty Foster tore the letter to shreds and burned it in the wood stove.

CHAPTER SEVEN

By the time Billy Hendrix arrived back at Calvin Cowles's store, his trip to Lotty Foster's house had become very interesting. Not only did he tell anyone that would listen that she ran him off yelling and screaming, to top it off he added that she ran after him with an axe. The story got a lot of attention, especially from the women. They gave him stick candy and lemonade to calm his nerves. Hoping to stop the talk, Calvin made light of it telling the boy not to worry about it.

"We've delivered the letter, and that's all we can do," Calvin said.

This did not stop the conversation, however. Many of the women had suffered the slurs and threats hurled at them by Lotty Foster over the years. Of course, they never took into account that it was their gossip that usually fueled the outbursts. The conclusion remained unanimous, Lotty Foster was one of the devil's daughters and they all knew it.

Finally, Calvin lost his patience with Billy. The store was busy and there was money to be made. He was not paying the boy to sit with the women and gossip.

"Stopped flappin' your jaws, boy, and get on over to the feed shed. I don't pay you to gossip. Now, go on and load up those sacks of cornmeal and flour for Mr. Saunders," he ordered.

He stood on the porch for a moment to make sure that Billy did as he was told. The boy knew Calvin meant business and ran to the shed.

"I can find myself another boy to help out easy enough," he warned.

Mr. and Mrs. White from Stony Fork were waiting inside. They had ginseng root to barter and it needed to be weighed. Working with furs, herbs and roots was Calvin's favorite part of storekeeping. Standing over six feet tall, he shook Mr. White's hand, and they began to barter. The kindly storekeeper was a nice looking fellow with steel blue eyes and graying hair that was balding on top. With a beard and mustache that was always neatly trimmed, he had a grand welcoming way about him that made his customers feel like family.

After Calvin finished up with Mr. and Mrs. White, he walked back out on the porch, spying J. W. Winkler, one of his regulars. Laughing, he watched as J. W. argued with Doc Carter on the porch. The old man was getting a tooth pulled that had bothered him for weeks. J. W. was a neighbor of Doc Carter's living just up the road from him on German Hill. He and the doctor went way back and Doc Carter had paid for it dearly. Doc was always pulling teeth or taking care of his bunions, warts, or sour belly. J.W. was always suffering from one ailment or another and to Calvin's knowledge Doc was never paid for his services. One would think that J.W. would be grateful for his friend's help, but he was anything *but*. On this day, when the tooth didn't come out quite as easily as J.W. thought it should, he tried to back out. Store customers were watching and laughing as the old man carried on and begged for a drink of corn liquor.

"J.W., I done told you, alcohol's just gonna make you bleed more. Dog days is coming, and then you won't heal right. You need to get this tooth out now," Doc Carter said.

Realizing it was late July and Doc Carter was right, several of the men who'd been watching, decided to help. They went over and held J.W. down. The last thing the old man needed was an open wound during dog days. The water would get stagnant and cause infection for people with wounds. They laughed and shouted words of encouragement while Doc Carter took his pliers and pulled. After several good tugs the tooth came out and everyone cheered. Everyone, that is, but J.W.

"Now, that wasn't so bad; was it?" Doc Carter asked.

"Hell, yeah, it was!" J.W. yelled, holding his jaw.

Doc Carter handed his ornery friend his tooth and throwing his arms up in exasperation, turned to go inside the store.

"That's what I get for trying to do you a favor! I should have let you suffer!"

Tooth pulling was just one of the many things that went on at Calvin Cowles' store. People came there for far more than dry goods and cloth for sewing. The store had a post office inside and was a place where trappers and wildcrafters could trade their fur and herbs. Calvin would hang animal hides and herbs up with animal traps, lanterns, candles—anything his customers needed. Women would travel to the store with family members or their husbands to catch up on the news, pick out cloth or meet with their friends to trade sewing scraps. Meantime, the men would play checkers or cards after they were done with their trading and catch up on news about the war.

Calvin even had a telegraph machine. Sometimes, traveling shows would stop there to perform. The justice of the peace in Elkville would hold court at Calvin's if he needed to. The store was located across from Colonel James Horton's house on Elk Creek. The store was a big wooden building with a wide front porch and storage sheds on either side. One was filled with feed and seed, the other with tools, sacks and buckets. Big barrels of pickles and salt fish were kept on the porch for sale, along with horseshoes, hoof picks and bridles. If anyone in Elkville wanted information or needed supplies to work the fields or tend the house, it could be found at Calvin Cowles's store.

Colonel James Horton and Calvin were great friends and spent many good times together as neighbors. History and politics were their favorite discussions. The war was currently their hottest topic. Although the two friends had opposing views, it did not strain their relationship. They actually seemed to enjoy having something newsworthy to debate. Although Calvin loved the south, he did not support the Confederacy. James Horton on the other hand did, and was crushed when his old friend Governor Vance was not re-elected for a second term. Calvin was grateful for the election of Governor Holden and was hopeful the states could come to a peaceful resolution soon. Too many men had already lost their lives. Calvin liked Zeb Vance—old fire-eater that he was, but Calvin liked Calvin better. Anything that could do Calvin or his family harm was bad; and the war, in his opinion, had proved harmful to everyone. So he and James Horton agreed to disagree.

Calvin loved Elkville. The land was lush and perfect for his growing fur and herb business. At first, his new bride, had been less than thrilled to make their home there. Relocating from Yadkinville had been hard on her. Her family was very close, and it was a long journey from Elkville to Yadkinville to visit. That meant she didn't get to see her family often.

He met Martha after his mother died and his father remarried. His father, Josiah, married a widow, Nancy Duvall. Calvin's new stepmother had a beautiful daughter named Martha. Calvin was surprised to find himself quite smitten with his stepsister and was fascinated with her interesting heritage. The petite descendant of French Huguenots, and a great niece of Kit Carson, Martha spoke fluent French. She was beautiful and bright and everything the young man could want in a woman. Calvin used his sense of humor and charm to woo her and the two soon struck up a courtship. He showered her with gifts and attention. By the time Calvin decided on Elkville for his fledgling business, Martha realized that if she wanted a life with him, she would have to leave her family. They married after a brief courtship and engagement. Calvin traveled to Elkville shortly after the marriage to make suitable living arrangements for his new bride. Martha stayed behind in Yadkinville with her family and waited patiently for his return.

About six months later, Calvin came back for Martha. As soon as she arrived in Elkville, she came to be a novelty to the other women in the community. She tried hard not to let it bother her, but sometimes it did. Her foreign accent and proper ways both fascinated and perplexed the women in the community. Martha tried to stay as focused on her own family as she possibly could.

Calvin was proud of his little corner of the world. He traded with the community and kept a journal detailing every herb, root and spice that was brought to him. He made notes about the effects that certain herbs or roots had on certain ailments. Many times when Doc Carter was busy with patients, customers would come to Calvin for a cure. He kept iodine in stock for goiters and suggested purple coneflower and goldenseal to ease the symptoms of consumption.

Calvin looked up to see Lotty Foster's girl, Anne, coming out of the store. She had a small poke tucked under her arm. Anne was a pretty young woman and not nearly as cantankerous as her mama. Lotty Foster was a woman he would never be able to figure out. Some said that years before, when she still called herself Carlotta, she'd been a different person. Sadly he wondered what kind of life Anne had at home. The stories that were told by the men at the store were not good.

Anne nodded to Calvin and walked past carrying the poke of dried apples and headed down the porch steps. Although she loved apple pies, it had seemed strange to Anne that her mama just up and decided to fix them. Lotty rarely cooked anything. She had given that job to Anne long ago. Anne wasn't sure, but it seemed to her that her mama had been anxious to get rid of her. As she passed by the women trading cloth scraps, she felt their eyes on her and heard their whispers. Sometimes when they did this, she would deliberately stare them down. A few times she had actually come out and let them know she knew they were talking about her; but, on this day, she didn't feel like having a confrontation. Everything had changed since Tom left for the war, and she was lonely and depressed. Instead, Anne chose to keep her eyes down and head towards home. As soon as Anne was out of earshot the women stopped their whispering. Betsy Scott was the first to speak.

"I wonder who Anne Foster's keeping time with now that Tom Dooley's gone off to war?" the petite brunette asked.

Betsy had large expressive eyes. They took in every detail of everything around her and lit up when she was excited—which was most of the time.

"I heard that the men that come to call at Lotty's house don't call on just Lotty anymore," Martha Gilbert added.

Jack Adkins listened to the women as he sat on a bench whittling outside the feed shed. He got up, put his knife in his pocket, and sauntered over to them.

"Well, wherever he is right now, don't think Tom Dooley is pining away for just Anne."

Ben Ferguson laughed at Jack. *Here he goes again,* he thought. He stood up, let out a big yawn and stretched. Ben considered playing another round of checkers, but walked over and slapped Jack Adkins on the back instead.

"Don't listen to old Jack here, girls; he's just jealous 'cause of Caroline Barnes. Caroline used to be sweet on Tom, ain't that right Jack?

Jack ignored the question.

"Tom did the right thing when he joined up to fight. He did what he had to do and I'm proud of him for it. Besides, I hear that Tom's a regular war hero now, Confederate through and through."

Jack Adkins was known to have a temper. He was a good fellow and nice looking. Everybody knew him to be as honest as the day was long; but he was a hothead; and Ben's comment irritated him.

"What's the matter with you, Ben? Have you lost your mind? Tom Dooley ain't never been nothin' but a no count, womanizin', lazy, son of a bitch! Probably layin' around right now playin' his fiddle and tellin' tall tales like he's always done."

Ben shook his head.

"Jack, you know you're just jealous because Caroline Barnes has eyes for Tom and not you."

All the women loved Ben and listened to him most of the time, when he had something to say. He was a good fella and known for his kindness. Jack Adkins even liked him but not when he defended Tom Dooley. It was obvious that Ben had made Jack angry.

"That's a lie!" he yelled. "Besides, I've been courtin' Caroline Barnes for almost a month now."

The women listened to the two men argue, enjoying every word. Finally, Betsy couldn't stand it any longer.

"Well now, Jack, I would have to say that Tom Dooley is a good lookin' man," she chimed in.

Gwendolyn Smith turned to the other ladies, rolling her eyes, and then looked back at Betsy in amazement.

"Pretty is as pretty does, Betsy Scott, and don't you forget it!"

Martha Gilbert hated it when Gwendolyn got on her high horse. If it weren't for their families being friends for so many years, she wouldn't tolerate Gwen at all. *The old biddy!* Martha thought. Gwen always dressed in dark clothes with big collars that made her look like a preacher. She wore her hair in a snood and her face was always frozen into a snarl of disapproval. Her appearance alone made the other women uneasy. Martha was convinced that if Gwendolyn Smith ever smiled, her face would crack. Old Gwen's sharp words didn't faze Betsy, though.

"Well, he is!" Betsy said, giggling. She turned to her friend Martha and gave her a nudge. "Martha, you even said he was."

All eyes turned to Martha Gilbert. Martha had meant nothing by the remark. She and Betsy had simply noticed Tom out plowing in the field one day. His shirt was off and she remembered that he turned to them and gave them the biggest smile. *He really did have a nice smile*, she thought. She'd simply remarked to Betsy that he was good looking and that was all there was to it. With Martha's husband Jonathan away to war, Gwen would be quick to raise her eyebrows now. Why Betsy had to run her mouth in front of Gwen, Martha would never know. She hadn't even thought about being with another man since Jonathan left, but Gwendolyn Smith could ruin a woman's reputation in no time. Her tongue was sharp and her spirit was mean.

"Well," she stammered not wanting to be backed down by Gwendolyn, "I would have to say that he is a good lookin' man."

Gwen shot a look at Martha Gilbert that would wilt daisies.

Ben just shrugged and laughed. "I got no problem with Tom."

This made Jack Adkins madder than ever.

"Well don't let your sweetheart get too close to him, Ben. He's got a way with women. Tom Dooley tells 'em whatever he thinks they want to hear, and then some."

By this time, the conversation had drawn a crowd. Hezekiah Kendall slapped Jack on the back.

"Is that what he did to Caroline?" Hezekiah teased.

Jack shook his head, still brooding.

"He's sly as a fox."

Calvin walked out of the store with Doc Carter and his Martha in time to hear most of the conversation. Concerned, he walked over to the group and gave them a warning look.

"Ya'll need to stop all this back bitin'. You don't want this to get back to Tom. He's a good ole boy, but he's got a mean temper when he's provoked. I saw him beat a man almost to death once. It still gives me chills just to think about it. The look in his eyes! It took three men to pull Tom off that fella."

Ben seemed to remember something about that.

"What was the fight about?" he asked.

Calvin stroked his beard and ignored his wife who was motioning for him to hush. Martha Cowles hated gossip and felt Calvin enjoyed it a little too much sometimes.

"It was over Anne Foster. The man was flirtin' with Anne here at the store. Anne knew Tom was watchin' and seemed to enjoy makin' him jealous. That girl's always flirtin' with somebody. Anyway, Tom just went wild. It was awful to see. The man was down from Happy Valley visitin' family. He had to stay awhile longer than he planned just to get strong enough to travel back home. I don't believe he's been back to Elk Creek since."

Calvin's story thrilled Gwendolyn Smith. She enjoyed talking about most anybody, but Lotty Foster and her daughter, Anne, were two of her favorite subjects.

She quickly chimed in. "That Anne Foster's never been nothin' but trouble. She's always flirtin' with somebody."

Martha Gilbert timidly shook her head in agreement.

"Well, she *is* as wild as Tom. You don't want no trouble from Anne Foster. Ask Caroline Barnes. Tom started callin' on Caroline and Anne threatened her. I don't know what Anne said to her, but Caroline's scared to death to even look at Tom now."

Everyone laughed when Martha Gilbert mentioned Caroline being scared —everyone except Jack Adkins. Caroline was such a nervous girl anyway. She was pretty, but not the sharpest pin in the cushion. She had long blonde curls that bounced when she bobbed her head, and she was always bobbing her head and going on about something. Poor Caroline was one of those girls that could talk all day and not say a thing. What Caroline did seem to have going for her, though, was a curvaceous figure. Poor Jack Adkins was so swept away by the girl's buxomness, it didn't matter to him if one single word of what she said made any sense. The ladies thought the whole situation was pretty funny.

Gwendolyn smiled a hateful smile as she started to talk about her favorite subject.

"Don't forget Anne's mama! And that poor little baby! That was the most horrible thing anyone could ever imagine. No matter what they decided in court, we all know she was guilty. Then Lotty ran off with that drifter. All of it broke her family's heart. I knew 'em well. When she came back, she was with child again and still no husband. People surmised that the drifter she left with was at least smart enough to not let her get a hold of him. Less than two years later, the Jezebel had another baby, a little boy, and who his daddy is, we'll never know. Maybe Mr. Triplette thought it was his, but how could anyone ever really know with Lotty Foster? Poor Mr. Triplette, like a fool married her and was dead in no time. She kept his cabin and dropped his name before he was even cold in his grave. Lotty Foster's mean as a snake and those children are lucky to be alive, if you ask me! Out of all of those younguns, Anne is the most like her mama. That girl is no good."

Martha Cowles refused to hear another word. Gwendolyn Smith was the most vicious gossip in Elkville.

"Hush girls! Don't you let old Gwen here pull you into markin' a young girl. Show some Christian kindness. If you had a mama like Lotty Foster, you might behave just like Anne — it's all she knows."

Miz Cowles put her hand on Martha Gilbert's shoulder.

"There but for the grace of God, go I," she quoted.

This made Gwen furious. Martha Cowles was always butting into her business.

"The girl is trash, Martha Cowles, and you know it! No better than her mama! I suppose a *Huguenot* wouldn't mind that kind of behavior, but folks around here won't put up with it!"

Martha Cowles ignored the personal insult. Gwen never missed an opportunity to remind her that she was an outsider. She managed to smile at Gwendolyn. Life had not gone as well for old Gwen, and Martha knew that. Gwen had settled in marriage. She married not for love, but for money and had proceeded to have two of the ugliest children anyone could imagine. They were all noses and crooked teeth. Marrying for anything but love was incomprehensible to Martha. She tried to pity the old crow, but it was hard to do and her anger got the best of her.

"When you talk about the man her mama ran off with Gwen, I remember it well. And I also remember another young girl who was smitten with that drifter," Martha retorted.

Gwendolyn stiffened. Her face turned beet red as the men laughed and snickered. Betsy tried to hide her smile as Gwen gathered her things.

"Those are lies! All lies!" she wailed. "I never even looked twice at that man."

Martha chuckled. She knew she had hit a nerve. Triumphantly, she watched Gwendolyn stomp off towards home. Martha Gilbert looked at Martha Cowles with an apologetic smile.

Looking after Gwen, Martha Cowles spoke once more to the ladies, "You ladies need to remember, never believe anything you hear and only half of what you see."

Martha Gilbert shook her head in agreement, but Betsy turned to Miz Cowles.

"No matter, Miz Cowles, you have to admit that Anne's life has made her hard. She can be vicious and cruel when she gets mad. They say she and her mama can conjure. If you get in their way, they can put an end to ya without even touching ya. Now that's what I heard happened to Mr. Triplette."

Ben Ferguson hated gossipy women. Women were as vicious as any pack of wolves could possibly be. He spoke up in Anne's defense.

"You can talk all you want, but I'm tellin' you right now, Anne Foster is somethin' to look at! Now I'm going home. I got work to do and a girl to visit tonight."

Surprised, Jack Adkins turned and looked at Ben.

"Who you callin' on, Ben?"

Ben grinned. "Well, it's not Caroline Barnes, that's for sure."

With that, he tipped his hat to the ladies, gathered up his seeds and small sack of cornmeal, and headed for home. *Some people seemed to thrive off of other people's bad fortune*, he thought.

Betsy Scott watched after Ben as he walked down the road. She elbowed Martha Gilbert and pointed in his direction.

"Ben Ferguson's a good lookin' man, too."

Martha tilted her pretty hazel eyes in Ben's direction and grinned.

Pursing her lips she put a finger to them. "Just don't be tellin' that to Gwendolyn this time, all right, Betsy? She thinks men should all look like *her* husband."

51

Betsy and Martha laughed and laughed as they thought about what it must be like to be under the covers with Mr. Smith. Then they spent the rest of the afternoon trying to get the thought out of their minds.

CHAPTER EIGHT

By the time Anne got home it was mid afternoon. The smell of biscuits baking in the wood stove greeted her as she opened the door. The crackling, grease-spitting sound of chicken frying turned her gaze to the old cast iron skillet on top. She was surprised to hear her mama humming at the sideboard. Lotty was chopping lettuce and onions to the tune of *Pretty Polly*. When Anne entered the house her mama put down the knife and motioned Anne to the dough box.

"I got the crust all rolled out for 'em," she said. "There's a little sugar and cinnamon in a bowl there. All you need to do is just sprinkle it over the dough and lay the apples down. Then you can shape the pies for me, all right?"

Anne shook her head in amazement. The atmosphere in the cabin was far too happy. Lotty was behaving like the kind of mama she'd always wished for, but now, it all seemed too good to be true. It reminded her of something a preacher at the store once said. He was preaching on the porch and told the crowd to beware. He warned the customers that Satan could be beautiful if he wanted to be. Anne suspected that was exactly what was happening in that house.

She proceeded to the dough box and began shaping the pies, dividing the dough into small balls and flattening each ball into a circle. Sprinkling them with sugar and apples in the center of each one, Anne folded the dough over the mixture, making crescents out of the small circles. Finally, she took a fork and crimped the edges of the pies to seal in the apples. Her mama would clean up the skillet after the chicken was done and fry the pies in butter.

The two women worked happily side by side. The good smells in the room made Anne hungry and soon she forgot to be suspicious. Mother and daughter laughed and sang until supper was ready.

Supper was a feast compared to what the Foster family was used to. A pot of beans and cornbread was the usual fare if they were lucky. After the meal,

Lotty shooed the rest of the family outside and asked Anne to help her clean up. The little ones went out to play and the boys went to the wood shed. They were told to chop wood. It would be important to do a little each day until cold weather.

When everyone was out of the house, Lotty told Anne about James' visit. Although, the story was a surprise, the fact that Lotty needed something from her was not. Anne had learned in her short years to be wary of her mama when she was too happy. Still, she sat down dutifully and listened as her mama told her version of the conversation.

Lotty finally got to the point and told her that James wanted Anne for his wife. When her mama was finished, Anne stood up and walked to the stove, putting some distance between them.

"And what did you tell him, Mama?"

Lotty looked uncertain as to what she should say. Anne had remained expressionless as she told her about James' proposal. She measured her words carefully.

"Well, I told him I would talk to you about it, of course. The decision would be entirely up to you," Lotty answered watching Anne's expression. Again, she couldn't get a read on her thoughts.

"Well thank you, Mama. Hopefully you won't mind telling him that I'm not interested."

"But Anne, this is the chance of a lifetime! How could you just . . . "

"Everyone in Elkville says you're crazy, Mama, and now I know you are for sure. James Melton is an old man!" Anne interrupted her mother. She tried to stay calm but her voice shook with anger. That her mama even considered it, made her furious. She would not be bartered.

Anne made her way to the door but Lotty got there first, blocking her exit.

"Anne listen to me! Just sit down and listen to me," Lotty demanded.

Reluctantly, Anne did as she was told. Lotty ran to the bedroom and came back with her hand mirror, giving it to Anne.

"I may not have done much right in my life, I know that, but I did have a beautiful daughter."

Anne turned from the mirror and shook her head. "Mama, please," she whispered.

Lotty walked to the window. The moon was out, lighting the yard outside. To get what she wanted she would have to share some private things with Anne. Before Anne returned from the store she had thought long and hard about what she needed to say to sway her daughter in the right direction. It was time to bring up the one subject that she knew would get Anne's undivided attention.

"I've never told you much about your daddy, have I?"

Anne looked at Lotty, in disbelief. As far back as she could remember, her mama had never talked about him. Anne shook her head.

"I was beautiful once. Did you know that? My hair may be auburn and yours dark, but beauty is still somethin' we share . . . among other things."

Anne ignored the remark. Anything her mother had done, she'd chosen to do. Anne had been forced to help with the men that came to call. She would not allow her mother to act as if they were kindred spirits — they were not.

"Your daddy was like Tom Dooley. He was good lookin' . . . a real charmer. I wouldn't listen when people tried to tell me that he had a string of women all up and down Elk Creek and Darby, or that he had a mean streak and liked to drink too much."

Lotty cast her eyes to the floor. Anne was amazed to see her mama was blushing.

"I wouldn't listen because I was in love . . . and there is somethin' so excitin' about being in love with a dangerous man."

Lotty's eyes misted when she spoke of being in love and it did not go unnoticed by her daughter.

"I ran away with him. I thought he would take me away from all my burdens. I was marked here after my first child died and I saw it as a fresh start with the man I loved. Still, it came with a price. Runnin' away like that broke my mama's heart, and I did love her so. I never meant to hurt her, but I did."

Lotty's voice shook when she spoke of her mama. Anne's mama was full of tricks and she knew them all — but when she spoke of Anne's daddy and her own mother the emotion seemed real. It was a part of herself that she had never allowed Anne to see.

"Everything was perfect — until I told him I was carryin' his child. After that, it all changed. He didn't want me anymore and although he didn't come out and say it right away, I knew he wanted to be rid of me. As my belly grew, it became painfully clear to me that I repulsed him. He took up with another woman when I was about seven months gone and I knew it was

55

time to move on. I went home. My mama was the only one that seemed glad to see me. Nothing had changed with my daddy. He'd cast me out after my first child and still said I was dead to him. Hell, he never really cared for me much anyway. He always loved the boys more than me. So, I went back to my grandma's cabin and made a home for us. I've been surviving the best I can ever since. My mama and your uncle, Will, were the only ones that would come to see me. Will didn't approve of my choices in life, but he still came. He used to bring your cousin to play with you sometimes. His girl, Laura, was a sweet child, but awful frail. She cried a lot, I recollect. Anyways, after awhile, I stopped seein' any of the family. I was alone and depressed. Then one day I finally decided I was gonna have to get hard or you and me was gonna starve to death. The only people I saw after that were the men that came after dark. One by one, your brothers and sisters came along. You know, the worst part about getting hard is that it changes ya. Not just inside, but outside, too. I went from bein' Carlotta to just plain old Lotty in the blink of an eye."

Lotty turned and walked towards Anne. Anne had seen that look many times, and it had always scared her.

She took Anne by the arm and drew her near. "You listen to me girl! I'll be damned if I'm gonna let that happen to you."

Anne pulled away. Lotty was hurting her, but she managed to stand her ground.

"I want to marry for love, Mama. Look how your marriage to Mr. Triplette turned out!"

Lotty shoved her back down in the chair.

"We do not talk about Mr. Triplette. Do you understand me? All you need to know is that we got a nice place to live out of that marriage. You and me and your brothers and sisters is all that matters. You best remember that."

Anne did not want to hear anymore. She turned away from her mama in disgust.

"Anne, do you hear me talkin'?"

"Yes, Mama, I hear you talkin'!" Anne was yelling now, trying to defend herself. "But do you hear me? I love Tom. I know I flirt and carry on some-times; and he does, too; but deep down he is the only one for me. It's always been that way. He's always been there for me."

Anne saw her mama's jaw set. Clearly she had taken Anne's remark as an insult.

"You've been there too, Mama, I know that, but it's different with us. I grew up knowin' our family was different from other families. When old Gwendolyn Smith and her gossipy old friends used to ask me about my daddy, I'd lie. I used to tell folks that he ran off and left us when I was little. They always thought I was too young to notice 'em grinnin' and whisperin'. It hurt me, but I learned a couple of lessons. First, people seem to enjoy askin' mean questions they already know the answers to; and second, it's easier if you don't let 'em see you're hurtin'."

Anne stood up and walked over to her mama. For all Lotty's flaws, she did love her. Putting her arms aound her, Anne hugged her tight.

"I learned to say, '*I don't have no daddy and I don't want no daddy . . . especially if he turned up lookin' like yours.*'"

Lotty laughed in spite of herself.

"That used to make Gwendolyn Smith so mad!" Anne giggled.

Lotty turned to Anne and touched her forehead to her daughter's.

"That is because you hit too close to home. It was the gospel truth and she knew it. Her daddy was *soooo* ugly!"

Anne laughed. Few people knew her mama the way she did. Lotty was tough on the outside, but there was still some good inside. She just didn't let it show. Growing up, Anne had learned to do the same. She reached out and lovingly took her mama's hand.

"I don't mind that you made me grow up different, Mama. You did what you had to do and no matter what anyone says, I know you kept us from starvin' to death—and I know you love me. But now is the time for me to choose how *I* want to live. I want my children to know their daddy, and I want to be in love with their daddy. Don't you see? Tom Dooley is my dangerous man, and things just might turn out right this time. I can't stop lovin' him mama."

Without warning, Lotty walked over and slammed her fist on the table. Anne jumped in surprise.

"It will not turn out right, Anne! You are going to do exactly what I did." She pointed her finger at her daughter. "You listen to me! You're gambling with fate; and I'm tellin' you right now, I've played those same cards before and I know you're gonna lose!"

She paced back and forth as Anne sat and watched.

"No matter what I have done to try and keep you from it, history is gonna repeat itself."

Lotty kicked the chair in front of her. "I won't let this happen again!"

The room got deathly quiet. Lotty could hear the children laughing and talking outside. They were happy and satisfied. Their bellies were full for the first time in a long while. Her desperation grew. She had to make Anne understand.

"Anne, keep on lovin' Tom; you don't have to stop. But let James Melton care for ya. Your hands can stay soft and your skin can stay white."

Anne looked at her mama's hands. They were the hands of an old woman, weathered and dry.

"He'll buy you nice store-bought dresses, and you'll have a nice house to live in. Gwendolyn Smith and that gaggle of gossips are just jealous, Anne. They all got plain-Jane daughters now, don't they? The prettiest dresses in the world couldn't make 'em beautiful. That's something only God can do, and they know it. This is your chance to show 'em all!"

Anne turned away from Lotty.

"I don't know . . . I . . . "

Lotty saw the doubt in her daughter's eyes. She pressed the girl harder, not giving her time to think.

"Tom left you here all alone, girl. Face up to the truth! He's just like your daddy. He wants to be taken care of, but he's not the kind of man that'll take care of you. James Melton is different. Whatever you want—whatever you need, he will give it to you. I'll even get your cousin Perline to come down from Watauga to work for ya. She sent me word just the other week that she was needin' money. James can afford to pay her. I swear to you, you won't have to lift a finger."

Anne was listening now.

Lotty continued. "She might even take your wifely duties off your hands, if you ask her just right."

"Perline is dog ugly from what I can remember. He's not gonna want anything to do with her."

Lotty laughed.

"She don't look that bad when she's cleaned up. Stranger things have happened. He could have you in the daylight to show off and Perline in the dark when nobody else is around."

Anne had begun to see the benefits of the arrangement—and her mama knew it. Lotty watched as she mulled it over and offered Anne the hand mirror again. This time Anne took it, taking a long look at herself.

Lotty pressed harder.

"Your looks will fade, baby girl; then what are you gonna do? Who'll take care of you then—Tom Dooley? Tom Dooley'll go to the next pretty little thing that turns his head . . . just like your daddy did. What are you gonna do when your hair fades and the wrinkles come? And keep in mind, babies will pull you down quicker than anything. They'll make ya thick. He'll keep you with child, and you'll let him because ya love him. Then he'll act surprised that you don't look as good as you used to. That'll be his excuse for the *other* women. But, if you marry James Melton, you can keep your looks *and* Tom Dooley. And believe me, as long as you can keep your looks, you can keep Tom."

Lotty leaned over and stroked her daughter's long dark hair.

"You trust your mama, Anne," she coaxed. "I know what men like him want—and it's not some fat little mama with a baby on her hip calling him to supper!"

Time away from Tom and harsh truths from her mama proved to be persuasive. Reluctantly, Anne shook her head. Lotty had won.

"I'll do it, Mama," she said with no expression at all.

Lotty hugged her daughter. "I'll send word to James."

Anne stood up and faced her mama. The two women eyed each other with a dead level stare.

"No, Mama. I'll tell him myself. You let him know that if he wants to marry me—he'll come talk to me face to face."

Without another word Anne went to the door and opened it.

"You best keep your promise, Mama, and send word to Perline."

With that Anne went outside and headed down the path towards the creek. Lotty watched her until she was out of sight.

It was the right thing to do, Lotty reassured herself. The next day she sent her son Pinkney to James Melton's house with the news. By that evening, she found a ham and some new shoes on the porch propped against the door.

CHAPTER NINE

Perline Foster grabbed her sack and climbed down from the wagon. When the dust cleared she looked around the little valley.

"Pretty, ain't it?" the man driving the wagon asked.

Politely Perline nodded and managed a smile. It was a very different view than the one she'd known. She had grown up in the mountains and was used to looking down into the valleys. Now she'd be looking up. The driver pointed to the cabin at the bottom of the hill and tipped his hat.

"That's Lotty Foster's cabin," he said. "Good luck, Missy." With that he grabbed the reins and headed for home.

Perline did not head down the hill right away. She was nervous and needed a few minutes to collect herself. She clutched her sack tightly to her chest and gazed down at the cabin. It'd been a long time since she'd had a bed to sleep in or a roof over her head. The sack she clutched held her only possessions: an apron, a shawl, a hairbrush that was her mama's and a quilt her grandma made for her the year before she died.

Perline's parents had been dead for several years. Sharecroppers, they left nothing for their young'uns when they passed. Perline and her siblings had to move off the property to make way for the new tenants soon after. Her brothers and sisters quickly scattered to the winds. She had not seen any of them since they were forced from their home. Her aunt and uncle agreed to take her in; and from the minute she walked through the door, she was made to feel like a burden to them. They treated her like the hired help and worked her hard. They were strict Christian people with very little tolerance for any kind of backsliding—and Perline backslid a lot. She was starved for affection and would get it any way she could. Her aunt and uncle had not been at all tolerant of the men who came to call on Perline. It wasn't long until she was thrown out of the house. After that, the sixteen year old would stay anywhere she could find a bed. By the time she sent word to her Aunt Lotty down in Elkville, she was desperate. Lotty was the only relative left that she could

60

think of that might take her in and was the last person her parents would have wanted their daughter to be with. Her mama had always told her that her daddy's sister was the black sheep of the family.

Perline never really expected to get an answer from her Aunt Lotty; but one day, surprisingly enough, a messenger was sent by James Melton to tell her she'd be moving to Elkville. The messenger relayed that a wagon would be on its way to fetch her in a few days. At the time she was sleeping in an old lean-to behind the local general store. She suspected the storekeeper knew, but he didn't run her off. She had mailed the letter to her aunt there and had gone faithfully to the store to check the mail every day for three weeks. As soon as word came, she packed up her few belongings and waited by the side of the road for two days. Perline was desperate and afraid she'd miss her ride. She didn't want to be in that lean-to when winter came. Working for James Melton was a good opportunity, and she planned to make the best of it.

Hunger finally gave Perline the courage she needed to head towards Lotty's cabin. Her stomach gnawed, and she felt sick. When she reached the yard, the door to the cabin opened and Lotty came out to greet her.

"Perline Foster, is that you?" Lotty yelled across the yard.

Perline tried to answer, but everything started spinning around. Her face felt cold and clammy; and when she tried to look at her surroundings — they were blurred. The last thing she remembered was a loud clap of thunder, and then darkness.

When Perline woke up she was lying in the grass. A wet mist covered her face and hair. Rain was drizzling down from the sky even though the sun was shining. She looked up to see Lotty's face.

"Come on, girl," she laughed, "we gotta get you inside and in better shape if you're gonna stay here. You're gonna have your hands full. Now get up and let's get in the house."

The sky rumbled again, and Perline jumped at the sound.

"Don't worry about a little thunder, Perline; it's just the devil up there beatin' his wife!"

Perline relaxed a little and laughed with her aunt. Her daddy used to say the same thing.

"Now you come on. James was wantin' to get married by the end of the week, but Anne would have none of it 'til you got here."

"I don't rightly know when I've felt that important," Perline answered trying to joke with her aunt.

"Well, let's get inside before it comes a downpour. James brought us a sugar-cured ham and some goods from the store. I've been bakin'! I was thinkin' just this mornin', this marriage is gonna be a good thing. It's gonna change our lives, Perline. We're all gonna be able to live easier now."

Lotty led Perline inside and guided her to a chair at the table. She went to the stove and brought back a big bowl of pinto beans and a small bowl of onions in vinegar and sat them down in front of her. Perline dug in. She was starving. In another minute Lotty brought Perline a big glass of milk and some cornbread. While Perline ate, Lotty went back to the stove and continued to cook. The taste and smell of the food and the warmth of the room made Perline sleepy. Her eyelids were so heavy she could barely hold them open.

Lotty turned around from the stove to tell Perline about James' cabin and found the girl sound asleep with her head on the table. *Perline was about the same age as her Anne*, she thought. *But by the looks of her, she seemed younger.* She was thin with dirty blond hair and a nose that was a little broader than it should be. Her best feature was her green eyes. For all Perline's flaws, Lotty had to admit Perline was interesting to look at. Watching her inhale the bowl of pintos, Lotty shuddered, thinking about her first few years alone with her babies. She knew all too well what it was like to be hungry.

"You sleep well, Perline. You got your work cut out for you," Lotty whispered. *That girl has no idea*, she thought.

CHAPTER TEN

When Anne came through the door, it slammed hard behind her. Perline's head snapped up from her nap. The minute she saw Anne, she knew things wouldn't be as easy as Lotty had allowed. Perline was shocked at how pretty her cousin really was. She had long dark curls, milk white skin, and large dark eyes—eyes that were blazing on that particular afternoon.

"Mama, where is Perline? You said . . . "

Anne stopped when she saw her cousin. She took a minute to size up the girl at the table. Perline tried to smile and stood up to greet Anne, but Anne just stepped back and stared.

"I was beginning to think you weren't comin'! Where you been?"

"I got on the wagon James Melton sent just as soon as it got there. I came as fast as I could."

"That fool, James, is slower than molasses," Anne replied. "Mama, have you talked to her? Does she know what's expected of her?"

Lotty shook her head and went back to her baking. She didn't argue with Anne anymore. The tables had turned since the agreement was reached and Anne was in control now. After she and James talked, her daughter had became a different person. James sent his betrothed and her family new clothes, shoes, and dry goods. Now with the wedding getting close, a sugar-cured ham had been delivered from the ham house up in Triplette. It seemed to Lotty that the more James gave them, the meaner Anne got. She almost felt sorry for him—and for Perline. She took a jug from the cupboard and poured a mug of shine. Turning to Perline, she offered her a drink.

"Thirsty, Perline?"

Perline gladly accepted the corn squeezings and drank them straight down. The homemade liquor burned her throat but warmed her belly and would hopefully calm her nerves.

Anne watched the two women for a minute. Without any warning, she started screaming at them.

63

"That's all I need is one more drunk in this house!"

Anne glared at Perline and she quickly put her glass down. Being new to the situation, she feared Anne would send her away if she was displeased. A full minute passed, and no one said a word. Finally Anne turned and stormed out of the cabin, slamming the door behind her.

"Let's get you settled, Perline," Lotty said, trying to ignore Anne. "You'll be needin' your rest. Anne never has liked workin' or cookin'. I suppose you've gathered she doesn't care much for James, either. You'll need to take care of him, too."

Perline *thought* she knew what Lotty meant by that. It didn't take a real smart person to figure it out; but still, she had not realized that this was part of the bargain until now. What was clear to Perline was that Anne was marrying a man she didn't love for his money. Hell, she didn't mind. A couple of days before, she didn't have a roof over her head or food to eat and now she did. That meant a lot to Perline. Lotty took her by the hand and led her to a straw tick she'd placed by the fire. She tucked her niece in and stuck a feather pillow under her head. It felt so nice to Perline to have someone tuck her in. As strange as this new situation was, she felt safe for the first time since her parents died. No matter what her folks had told her about Lotty, her aunt had already treated her better than her Christian kinfolk. The shine Lotty had given her was working. Her eyes became heavy, and it was difficult to think clearly. As Perline drifted off to sleep, she thought she saw Lotty in the distance; but she couldn't tell if it was real or just a dream. Lotty was dancing around the room, all smiles and chanting something. It sounded so strange Perline convinced herself it was part of a dream. The last thing she remembered seeing was the blurry image of a crow's foot—and then it was lost.

Perline Foster fell into the deepest, most peaceful sleep she could remember having in a long time.

CHAPTER ELEVEN

Perline opened one eye and looked into the angry face of her cousin. Anne was shaking her.

"Get up," she snapped. "Let's get this over with."

Apparently, James and Anne were eager to commence with the marriage and decided not to wait another day. Anne stood there glaring at Perline in a white dress. It was simple, but pretty—with lace around the neckline and cuffs. Her dark hair was swept up with white spring flowers scattered in her curls.

Perline stood up and Lotty immediately whisked her away to the bedroom. She pointed to a blue calico dress laid out on the bed.

"That's for you," she said. "Now hurry and wash up. I put some water in the bowl on the dresser. Get a move on. The preacher will be here soon."

Perline did as she was told. She went to the wash basin on the dresser and picked up a cloth beside the bowl. She dipped it in the water and slowly began to wash herself. The water was cold, but it felt good to clean up. She had not bathed in weeks.

After she finished washing up, she took the dress from the bed and slid it over her head and buttoned it up. It was a little loose but Perline didn't care, it would do. It was clean and nicer than anything she'd ever worn. Making her way back to the fireplace she found her sack. Reaching inside, Perline pulled out her mama's hairbrush and with great care, began to untangle the knots in her hair. No matter what else happened to Perline on any given day, brushing her hair was her one girlish ritual. It made her feel closer to her mama. This morning Perline's hair was tangled more than usual. The wagon ride from Watauga had been blustery.

"The preacher's here," Lotty announced looking out the window.

Quickly, she herded Anne and Perline out of the house. A crowd of neighbors were outside. Women were placing food on the table, and the men were gathered around talking to the groom. The preacher joined the men in conversation for a little while.

Finally, the preacher made his way to the porch, raising his hand to silence the crowd.

"I reckon we can commence now," he announced.

The guests fell silent. Anne walked over and stood by James. Anne's brother Pinkney stood beside her. He would represent the family and give his sister away.

Lotty nudged Perline and pointed for her to stand behind Anne. Reluctantly, Perline joined the wedding party. She kept her head down and tried not to draw any more attention to herself than she had to. The preacher recited the vows and James and Anne placed gold rings on each other's fingers. It made Perline sad to see such a beautiful gesture and know it meant nothing to Anne. When the preacher finally announced them man and wife, James reached over to kiss his bride only to have Anne turn her head. The poor man was barely able to brush the side of her cheek. If he was embarrassed by her actions, he didn't show it. Instead, he turned with his new wife and waved to the crowd of onlookers.

After the wedding was over the crowd cheered and clapped for the new couple. It was not a particularly joyful cheer, but Perline believed the group did it for James' sake. Lotty didn't seem to notice. She was having the time of her life. She had invited some of her male acquaintances over to play music. There was plenty of food on the table and wildflowers all around. James looked nice. He was all dressed up in a suit that fit him just right, and his sandy hair was slicked down. When Perline stood next to him at the cider table, she noticed that he smelled nice, too. James seemed to be a quiet man, soft spoken and humble, and Perline didn't think she'd mind taking over the wifely duties at all. She'd done much worse than James Melton.

James' brother, Julius, and his wife were there along with James' sister Sarah, and her husband. Julius seemed fine with the whole thing, but Sarah was not. She did not approve of Anne. James' sister had blonde hair and blue eyes like her brother, but she was pretty and not at all like him in her ways. Sarah was quick to say what was on her mind. When James told her and Julius about the wedding, she quickly let them all know how much she disapproved—especially poor James. Anne knew how James' sister felt about her, and the two women exchanged many a heated glance during the festivities. James' new bride seemed to enjoy the fact that Sarah was upset and would taunt her with little grins when he wasn't looking.

Later in the afternoon, the shine came out and the men started popping corn over an open fire. More people came by to visit. Most of the rowdier guests were friends of Lotty's. Perline didn't meet one friend all day who introduced themselves as a friend of Anne's. She thought that was sad. The rowdier the crowd became, the more Anne withdrew.

Around dusk, Perline saw Anne go inside, and she decided to follow.

"Sure is a nice gatherin'," Perline said.

"Nice for who?" Anne pouted back.

"I thought you wanted this, Anne. Your mama said . . . "

"The only thing I want is to keep Tom Dooley." Anne bowed her head. "And to make sure my family's taken care of. That's all I have ever wanted, really. Mama says to keep Tom, I have to keep my looks. I suppose she's right. If I'm not careful some younger girl will come along someday and turn his head."

Perline had heard about Tom Dooley from Lotty. Perline thought Tom must be something special if Anne was so taken with him. Although her cousin was hard to get along with, Perline admired her beauty and her situation.

"Your mama wants me to be a blind for you and him when he comes back from the war. "Lotty told me, '*You cover for Anne so's she can keep her marriage to James and still see Tom.*'" Curious now, she asked, "I barely remember him from when we was all little. Did he turn out to be good lookin'?"

Anne smiled for the first time that day. She leaned against the kitchen table and closed her eyes.

"Yes, he did, Perline. Yes, he did! I miss him. He's the only real friend I've ever had, and I miss him every day of my life."

Perline tried to imagine what it must be like to love someone so much. She felt sad for Anne and excited at the chance to meet Tom when he came home.

Anne must have sensed what Perline was thinking. She turned around and looked Perline square in the eyes.

"I'm happy to feed you and give you a place to stay, Perline. I'm even happier to share my new husband with you. But you hear me, you ever touch Tom Dooley, and I'll kill you."

Without another word, Anne walked outside. Perline got the message loud and clear. She was happy to have a place to live and a man when he wanted her. She decided to put Tom Dooley out of her mind.

The wedding party got pretty wild after that. It was late when the group walked the newlyweds and Perline up the road to the Melton cabin. Anne dutifully walked on one side of James, and Perline walked on the other. Lotty and her friends walked behind, carrying Anne's things. Julius and his wife walked with the crowd, too, but Sarah made her husband take her home. She said she couldn't bear another minute.

The rowdy crowd serenaded the newlyweds with loud drunken songs and the banging of pots and pans when they reached the cabin. They toasted the bride and groom with mugs of shine. Several of the fiddlers shot their rifles in the air as Anne allowed James to carry her over the threshold. With a few cheers and some jeers, the crowd finally left, heading back to Lotty's. Most of them would stay up all night. Perline wished she could go, too. The Melton cabin was quiet after everyone was gone except for the far-off sounds of the fiddles.

The music reminded Anne of Tom. She took a long look around her new home. It was larger than her mama's cabin. The furniture was good and sturdy, and there were more windows than she was used to. It was nice and clean.

"Can I get you anything, Anne?" James asked.

"No, thank you, James," Anne replied coolly. "I'll be goin' to bed now."

James moved towards Anne, and she quickly put out her hand to stop him.

"We have an agreement, James, and you know it. I don't know if you thought I'd get all soft after all the gifts and the weddin', but I'm here to tell you that I meant what I said. Now, go on to bed and leave me be."

Anne walked into her new room. She pulled down the new quilt James' sister-in-law had made for the couple as a wedding present. It was a wedding ring pattern. The poor woman must have worked night and day to finish it. Sick and tired, Anne sat on the edge of the bed and looked out the window of her tiny room. The moon was out, and the stars were twinkling above the ridge.

Protectively, she put her hand to her belly. It was protruding just the tiniest bit.

No child of hers would go hungry, she thought.

James Melton held true to his word. He nodded to Anne and walked into the other bedroom on the other side of the cabin. James' new room was added as part of their agreement.

Perline didn't know what to do exactly, so she just sat by the fire for a time. After Anne was settled and down for the night, James came to the door of his bedroom and motioned for Perline to come in.

Perline started working for the Meltons right away.

CHAPTER TWELVE

Spring melted into summer. There was plenty of rain. Perline spent a lot of her time helping James in the garden and was happy to do it. Any time that she could do something to insure that her belly would stay full, she was glad to work. James was kind enough and as much of a gentlemen as he could be, given their arrangement.

Anne was a different story. From the day she moved into James Melton's cabin, she was never satisfied. Anne was like a hungry child that couldn't get its fill. The more she was fed—the hungrier she became. James bought her nice clothes and made sure that Perline cooked whatever Anne decided she wanted to eat. It was obvious to Perline as she watched James, he believed deep down that if he could spoil Anne enough, she would come to love him. The sad truth was there wasn't enough spoiling in the world for Anne Melton.

Anne never allowed Perline to get close. Perline had hoped that her cousin would be like family to her. She desperately wanted to feel that she belonged somewhere.

Her Aunt Lotty wasn't much better. As soon as the marriage was final, Lotty went back to being her old selfish self. She was wild and drank too much most of the time. Her bargain with James had paid off, though. James saw to it that his mother-in-law didn't go hungry after the marriage and that she had decent things to wear and shoes on her feet. Still, Lotty was kind to Perline when she needed her. She was never really mean, although she had a reputation with the other women in the community as being wild and dangerous. The only thing that scared Perline about Lotty was the memory of her dream—the one she had on her first day in Elkville before Anne's wedding. She didn't remember much about it except that it had scared her. It stayed with her, like a warning. The rumors scared Perline, too—especially the talk about Mr. Triplette. His death was still a mystery. It was safe to say that, in ways, Lotty scared the bejesus out of Perline. She got the feeling without ever being told that crossing Lotty would be the wrong thing to do and to cross Anne would be to cross Lotty.

In the Fall, Perline and James put up a good crop. Anne watched mostly from the porch, her belly growing bigger with every day. Perline canned corn, beans, tomatoes, and collards. She put up several quarts of pickles and pickled beets. That was a real luxury. Salt was scarce, but somehow James managed to get some. He said he loved pickles and it was worth every penny. She was even able to bury some cabbage for sauerkraut later on. *Sauerkraut and pork was as good as it got*, Perline thought. Of course, the time had to be just right for kraut. It had to be buried when the signs were right and when she wasn't bleeding. Everybody knew a woman couldn't can kraut when she had the curse. It would go bad and stink. In fact, anything a woman canned during that time would spoil. The Bible clearly said that when a woman bled, she was unclean. Perline had learned that from her grandma.

So, she waited for the signs of the moon to turn to the head and then she chopped up some cabbage and fixed James some kraut. Perline put it in a big crockery jar and covered the crock with a plate. She held the plate on top with a heavy rock so the kraut wouldn't spew over while it was working. She buried it and they waited. James seemed to enjoy watching Perline work. When the kraut finally came out of the ground and was ready to eat, he complimented her and told her later it was worth the wait. She buried apples, too, and put straw over them. They would have some fruit for Christmas time. She also strung apples up to dry in the attic for pies, along with strings of green beans. Leather britchey beans were good eating in the wintertime. James was gonna go to the store and buy a sugar-cured ham and some molasses. The Hambys that lived up from Cowles' store kept bees. She went up to see them one day and bought four jars of sourwood honey. Honey made the best pies and cakes in the world. But her favorite way to eat it was right out of the jar on a hot biscuit with some butter. She'd never had this much food guaranteed and stored away before. Life with the Meltons was strange but secure for Perline, and she was content.

When Anne's baby finally came, the food was stocked and ready for winter. It had been a long labor—a full day and a half. For all Anne's delicate features, she had been anything but delicate in labor. Anne was fierce. Lotty had delivered the little girl with Perline's help. Watching Anne hold the newborn was the first real kindness Perline had ever felt from her cousin. Holding the beautiful child with its dark curls and eyes, Anne wept for joy and held her with as much love and tenderness as any mother possibly could. James never questioned Anne about the child she carried. And when the baby girl was born he immediately accepted her as his own.

When spring rolled around again, the strange little family had been together long enough to know each other well and a pattern was set amongst them. After supper, Anne would go to bed alone and James would go to his bed alone. When he thought Anne was asleep, he would motion for Perline. It wasn't every night, but that was fine. Some days Perline was so dog-tired she was asleep before her head hit the pillow. She suspected there had been a few nights James had found her that way and been kind enough to let her be. James never mistreated her or said anything unkind. He never said anything, period. Sometimes Perline wondered what went on in that man's head.

Time passed; and before Perline knew it, a year and a half had come and gone. Anne became more demanding, and James became more withdrawn.

Perline tended the house and cooked and sometimes cared for the little one. Neighbors had counted the months as soon as Anne had given birth and took much enjoyment out of noting that the months came up short. No one around the Melton cabin seemed to care, though.

Little Mary Beth was a beauty, just like her mama.

CHAPTER THIRTEEN

It was a beautiful spring day in 1865. Laura Foster walked down the trail with her daddy to the store. Will Foster had demanded that his daughter come with him, even though she'd told him over and over that she had weaving to do. She and her Aunt Mary did a lot of weaving for people in the community. Homespun cloth was the most affordable thing to use in hard times, and it held up better than store-bought. Laura and her Aunt Mary had more orders than they could fill.

Laura strayed from the path and found herself near the creek bank. She loved to walk along the water's edge and daydream.

Will Foster was clearly getting impatient with his daughter. "Come on, girl. Quit your gommin' around. I got things to do today," he yelled from the path.

Laura laughed. "I'm comin', Papa."

Will walked towards Laura watching her with amusement. She'd grown up overnight and turned out to be a pretty girl. She was the apple of Will's eye. The trouble was she knew it, and he had to work hard to hide it. He didn't want a girl so struck on herself that she would have a hard time finding a husband.

"Your head's always in the clouds, and you're always daydreamin'. Well you won't have time for that much longer. You're getting' close to marryin' age, and you need to find yourself a husband. Cookin' and cleanin' for a husband will keep you from wastin' your time."

Laura tried to ignore her daddy, but Will kept on.

"I hear Bob Cummings is lookin' for a wife, and I hear his eyes are set on you."

Irritated, Laura answered her Papa. "Bob Cummings is a nice man, but he ain't the man for me."

"And just why is that, Miss high and mighty?"

Laura made a face. "He's a school teacher, Papa. He acts too much like a girl. His hands are soft, and he talks real proper. He's not like the other men I know, and he makes me uncomfortable."

His girl was throwing away a good life as far as Will Foster was concerned. He liked Bob.

"The reason he don't act like the men around here is because he has some learnin'. School teachin' is an honest profession. Besides, he can afford to pay some poor old fool like me to do the hard work for him. I wish I could do that. My old back is plumb wore out. If you married Bob, you could get some learnin' yourself and be a proper lady. No man around here can do that for you. I'd be proud to call Bob Cummings my son-in-law."

Laura walked away from her father and picked up a rock on the creek bank. She skipped it across the creek. Sunlight danced on the tiny streaks of copper in her chestnut hair. It was long and pulled back with a ribbon tied at the nape of her neck. She turned to her daddy.

"I'm gonna fall in love someday. The man of my dreams is gonna find me, and when he does he'll sweep me off my feet and treat me like a princess. He's gonna know all the right things to say, and he's gonna think I'm the prettiest thing he ever saw. And I'm gonna know him when I see him. It'll be love at first sight. He'll look at me and grin and give me a wink, and I'll know it's him."

Will Foster laughed out loud.

"How do you dream this up, girl? I've spoiled you for sure."

Laura came over and kissed her daddy on the cheek. "Maybe you have spoiled me, Papa. But I'll know him when I see him, and I can tell you right now, it ain't Bob Cummings."

She winked at her papa. "You just wait; it'll happen."

Will quickly forgave her for her foolishness. She was young and she'd learn, he thought. He kissed her on the forehead.

"I'll wait, little girl. I'll wait about as long as it takes me to get a switch to your lazy behind."

With that, Will snapped a switch from a nearby bush and shook it at his daughter. Laura laughed at her Papa's playfulness and ran off in the direction of the store, with Will following close behind.

CHAPTER FOURTEEN

When Will and Laura got to the store, there was a crowd as usual. Several of the men were sitting by the feed shed playing cards. The mail pony had just finished making its monthly delivery to the store. Calvin kept mail for all of the Elkville residents. He delivered the mail to them when they came to trade. For those he didn't see as often, he would have one of his young store helpers deliver a letter or package — especially if he felt it needed immediate attention. Will wondered if there would be any news about the war. The community had received so little information since Stoneman's men destroyed Calvin's telegraph machine during the raid. The Yankees had torn down or burned just about everything they'd come in contact with. They would have burned down the courthouse in Wilkesboro, too, if Calvin hadn't made a trip to town in an effort to persuade them not to. During the raid, the old storekeeper stood on the steps of the courthouse and pleaded with the Yankees to spare it. He knew a lot of the Union soldiers because he still traded with them and spoke to them as their friend. His plea worked and the courthouse was spared, but when he returned to Elkville from Wilkesboro, he found his telegraph machine smashed to bits.

Mary Dooley and her daughters were making their way down the porch steps as Will and Laura approached. Mary noticed the young man on the mail pony as he started to ride away and ran to him.

"Any news from the war?" she asked.

The boy shook his head and Mary's shoulders drooped. *No news, is good news*, she tried to convince herself.

Ben Ferguson walked over to her.

"I hear the war'll probably be over soon, Miz Dooley."

"Oh, I hope so, Ben. I do hope so."

Martha Gilbert came by and hugged her. "I hope so, too, Mary. I know you miss your boy, and I miss my Jonathan. I don't know how much longer

74

I can keep up the farm without him. The boys do the best they can, but they're still awful young."

Betsy Scott joined in.

"Jonathan and Tom will both be home soon; I know they will. We just have to have faith, that's all."

Martha turned to Betsy and hugged her. "Bless your heart, Betsy; you're right."

Mary nodded to the women. "I say my prayers every mornin' and every night," she told them.

With that, she motioned to her girls. "Well, I need to be goin'. Y'all take care."

Anna and Eliza helped their mother carry her things. Anna took most of the load. She was used to taking up the slack for Eliza. Her little sister had been born with a limp. One foot turned in slightly. It wasn't much of a hindrance, but it made balancing hard for her sometimes. Anna was a good daughter. A few months before, she'd married Cajah Hendrix. She and Cajah had been sweethearts since they were children, and their marriage had seemed to be the most natural thing in the world. Mary Dooley was so pleased. Cajah and Anna tried to help Mary as much as they could. With no man around, the older woman found keeping up the farm to be too much for her.

Everyone waved goodbye, and the Dooleys headed down the road for home.

James Foster came out of the store in time to see his daddy and sister approach.

The fifteen year old boy had grown impatient waiting for Will and Laura.

"It's about time you got here. I was beginnin' to think somethin' had happened to ya."

Will patted his impatient son on the back.

"I'd 'a been here sooner, but your sister's been lolly gaggin' around."

Laura smiled and rolled her eyes to the sky. Trying to ignore them, she walked over to talk to Martha Gilbert and Betsy Scott.

"If that had been me, you would have tanned my hide. You spoil her rotten, Papa."

Will looked at his son and spoke in a serious tone.

"I hope that's not a problem for you, boy. She looks too much like your mama for me to treat her any other way."

75

James knew there was no use trying to argue with that. His daddy was crazy over his sister, and had been just as crazy over his mama.

"Aw, never mind," he said. "I ain't much better at tellin' her no than you are."

Calvin stepped onto the porch of the store and spied Will Foster.

"Will Foster! Glad you came today," he shouted.

Will noticed that Calvin was thinner than he'd seen him in awhile. Poor man. He'd just gotten back to Elkville a few days before. Some of the Confederates had heard he was still trading with the Yanks, and they had him arrested and thrown in jail. Some of his own neighbors had called him a Yankee sympathizer.

Calvin's old friend, Colonel James Horton, had gone to Wilkesboro and used their telegraph to contact Governor Zeb Vance. Vance had come to Wilkes County and used his persuasion to get Calvin released. He accompanied Calvin back home to Elkville. On the way, Vance chastised his friend and warned him about future trades with the Yanks until the war was over. Vance knew what he was talking about, too. He'd spent some time in Old Capital Prison in the District of Columbia for his allegiance to the Confederacy. Vance hadn't been as lucky as Calvin. He was there for eleven months before he was paroled. Vance had told Calvin, *"You best be on the same side as the place you're spending time in. We got thrown in jail for opposite reasons because we were both stupid enough to say what we thought in the wrong place. Be careful, Calvin."*

Those were just two stories Will knew of. A lot more folks had been accused of worse because of the war. It was a dangerous time. Will preferred to keep quiet about what he thought. As long as he could farm the land, the sharecropper was happy.

Will felt sorry for Calvin. His family had moved to North Carolina from Connecticut, and he understood how he would be attached to both sides. The war had been hard for everybody, and Calvin was no exception. The storekeeper stepped down from the porch and ran to meet Will.

"That cloth you ordered came in just now on the mail pony."

Laura whirled around in the middle of her conversation with Betsy and Martha.

"Cloth? For me?"

Will nodded with pride.

"Oh, Papa!" she yelled, as she rushed down from the porch to hug her daddy. "I've never had anything but homespun in my life. I can't believe it."

Calvin pretended to be shocked when he saw Laura. "Now, who is this you got with you, Will?"

Will laughed.

"You know who this is, Calvin. This is my daughter, Laura."

Calvin put his arm around Will.

"Laura? Naw! Why I can't believe my eyes. Child, you were just a little thing when I saw you . . . oh . . . how long has it been? Why look at you! You're all growed up." Calvin turned jokingly to his friend. "She's awful pretty, Will. Thank the Lord she took after her mama and not her ugly old daddy."

Some of the men playing cards overheard him and started shouting words of agreement.

"I'll have you know, Calvin," Will said, "that I was a looker in my day."

"More like the end of days," Ben Ferguson yelled.

The men playing cards whooped and hollered.

"Ben Ferguson, you're one to talk. When you were born Doc Carter slapped your mama."

Everyone was laughing now, ladies too.

Ben grinned. "All right now, Will, you leave my mama out of this, ya hear?"

Martha Cowles scurried over to Laura and took the young girl by the arm.

"That's enough, you two. Let the girl have a compliment and enjoy it. Laura, ma cherie, come in and let's see the cloth your Pa Pa ordered. It matches your eyes. You are going to look trés jolie when your aunt gets hold of this, non?"

Laura shook her head in agreement and let Miz Cowles lead her inside to look at the cloth. She'd always loved Martha Cowles. She was such a feisty little thing and always fun to talk to. Laura craved female companionship and with the exception of her Aunt Mary, she had very little. It was hard on her living with just her daddy and brother sometimes.

Bob Cummings stood back and watched Laura. From the minute she had arrived the schoolteacher's eyes had been glued to her every move. Shy and nervous, he stepped forward to make his feelings known.

"She already looks like a little doll, Miz Cowles."

Irritated, Laura tried to ignore Bob.

Laura's snub did not go unnoticed. Embarrassed, Bob stepped back and pretended to look interested in the card game the local men were playing.

"Wait 'til you see it," Martha called out. "It could be a dancing dress. You dance, Laura, non?"

Laura grinned and answered, "Yes, Ma'am."

The men watched Miz Cowles and Laura walk into the store. Jack Adkins laughed once they were inside and out of earshot.

"You better get your shotgun loaded, Will. That girl is ready for courtin'."

Will shook his head and walked over to Jack Adkins. He crossed his arms and gave him a threatening look — the kind that only a father can give.

"God help me, I know," he answered in his sternest voice, trying to conceal a grin.

Jack Keaton stood away from the others and listened to the conversation. He leaned against the porch of the feed shed. He and Will had not been on the best of terms for awhile. Jack had courted Laura for a few months but the relationship hadn't ended well. Laura grew tired of Jack before he'd grown tired of her, and he didn't like being cast aside. When he tried to come back around, Will had come out of the cabin and asked him to leave.

Laura's brother, James, pulled his daddy to the side. "I just want to ask you one thing. How did you pay for that cloth?"

"Don't you worry about it, James. I promise you won't starve to death."

James shot his papa an angry look. People had always teased him about being fat. He had even asked Doc Carter about it once. Doc told James it wasn't his fault. He believed James had a condition. Will, however, was not convinced. He still teased his son about eating too much, every now and then.

Laura and Miz Cowles returned with Laura's new blue cloth. She ran to her daddy and hugged him.

"Thank you Papa! It's so beautiful!" Laura kissed Will on the cheek. "Do we need anything else?"

"No, darling, not this trip. I got what I came for. Thank you, Miz Cowles, for all your help."

James rolled his eyes. "Like I said, we're gonna starve to death."

Will pointed James jokingly towards home.

"Come back and let me see that new dress, Laura," Martha called to Will's daughter.

"I will, Miz Cowles," Laura answered.

"You take good care of it. There will be some dancin' goin' on in the fall when it's time to boil down the molasses. No respectable young mademoiselle would want to miss a molassy boilin'."

Laura hugged her and replied, "Me and my new dress will be there, Miz Cowles."

Will looked at Laura and grinned. She was so much like the young girl he had married years before. High cheekbones and beautiful round eyes, she was the spitting image of her mama. When she smiled, there was a tiny space between her teeth that, in some odd way, suited her. She had a look about her that was all her own. She stood out. He loved her so much it hurt, and he wanted her to have a good life — she deserved it. Will firmly believed Bob Cummings could give it to her. Doggone it, he liked that man. No matter how much he liked him though, his choice for Laura was clearly not going to be hers. Laura had a mind of her own.

"Oh, Lord, help me get through this courtin' phase without 'a killin' nobody," he said partially joking.

Will and his two children started off on their way home. The trip would be a good two hours on foot. Calvin knew they would just make it back before dark.

Calvin's wife had been just as surprised as James Foster at the purchase Will had made for his daughter. She pulled Calvin aside.

"How on earth did Will Foster ever afford that cloth, Calvin?"

Calvin pulled out a worn pocket watch from his vest and held it up for Martha to see. It was yellow gold with beautiful etchings on the casing.

"I'll trade it when the Union comes through on their next pick up of fur and herbs."

Martha slapped him on his shoulder.

"You old goat! How could you?"

Calvin shook a warning finger at his wife.

"I'm a businessman, ma cherie. He wanted that cloth for his daughter more than he wanted this watch. He didn't even flinch when we struck the deal. That tells me if I hadn't done it, he would have gone and traded it at the store up on German Hill. Besides, anymore, if you have anything worth anything and those damn bushwhackers find out, they'll take it while you are sleeping or worse."

Exasperated, Martha scolded her husband. "You are going to keep on until they string you up by your heels one day, like Lewis Absher did that Yank. Tu est trés enervante!"

"No, Martha, I am not irritatin', and you speak English when you are insultin' me. Besides, there's no proof that Lewis did that."

"None except that he ran off to Tennessee to wait things out. He knew that he could stay up there for seven years and come back here free and clear of any crime. It's the law. Do you know how long it must have taken that man to die, hangin' by his heels? Calvin, I'm scared for us sometimes. You need to choose sides."

Calvin loved her so. In later years, he would remember this conversation with much sadness. It was a fever and not bushwhackers that would someday part him from his Martha. He put his arms around his petite wife and kissed her.

"Now, why would I go and do a thing like that? I just got out of jail for speaking my mind. Look around you, Martha. The mountains are divided in this war. Union and Confederate livin' side by side. Our neighbors are killin' each other." He held her tighter and spoke to her tenderly. "No, darling. The only side I'm on right now is our side. If we don't starve to death like the rest of the folks here in Elkville, we just might make it. I'd like for us to be some of the few around here to die of old age. I would think you might like that, too."

Martha stood on her tiptoes and tenderly kissed his cheek.

"Oui," she said.

"Je t'aime, ma cherie," Calvin whispered.

"Je t'aime," she whispered back.

CHAPTER FIFTEEN

Reluctantly, Tom signed his name to the United States pledge of Allegiance and dated it—June 11, 1865. It was a requirment of each of the prisoners before they were set free. *It didn't matter*, he convinced himself, *he knew who and what he was no matter what kind of paper they made him sign.*

Finally, the gates of Point Lookout opened and the prisoners walked onto northern soil as free men. Most took off right away—heading back to their different home states.

Tom decided to spend some time in Maryland before he started for Elkville. He needed to get his thoughts together and rest. He was able to find enough field work for food and a place to sleep. The Yanks did not treat him well, but he didn't care. He needed to get his strength back. Pride would not allow him to return to his girl as he was. He had told Anne the last time they saw each other that he would come back the kind of man she could be proud of. Now, that the war was over and he was finally free, that was exactly what he intended to do. When he was strong enough, Tom started the long trip home by hopping a northern boxcar. He would do that many times until he reached the southern part of Virginia. After that, he'd be on foot. Most of the southern railroads had been destroyed, so he would have to walk the rest of the way. Hopping boxcars was tricky business. The Yanks didn't take kindly to Confederates riding their trains. He barely escaped discovery on several occasions. The men that were caught were usually beaten or put in jail.

It was late September when Tom crossed into North Carolina on foot. Shortly after he arrived in his home state he ran into Jonathan Gilbert, Martha's husband. It was good to see a familiar face. Tom and Jonathan had grown up together in the small community of Elkville, and the two men decided to make the final part of their journey together. The South they walked into shocked them. Wreckage and ruin blanketed the countryside. Southerners along the way were as gracious as ever, but thinner and quieter than Tom remembered.

Tom and Jonathan were still a long way from home. The two men talked and shared their war stories along the way to pass the time. It had been a long war for both of them, and they were anxious to get back to their loved ones. The only pair of shoes Tom had was falling apart. He took some old strips of cloth from his backpack and tied them around the toes hoping this would keep the soles of his shoes from flapping as he walked. Jonathan had taken old rags and burlap and tied them on the bottoms of his feet. His boots were long gone.

Jonathan talked about Martha most of the way home.

Tom talked and thought about nothing but Anne.

CHAPTER SIXTEEN

The day before Colonel Horton's annual molassy boiling the Meltons arrived at the store to do some last minute trading. Perline needed to add a few notions to Anne's dancing dress to finish it.

Although Perline was the seamstress and had a good eye for dressmaking, Anne made her wait outside while she chose the lace and ribbon herself. Perline knew from past experience that Anne would take her own sweet time; and as a result, she would be up all night finishing the dress. Anne was spoiled rotten, and Perline resented the fact that she was the one who had to suffer for it. Her pouting was interrupted as Billy Hendrix and one of his friends came out of nowhere, running towards the store and yelling their fool heads off.

"Confederate soldiers comin'! Confederate soldiers comin' down the road!" Billy yelled.

"Who's comin'?" Perline yelled back, still irritated.

"Tom Dooley! It's Tom Dooley and Jonathan Gilbert, come back from the war!" Billy shouted.

For no apparent reason Perline's heart began to race. All of the anger and resentment that had been working on her just minutes before fell away, and she found herself so excited she could hardly breathe. There was commotion all around—some of the men on the porch started cheering and the ladies clapped and waved. The Meltons and the Cowles came out of the store to see what was going on. In all the excitement Perline turned around and caught a glimpse of Anne's face, pale and shaken, staring out. Perline followed her gaze, and that's when she saw him. Through all the dust and dirt and shoddy clothes, Perline saw the man that had captured the heart of Anne Melton. He was wearing a Confederate jacket and cap and had a bundle strapped to him with a fiddle. Smiling, Tom waved to the crowd as old friends stepped up to shake his hand or slap him on the back. As he greeted them—he scanned the crowd, clearly looking for Anne. When he finally spotted her he started to move in her direction, but something in her expression made him stop.

Intuition told him something was wrong. Looking closer, he noticed Anne's hand on James Melton's arm. The Confederate soldier planted his feet and waited to see what would happen next.

Calvin Cowles broke the silence.

"Tom Dooley!" he yelled. "You're a sight for sore eyes, son!"

Calvin ran to Tom, giving him a big hug. "We're proud of you, boy, real proud."

He grabbed Jonathan and hugged him, too.

"Thank you, Calvin," Tom answered, never taking his eyes off Anne. "I'm glad to be back home."

"Well, now," Calvin said. "Nothin's changed much. A few have died . . . some got married. Your sister Anna did and . . . uh, I believe you know James Melton and his wife, Anne, here."

The murmers and whispers did not go unnoticed by Tom. He felt embarrassed and confused, but he managed to look James in the eye and keep his emotions in check, just the same.

Anne remained frozen on the porch. Through tear filled eyes she stood staring straight ahead—jaw set. Her lips were trembling, and for a moment, Perline wondered if she might actually cry. Looking down, Perline saw Anne's fists were clenched at her sides. Tom's face could not hide his feelings. It was easy to see he was hurt and thrown completely off guard. The Confederate war hero, coming home to his girl, looked defeated. Still, he tried to save face and in front of the onlookers, walked over to James Melton and extended his hand.

"You did real good there, James. Anne'll make you a fine wife."

James nodded. "She already has."

There was an uncomfortable silence.

Martha Gilbert rushed out of the store with Gwendolyn and Betsy. She ran to Jonathan and threw her arms around him almost knocking him to the ground. Jonathan hugged her so tight her feet flew up in the air. The two stood in the middle of the crowd and kissed each other as if they were the only two people on earth, and everyone cheered. Anne and Tom watched the happy couple. Martha Gilbert did everything that Tom had dreamed Anne would do when she first saw him again. Anne had dreamed the same dreams. Both Tom and Anne lowered their eyes from the sight.

Bubbling over with excitement, it was Perline that brought Tom and Anne back to reality. She stepped forward and as daintily as Perline Foster could, held out her hand. Surprised, he took it, not knowing how to react.

"Hello, Tom," she said in a voice that he thought too sweet to be real. "I'm Anne's cousin, Perline. You remember me? I ain't seen you since we was little, but I do remember you, now that I seen your face. I've been workin' for the Meltons since they got married."

She leaned into him with a knowing look.

"I've heard all about you—heard you play a mean fiddle. The Hortons are having a molassy boilin' tomorrow night and I'm plannin' on bein' there. Why don't you come and bring that fiddle of yours? I'd love to hear you play," she said in her flirtiest tone.

Tom looked at Perline and wondered why she was behaving like that. He did not remember her. Looking at her it was easy to see why, he thought. She was not somebody he or anyone else would give the time of day to.

Perline looked back at Anne and knew there was nothing her cousin could do in front of all those people. Her hands were tied by marriage vows. Even if it meant a beating from Anne when they got home, it would be worth it. Anne had been horrible to Perline lately, much worse than usual. When they got home, she'd tell Anne she was only doing what Lotty told her to—which was partially true. Perline had been told many times that when Tom came home she would need to cover for the couple so that people wouldn't see the truth. Her Aunt told her, *you be the blind for Anne and Tom.*

About that time, Mary Beth stepped out of the store with one of Martha Gilbert's little girls.

"Mary Beth, come on down here. There's somebody here you should meet," Perline yelled.

Surprised, Tom watched the little girl toddle over to Perline and take her hand. She was wearing a little blue calico dress and eating a stick of horehound candy.

"Mary Beth, say hello to Tom."

"Hello," she said, hiding behind Perline's skirts.

Tom looked curiously at the dark eyes and curls. Cold recognition washed over him.

"How old are you, Mary Beth?" he asked.

The child held up four tiny little fingers.

"Mary Beth, come here right now!" Anne yelled.

Turning to her mama, the little girl did as she was told.

"That's right," Perline yelled after her. "You go on to your mama!"

But when she got there, the child held up her arms to James Melton instead. James picked her up and lovingly held her. Tom watched in pain as she put her arms around James' neck.

Jonathan and Martha happily made their way into the store. Tom stood awkwardly looking at the Meltons and Perline, not knowing what to do next. It was Calvin who finally broke the silence.

Well look here! It's my old friend Will!" the storekeeper announced. "What brings you out today, Will?"

Will laughed and slapped Calvin on the back. "I been told that a dancin' dress ain't no good if your hair's not right and you don't smell pretty."

Laura blushed and scolded her Papa, "Hush, Papa! You're embarrassing the daylights outta me!"

"Well it's the gospel truth or I wouldn't be here," Will said. He turned back to Calvin, "You got any lavendar water, Calvin? This girl's gonna die without it and a pretty ribbon for her hair."

Laura walked away from the two men and made her way to Miz Cowles on the porch. She refused to say another word to her Papa. When she reached Martha, she shot her father a warning glance to be quiet; and that's when her eyes met Tom Dooley's. Still angry, she managed a polite smile at the soldier and tried to figure out why he looked so familiar. Tom politely nodded back.

Jack Keaton had been sitting on the edge of the porch whittling when his cousin, Tom, came home. He felt bad for him. Tom had left for war; and while he was gone, had lost his girl. Jack had stayed home and still lost Laura Foster. Jack had known Tom since they were little. Tom's mama was a Keaton before she married Tom's daddy. Like his cousin, Jack was good looking. He had curly hair like Tom's, but lighter. He was bigger built, but anyone could definitely see the family resemblance between the two.

When Laura came into the picture, Jack lost interest in what was happening with the Meltons and turned to watch her. *She was all smiles and innocence in public*, he thought. He wondered what people might think if they knew the real Laura—the one that used to meet him in the Winkler's barn late at night. He had enjoyed that. She wasn't the smartest girl he had ever met, but brains had not been high on his list at the time. When Laura told him she didn't want to see him anymore, he was caught completely off guard. She'd never given him any sign that she was tired of him and Jack found himself genuinely hurt by her rejection. Jack had cared for her more than he'd realized. Adding insult to injury he later found out, through

Jack Adkins, that she was seeing a fella near German Hill. She had simply changed her mind and dumped him without so much as a "I'm sorry." Now he watched her looking at his cousin, all smiles. *Tom needed to stay away from that one. She was trouble*, he thought.

"Well, now, Calvin, who do we have here?" Tom asked, speaking bolder and louder than usual. It was Martha Cowles that answered him.

"This is Laura Foster, Tom."

Tom approached Laura.

"This is Laura Foster? Are you sure, Miz Cowles? The last time I saw Laura Foster, she was just a little thing."

Tom turned to Anne on the porch.

"But this ain't no little girl, Miz Cowles. This pretty little thing is a woman." He looked at Laura and winked.

Laura watched in a daze as the man of her dreams took her hand and kissed it. The wink, the smile, it was all there just like she knew it would be.

"I'm Tom Dooley, Miss Foster. I don't know if you remember me or not, but my family used to trade with your mama. We used to buy cloth from her and your Aunt Mary."

Laura remembered him and nodded.

"You and Jack Keaton over there used to pick on me." Laura gave a nervous glance toward Anne and Perline.

"Well, pretty lady, if you'll give me half a chance, I'll make it up to you as best I can."

Again, he turned and looked at Anne.

"Are you goin' to the molassy boilin' tomorrow night?" Tom asked.

Laura beamed with her answer. "Yes, I am."

"Well, I just might see you there."

Perline was fuming. In all the time she had been in Elkville, she had only been with one other man besides James. Jack Keaton was fun to be with sometimes and came to see her once in awhile. It was through Jack that Perline had heard about Laura Foster. She'd never met her, but she hated her just the same. Jack was still lovesick over Laura, and Perline knew it, no matter what he said. Now, Tom Dooley was home; the man she had waited and waited to meet was finally there, and Laura Foster was in the way again.

Unexpectedly, Anne stepped off the porch and stood by Perline.

"So, does this mean you'll be comin' to the dance tomorrow night, Tom?" Anne asked. "It would give you a chance to see everybody again. We've all missed ya. Maybe you and I could have a little talk. You don't mind, do you, James? Tom's an old friend."

James held on to Mary Beth and nodded his consent.

"No, Anne, I don't mind," he answered quietly.

Tom looked at Anne and Perline. They were both angry and he was glad.

"Well, I didn't know nothin' about no dance 'til just now, and I am awful tired. But I just might have to come now that I've met Miss Laura Foster."

He looked at Laura and winked.

"Besides, I've always liked Colonel Horton. He's a good man." He turned and looked Anne straight in the eyes and added, "True to his word."

Anne cast her eyes down and away from Tom's.

"Maybe we should have that talk tonight, Tom. Why don't you come by after supper?"

"I'll just have to see about that. I want to get home and get rested up for tomorrow night. I'm sure with all the dancin' and drinkin', I'll need it." Tom looked at Laura again and grinned.

He made a promise to himself right then, that he would not meet Anne that night. Tom remembered all too well what happened in Wilmington with Elizabeth and her husband. Married women were nothing but trouble and Anne was just like Elizabeth now. His mistake that day was looking back at her. He told himself not to, but he couldn't help it. Time had only made her more beautiful and his resolve quickly weakened. His heart took over his head. Before he was out of sight, he knew that he'd break his own promise before daybreak.

"We live out on Reedy Branch, Tom. Just down from Mama's."

He turned his back to her and answered loud enough for her to hear, "I said maybe."

Turning to Laura, he tipped his hat and gave her a wink and a grin. "I'll see you tomorrow night, Miss Laura."

Tom turned and started walking towards home. Calvin asked Hezekiah Kendall if he would fetch his wagon out back and catch up with Tom. The poor boy needed a ride, he thought. He was a Confederate soldier, going home to be with his family. The kindly storekeeper would make sure Tom did not have to travel home on foot.

Calvin shook his head as he watched Tom leave. "There goes a broken-hearted man, ma cherie."

Martha Cowles nodded. No matter what else happened in Tom's or Anne's life, she would always remember them before he left for war. So beautiful and young—and in love! *Fate and time could be cruel*, she thought.

Laura Foster watched Tom until he was completely out of sight. Anne and Perline stood behind her and sized up the competition—strangely united.

Jack Keaton threw down the stick he'd been whittling and put his knife away. He would make a point of visiting the Foster cabin the next day. Laura would be a fool to cross paths with Anne Melton and he planned to tell her so. *Women were not worth the powder to blow off their heads*, he thought.

CHAPTER SEVENTEEN

Tom's ma was on the porch scrubbing clothes on a washboard when Hezekiah drove up with Tom. It took her a minute for the reality of the situation to sink in. She had dreamed of this day for so long that when it finally came, it didn't seem real. It took seeing her son get off the wagon and hearing the sound of his voice for it to finally register. Tom looked at the woman on the porch. Her hair was grayer than he remembered, but the kind eyes and warm smile were those of his mother.

"I'm home, Mama," he declared. The tears he fought back so hard at the store broke free and ran down his cheeks. "How's my best girl?"

The next thing Mary Dooley knew, she was holding her son as tight as she could hold him. She was in such a state, she didn't remember how she got from the porch to her son. Her son was home, and she was filled with such emotion and overwhelming joy that nothing else mattered.

Eliza came to the door of the cabin and saw the two of them by the wagon. She grabbed her crutch and quickly made her way to her brother. After hugs and kisses and more than a few tears, the little family crossed the yard to the cabin.

When they reached the porch, Ma Dooley looked back and thanked Hezekiah for bringing Tom home.

"Would you be so kind as to go by and tell Anna and Cajah the news?" she asked. "It's on your way. Tell 'em I'm gonna cook a big supper tonight and I'll be needing some help."

Hezekiah nodded. "I'll be glad to do it, Miz Dooley." It was nice to see Mary so happy again. He liked the Dooley family. They were good people.

As the wagon drove off, Mary and Eliza led Tom into the cabin. Mary put some wood in the fireplace. Tom needed a nice warm bath, and she quickly sent Eliza to the well.

"It won't take long to heat up some water in this kettle," she told him. "You need a nice hot bath and a good nap. When you wake up, I'm gonna have supper cooked for ya. When Cajah gets here, I'll have him catch one of my hens and wring her neck; and then I'm gonna fry her up and fix some collards and biscuits. You could stand to put a little meat on your bones."

"Lord, it's good to be home!" Tom laughed, hugging his mama.

When the water was warm, Tom's mama poured it into a large tub on the back porch.

"When it cools off, you let me know; and I'll add some more hot water to it. I done started heating up some more."

Tom crawled into the tub and sat down. His mama handed him a bar of lye soap and hurried back into the house. Tom's back and feet ached and the warm water felt good. He sank down in the tub until the water touched his chin. Relaxed, he let his guard down enough to think back on what happened at the store. Tom had carried the memory of Anne all through the war. Seeing her face, remembering the sound of her voice was what kept him walking those last miles home when it was hard to put one foot in front of the other. What would he do without her?

At the table during supper, Eliza and Anna talked about the molassy boiling. Both of his sisters were excited, and they begged Tom to come with them. It sounded like fun, but Tom wasn't sure that he would be up to seeing Anne again so soon. He told the girls he might need to stay home and rest.

The table was laid out with all of his favorite foods—fried chicken, biscuits, collard greens in fat back, pork ribs, corn on the cob, mashed taters and gravy. He ate until he couldn't eat anymore. When his mama brought out the fried apple pies, Tom wasn't sure where he would put them, but then he saw the sparkle in her eyes; and somehow he was able to find the room.

Lying down on the bed after supper, Tom wondered if he would be able to sleep with so much weighing heavy on his mind. Luckily, sleep came fast. Tom closed his eyes and was lulled by the familiar sounds of Reedy Branch outside his window. He drifted off cushioned by feather pillows and warm quilts, comforted in the familiar surroundings of home.

Mary Dooley stood at the door of his room and said a little prayer. She thanked God for sending her boy home to his family. The sound of his gentle breathing filled her ears as she watched him. Her son was home and she wept for joy.

CHAPTER EIGHTEEN

Lotty sat straight up in bed and wiped the sweat from her forehead. Her heart was beating so loud she was certain the man beside her would hear it, too; but he was sound asleep.

Quietly, she got up and tiptoed to the window. Bright moonlight made it easy to see outside. The man was not there. Even though she knew it was only a dream, she shuddered remembering it. Lotty was smart enough to know that only fools ignored the messages of the spirits, and the images in her mind were so powerful that she knew it was a warning.

It had been years since Lotty had dreamed about him. So much time had passed that sometimes it was hard for her to remember his face at all. But tonight, he'd come back to her while she slept, clear as day.

She was standing on the front porch when she saw him. Up on the ridge above the house, he stood. The sun was setting behind him and silhouetted him in shades of gold.

At first, Lotty assumed he was beckoning to her; but when she turned around, she found Anne standing behind her. Fearfully she realized it was her daughter he wanted. Anne was wearing a red dress and looked as beautiful as Lotty had ever seen her. She tried to talk to her; but Anne didn't hear her, walking past Lotty towards the ridge. A blanket of flowers covered the ground at Anne's feet, leading her towards the top. Her daughter was barefoot. Lotty watched as Anne's delicate feet stepped on the carpet of petals.

Looking around, Lotty noticed the landscape was starting to change. The sky turned to deep pinks and orange. Mud appeared where the carpet of flowers had been, and she watched Anne step into it unaware. With every step, the mud crept higher on Anne's feet . . . to her ankles . . . her shins. Still, Anne kept walking up the hill.

The sky turned blood red and Lotty knew if Anne went over that ridge, she would be lost to her forever. She tried to step off the porch, but the planks wrapped around her feet and tied them to the spot where she stood. Vines sprang up, entan-

gling themselves in the porch posts and rails. Frantic, Lotty screamed Anne's name, but no sound came out. The man on the ridge looked at Lotty and smiled. Lotty knew that pure evil hid behind the handsome mask he wore.

As Anne reached the top of the ridge, the man who'd once been the love of Lotty's life reached for their daughter. Anne took his hand and smiled. She seemed so happy. Lotty watched feeling sick to her stomach as her girl made the mistake she knew so well. She found her voice in time to scream to Anne, "Don't go! Please come back!" But Anne did not hear her mother. Lotty's dangerous man nodded to her as he guided Anne. It was then that his looks begin to change. Confused at first, she wasn't sure who was taking her girl away, but as Anne faded from sight she realized who it really was.

Lotty Foster had been home with company all day. She hadn't seen or talked to anyone else, but a profound and deep certainty told her he was back. Lotty knew Tom Dooley was back in Elkville, and trouble would follow. Shaking, she made her way to the washbasin and splashed cold water on her face. Trembling hands found a small bottle of nightshade leaves on the shelf above the basin. Taking it with her, she went to the stove and boiled some water. When the water was ready, Lotty poured the water into a mug and took a few leaves from the bottle and placed them into a muslin steeping bag. When she could see the water was dark enough, she took the steeping bag out and drank the relaxing herb straight down. She sat in a chair by the stove and waited to feel its effect. After awhile she began to yawn, and it became hard to keep her eyes open. Relieved, Lotty knew the nightshade had done its work. Quietly she crawled back in bed with her friend and scooted up next to him. His body felt warm and safe. She was grateful for his company. Lotty Foster was known for being tough and mean. Many folks told tall tales of her drinking and the men she kept company with, but few really knew her. No one knew the things she protected inside her, locked up tight.

But Lotty knew. There was a little girl hiding there—*a little girl who was still afraid of the dark.*

CHAPTER NINETEEN

Tom was surprised at how easily he managed to fall asleep after supper. He had been blindsided at the store by Anne's marriage to James Melton. All the dreams he held onto during the war had vanished in seconds. Tom was mad and hurt, and that did not make for a good night's sleep. Still, the warm bath, good food and sheer exhaustion won out; and he was asleep before the sun set that evening.

Having gone to sleep so early, he awoke in the wee hours of the morning. Looking out his bedroom window, he could see the stars were out and the moon was still high in the sky. He tried to push Anne from his mind, but could not and in minutes, was dressed and on the path to James Melton's cabin. Walking in the dark he convinced himself that his only reason for meeting Anne was to find out why she hadn't waited for him. His heart ached, and there was such a deep gnawing sense of loss inside him. Tom convinced himself that the girl at least owed him an explanation.

As he got closer to Anne's cabin, he looked up on the hill and saw light coming from a window at Lotty Foster's. He wondered what no good she was up to. Angry, Tom looked away. Anne had been wrong not to wait for him; but in his gut he knew Lotty Foster had something to do with it.

As he reached the Melton cabin, Tom stopped and looked around the yard. At the edge of the woods on James' property he saw Anne's bleached white gown through the trees, and suddenly nothing else mattered. Tom forgot his anger—he forgot his pain—and ran to his girl. Grabbing her, Tom kissed her on the lips passionately. After a moment he stopped. The kiss felt wrong. Tom grabbed who he thought to be Anne by the shoulders and held her back to get a better look. In the moonlight he stared into the cat green eyes of Perline Foster. Perline looked back at Tom and giggled.

"You should be more careful who you're kissin', Mr. Dooley," she flirted.

From the minute he met Perline at the store, Tom had disliked this girl. It had been evident from the first that the little troublemaker seemed to enjoy the pain and embarrassment she caused. Tom knew Perline would delight in telling Anne about this when it was to her advantage. Repulsed, he decided to ignore her.

"Where is she?" he demanded.

"I swanee you're impatient ain't ya?" Perline laughed. "You could at least try and be nice to me. Anne's had me out here waiting for you for hours." Perline leaned in for another kiss.

Tom pushed her away. "Just go get her, Perline," Tom ordered.

Perline stepped back and glared at Tom. "Fool man!" she snapped. "I'll go and get your married girlfriend for ya." Turning, she began muttering to herself and stomped off to the cabin.

A few minutes later, Anne opened the door and stepped outside. Tom watched her as she peered into the woods looking for him. Stepping out just enough for her to see him, he waved to her. When she saw him her face lit up. Time melted away and Anne ran to Tom with the same reckless abandon he remembered so well. She wasted no time in saying hello. Greedily, she grabbed him, kissing him over and over. Remembering why he came, Tom pulled away, resolute. He wanted to let go and be with her but he wanted answers more.

"I've come here for answers, Anne. I need to know why," he said.

Anne was shocked by his rejection. She tried to start an argument to avoid the question.

"You're late," she argued, trying to ignore his question. "Supper's been over and I've been up all night waitin' for you!"

"It don't matter if I'm late or not and there ain't no use changin' the subject. I want to know why, Anne. You tell me why!"

Anne's expression hardened. "I did what I had to do. Remember, you left me here all alone to fend for myself, so I did. Besides, I did it for us, in a way. I did it for you."

Her words angered Tom. "You did it for me? Well, tell me, Anne, what else did you do for me besides leave me for another man?"

Anne's anger quickly faded. She needed to make him understand. For three and a half long years she had prepared herself for this moment but now that Tom was finally home, Anne couldn't find the right words to say.

"He's got money, Tom. I don't have to work on the farm and get all old and worn out like Mama did. I can keep myself lookin' nice so you won't get tired of me."

As soon as the words were out of her mouth, Tom knew. Lotty was behind this.

"What else did your mama tell you?"

"Mama didn't do all the convincin', Tom."

"The Hell she didn't," he yelled.

Rage filled him. Anne had thrown away everything they had together because of some fool notion her mama put into her head. Tom grabbed her by the shoulders and shook her. He was angry enough to scare her now.

"Why did you have to go and do this?" he demanded.

Anne broke free and staggered away from him. As she did, she happened to look up and see Mary Beth standing in the doorway. She walked out of the woods far enough for the child to see her.

"Mary Beth!" she yelled in her angriest whisper, "you get on back in that house and go to bed before I skin you alive."

Mary Beth stood there in her little white nightgown and gave her mama an angry look. She pointed to the door. Tom was surprised and touched by her forcefulness. She was clearly motioning her mama inside. The child refused to budge until her mama started to move towards her. When Anne did, Mary Beth flashed a defiant look at her mother and stomped back inside.

"You shouldn't talk to her like that," Tom said when the child was gone.

"It's nothin' to you," Anne answered.

"The Hell it ain't. I saw her at the store today, Anne. I got a real good look. That little girl is my blood and you know it." Anne's silence was answer enough for Tom.

Everything felt as if it was falling down around him—Anne's marriage, the little girl with the dark eyes. Tom moved away from her and leaned against a tree.

"Nothing feels the same. It's funny, all I could think about while I was gone was gettin' back home to you and Ma and the girls. Now, I wanna be anywhere but here."

He slid down the tree and sat, head in hands. Anne walked over and sat down beside him, gently putting his head on her shoulder. She stroked his hair as she comforted him.

"James Melton is an old fool with lots of money," she whispered. "He doesn't touch me, Tom, I swear. That's what Perline is for. James is in there asleep right now with Perline. She knows her place."

Tom looked up at her. He could smell lavender in her hair and felt the silkiness of her skin.

Anne took his face in her hands and looked deep into his eyes.

"You and I are still the same," she cooed. "We will always be the same, no matter what happens—just you and me. I've forgiven you many times, Tom. Caroline Barnes is just one of many and you know it. None of them could ever tear us apart and James Melton won't either."

Pulling back from him, she loosened the front of her gown. Tom watched as the gown fell off her shoulder. All the promises he'd made to himself melted away. Greedily, he pulled the gown off her. Anne's breathing started to quicken as Tom brushed his lips against her bare shoulder. She closed her eyes, as his dark curls brushed against her skin. Pulling away, Anne picked the gown up off the ground to cover her and pointed to the cabin.

"I put some quilts in the attic," she whispered.

Yanking the cloth from her fingers, Tom pulled her roughly to him.

"I don't want no quilts in no attic," he murmured.

Perline could just make them out from the crack in the door as she stood watching. She had not gone back to James Melton's bed that night. Instead she stood and watched as the two fell into the shadows of the trees. Perline touched her lips.

They still burned from his kiss.

CHAPTER TWENTY

Laura Foster woke early. She ran to the window and looked out. The sun was coming up and she was happy to see a clear sky. With no rain in sight, the weather would be perfect for Colonel Horton's molassy boilin'. Happily, she made her way to the closet and pulled out her new blue dress. Her Aunt Mary made it for her the month before. It was soft blue with lace on the collar and sleeves.

She picked up her hand mirror from the top of her dresser and carefully studied her face and hair. *How should she wear her hair tonight*, she wondered, *up or down?* She always looked forward to Colonel Horton's annual molassy boiling, but this time would be different. Tom Dooley told her at the store that he would see her at the dance, and she wanted to look especially pretty.

There would be enough food to feed Lee's entire army. Fiddlers would come from all over to play, and there would be plenty of dancing and courting going on. Her daddy told them he heard that Colonel Horton planned to roast at least five pigs, and his farm hands were getting up at the crack of dawn to fix the barbecue. Aunt Mary was making sweet tater pies, and Laura had baked an apple stack cake the night before. As she peered out of her bedroom window, Laura could barely make out her daddy and brother standing by the barn. She needed to hurry. They'd already done their morning chores and James was holding the morning bucket of milk.

Laura went to the kitchen to start breakfast. Before she could do anything else, Will and James needed to be fed. After she mixed the dough and patted out the biscuits, she put them in the oven and hurriedly scrambled eggs and boiled grits. Once the red eye gravy was on the table, she went to the porch and called across the yard to her daddy and brother. Impatiently, she waited for them to finish eating. After everyone was through and breakfast was cleared away she put on her shawl and went outside to take a walk. She needed to do some thinking.

The path Laura chose was not used as much as some of the others. It was a quiet path, perfect for thinking. As she walked she tried to remember every detail of her meeting with Tom Dooley at the store. He'd been all that she could think about since. That grin, the wink, the smile that gave her goose bumps; he was everything she'd ever dreamed a perfect man should be. When he winked at her, she knew he was the one. Bob Cummings and Jack Keaton never made her feel the way she felt when she saw Tom Dooley. *Tom Dooley*—even his name made her smile.

From the very minute she saw him, she knew there was something between them. She could feel it. The attraction was so strong for her she felt embarrassed, looking around to see if anyone else had noticed. No matter how silly her father or brother might say she was, *a woman knew when she found the right one*. She wished her mama was still alive to talk to. She would've understood when Laura said what was in her heart. The men in Laura's house would never understand a woman's intuition.

It was almost time for the mid day meal when she returned. She was surprised at how late it was; the time had flown by. Laura ran to her room and pulled the new dress from the closet. Whirling around the room she laughed and danced. It was finally time to get ready for the party.

CHAPTER TWENTY-ONE

Standing in the bedroom, Perline sewed the final button on the dress and checked the bodice with Anne wearing it. Anne had insisted the bodice be skin tight to show off her tiny waist and full bosom. When Perline was done, Anne ran to the mirror on her dresser and took a long look at herself.

"Perfect," she said.

Anne was as happy as Perline had ever seen her.

"Red is your color, Anne; that's for certain."

Perline secretly wished she could rip the dress to shreds; but then she'd have to answer to James; and she might end up with no food and no place to sleep again. Gazing into the mirror, Anne pulled her hair away from her face. Perline quickly secured it with tortoise shell combs, letting the rest of Anne's hair fall down her back.

Perline knew what was next. Anne dipped a handkerchief in some pokeberry juice and patted her lips. It turned them scarlet red like her dress. As much as she had learned to hate Anne, Perline couldn't deny her beauty.

When Perline was little, her mama had cleaned for a wealthy family in Watauga. The family's little girl owned a doll that looked just like Anne. The doll had dark curls, a porcelain face, and its lips and cheeks were scarlet red. Perline loved the doll and asked her mama for one of her own. But her mother explained that this could never happen. A doll like that cost more than they made in a month, she told her. About a week later, her mama gave Perline a cloth doll she'd made especially for her. Perline studied the doll with its rag face and little bonnet that hid the fact that it had no hair. It was plain like her, she thought.

Ashamed of the doll and herself she grabbed it and ran to the barn. Looking around, she removed the plank that bolted the door and went inside. Perline made her way to the ladder leading to the loft and climbed up. When she reached the top she found a comfortable corner and nestled down in the hay. It was quiet there and peaceful. It was her safe place. There in the quiet of the loft, Perline cradled the rag doll her mama had lovingly made for her and wept. She rocked the doll back and forth and sobbed. *She was nothing more than rag and stuffing herself*, she thought. The next day when her mama went back to clean for the wealthy family, Perline went with her. When she was certain that no one else was around, she went to the little rich girl's room while her mother served the mid day meal to the family. Quickly, she found the porcelain doll and stuffed it underneath her skirt. After the meal was over and put away, Perline and her mama finished their chores and headed for home. That evening, after supper, the little thief took the stolen doll outside and went around behind the shed next to the barn. Perline found her daddy's axe where he always left it, stuck in an old stump. She pulled and tugged with all her might until the axe broke free. Perline carefully placed the porcelain doll on the stump and raising the axe above her head, brought it down with all her might, smashing the pretty thing to bits and pieces. Glad to be rid of it, she scooped the broken bits into her apron and buried them in the woods. Once the porcelain doll was gone, she found that her rag doll didn't look as plain. Perline remembered the dolls as she watched Anne in front of the vanity mirror and wished to be rid of Anne, too.

"Perline," Anne said, "I want to do something for you."

Anne walked to her closet and pulled out a bright green skirt and a calico green blouse. "Wear this, if you want. I hope you find somebody special tonight."

"I'll wish on it, Anne," Perline said.

Perline knew what she would wish. She took the dress off the bed where Anne had laid it and held it up. Perline and Anne were about the same size; it just might work. Maybe if she washed up and fixed her hair, Tom would take notice. The green would look good with her eyes. Self consciously she brushed the dirt from her left cheek and tried to imagine her hair swept back from her face.

The two women spent the afternoon primping and working on their hair. James stayed out of the house for most of the day, working in the fields. He came back by mid-afternoon to wash up.

The hours passed by slowly. When James walked in and told them it was time to go, Perline finally allowed herself to get excited. She was surprised at how nice he looked and smelled.

Perline took out a big basket and packed it carefully with the green beans she had fixed, two jars of pickles, and two jars of pickled beets. James was proud to be taking Perline's pickles. He said it was a sign of wealth to have enough salt to make them. *The strangest things made him happy,* she thought. As quiet and timid as James seemed, he liked for people to know he was successful. He helped Anne into the wagon. Perline watched as Anne put a tiny foot up on the wagon's sideboard. James had polished the new shoes he'd made for her and they shined in the sunlight. When he was sure Anne was settled, Perline climbed into the back of the wagon by herself. For all the special care she'd taken with her looks and all the time she'd spent in his bed, James didn't even notice her. He got up and took the reins, sitting proudly beside his little porcelain doll.

With a "giddyup," the foolish man steered the pair of horses in the direction of Colonel Horton's farm.

CHAPTER TWENTY-TWO

The Horton farm was alive with activity. Lanterns, torches and camp-fires lit up the night sky all around. The fiddlers were on the porch playing and singing like they were possessed. Long plank tables were set up outside, piled high with bowls of green beans, squash, pies of all kinds, cornbread and hush puppies. Some couples were already dancing. Several of the ladies were seated at a big table down by the lily pond. Behind the barn, a large group of men was gathered, drinking shine. They tried to stay out of view as best they could to avoid being chastised by their wives and girlfriends.

Will Foster hugged his daughter and looked sternly at both of his children. "I'm goin' over to talk to the men folk for a bit. Y'all mind your manners, ya hear me?"

"We hear ya, Papa," James said.

Will Foster turned to James and ordered, "You watch out for your sister tonight, boy. She looks too pretty not to be looked after."

"I will," James said. "Don't you worry about a thing."

James and Laura walked around and talked to some of their friends. When Will was safely out of sight, they nodded to each other as brothers and sisters often do, and went their separate ways. Relieved to be on his own, James made his way to the barbecue table. Laura was glad to be rid of him. She wanted to be alone when she ran into Tom.

Nearing the barn, Laura could hear the men laughing. She knew they were telling tall tales and drinking. Amidst the trees and woodpiles, they sat around a campfire drinking hard cider. Each one of them tried to outdo the other with their stories. *It would get wilder and louder as the night went on,* Laura thought. *It always did.* Some of the storytellers were eating plates of barbecue. Laura strained her eyes and ears searching for Tom, but he was nowhere in sight. The light was dim, and the crowd and smoke from the campfire made it hard to see who was who. Laura recognized her uncle's voice. J.W. was enjoying his cider as usual. She quietly inched closer, trying not to be seen.

A piece of lace from her dress snagged on the barn wall and she pulled it free, taking special care not to tear the precious blue store bought cloth. Covered by darkness and shadow, Laura eavesdropped on the men. They would be angry and run her off if they found her there. Man talk was not meant for women to hear.

"It's true," J. W. was saying. "They was burnin' down the barns and all the outhouses. They was getting' ready to torch the place."

Ben Ferguson and Jack Adkins along with some of the others were making fun of J.W. They were calling him a crazy old man and laughing. It was Colonel Horton who quickly came to his defense.

"J.W.'s right." The Colonel said. He leaned over to J.W. and asked him to pass the jug of shine.

"The Colonel leadin' the charge left Fort Defiance standin' because he saw that Rufus Lenoir was wearin' a Masonic pin on his lapel. Turned out that the Yank Colonel was a Mason, too. Rufus told me so himself. Don't you know old General Stoneman was mad as Hell when he heard about that."

Jack Adkins jumped into the mix. He'd been drinking and was angry. Laura laughed to herself as she listened. Poor Jack was *always* angry about something. He was nice looking, with big brown eyes and sandy blonde hair. But he was a big fellow and could be a real bully, making him hard to handle at times. Jack cut a wide path when he was mad.

"I don't know why he should be," he yelled. "Stoneman left us with nothing. That raid took most of our good homes and even Calvin's telegraph machine. Stoneman did such a good job, he didn't even know that General Lee had surrendered at Appomattox, and the war was over for three or four days. I don't know about you, boys, but my family's pretty hungry right now. My mama's rail thin and my sisters . . . " Jack shook his head, raised his glass to his buddies, and yelled, "Here's to General George Stoneman . . . may he rot in Hell!"

The crowd went wild with cheers and jeers. It was pretty clear that the men were all feeling the effects of the shine. It was also clear that even though the war was officially over, the men still felt divided from the North. Ben Ferguson laughed at his old buddy.

"You are depressing to be around, Jack. I'm gonna go and find me a girl," Ben said.

Ben left the others laughing like he always did. He was a good-natured fellow. *Of course he had to be*, Laura thought. He had endured a lot of teasing growing up. He was handsome, really; but when he was younger, he'd been teased unmercifully for his shock of bright red hair. No matter what, Laura thought, he had some of he prettiest blue eyes she'd ever seen.

Laura heard Jack tell him he ought to go talk to Laura Foster. It felt strange, hearing the men talk about her. She heard Ben tell him, "No."

"I saw Tom Dooley talkin' to Laura at the store yesterday, Jack. I believe I'll wait on that one. I know how Tom is, and I don't feel like getting' my nose broke tonight."

This pleased Laura to no end. It meant other people noticed the attention Tom had given her. It wasn't just her imagination or the hopes of a foolish girl.

Jack continued his rant. "Just how many women does Tom Dooley have to have? Why, if I never saw him again . . . "

"What's goin' on fellas?" she heard Tom ask.

Watching Jack, she hadn't noticed Tom walking over to the group. Laura jumped at the sound of Tom's voice. Chill bumps rose all up and down her arms.

"Nothin'. Not a damn thing!" Jack yelled, slamming his cup down on a barrel.

Jack Adkins stormed off past Laura around the corner of the barn in a huff. She was grateful he didn't notice her.

"What's wrong with Jack?" Tom asked.

"Aw, some of us don't have the luck you have with women, Tom," Ben answered.

Tom laughed out loud.

"That's not luck, Ben. That's talent."

Amidst the jeers and cheers from his buddies, Tom took a big swig of shine and started walking in Laura's direction. Laura knew she needed to move. The last thing she wanted was to be discovered. Carefully and slowly, she rounded the corner of the barn. Laura looked up just in time to avoid running straight into Tom.

"Well, hello, Mr. Dooley. Do you remember me?" she managed to blurt out, trying to cover the situation with humor.

Surprised to see her, Tom laughed at her remark.

"Remember you? Why, pretty lady, you are all that I've thought about since I met you at the store."

Bob Cummings watched from a distance. He had been keeping an eye on Laura ever since she arrived. By the smiles and laughter, he could tell they were flirting with each other and it made him angry. Gathering his courage he walked over to them. Big gatherings made the little schoolteacher uncomfortable. Still, he had come especially to see Laura and Tom was ruining his plans. Coming up behind the two he tapped Laura on the shoulder.

"Laura, would you like some cider?" Bob asked.

Laura turned to see Bob standing there staring at them. He looked so out of place in his fancy duds. She tried to be as polite as she knew how, but she was not going to let Bob get in the way of her time with Tom. It was too important to her. Besides, she'd never encouraged Bob in the least. Laura did not believe that a girl belonged to a man just because he decided she should. A woman should have her own say in the matter. Laura made up her mind to get rid of Bob as fast as she could.

"Why, thank you, Bob. I would. How about you, Tom? Would you like some cider, too?"

Tom was embarrassed for Bob. He hadn't known that Bob was interested in Laura when he was flirting with her at the store. Had he known, he wouldn't have carried on so with her. Men generally save that kind of insult for their enemies. Seeing that Bob was clearly embarrassed, Tom tried to smooth over the situation.

"Well, Laura, I . . . " Tom started.

Before Tom could finish, Bob interrupted him.

"I don't aim to get but one glass, Laura," Bob said firmly.

Tom waited politely. He realized there was nothing he could say now. It would be up to Laura to handle Bob. He did not aim to get personal with anybody right now. After all, he'd only been home a day. Besides, there were plenty of women to go around. Laura was pretty; but he suspected with an innocent like her, he would have to pretend to fall in love; and he just didn't have the energy or the inclination. Other women wouldn't be as much trouble. Of course, they wouldn't be much of a challenge either, and Tom did like a good challenge. Tom had no idea how determined Laura was.

To his amazement, Laura snapped at the schoolteacher, "Then, I'm not thirsty, Bob."

The men at the barn murmured and watched. Some laughed. Poor Bob skulked off behind the barn. Jack Keaton was back there smoking a pipe of tobacco. He had been watching Laura since she got to the party, too. Laura had seen him in the distance several times, but tried to ignore him. *Misery loves company*, Laura thought. Seeing the two together, she could only imagine what they would say about her, but she didn't care. She turned to Tom and smiled.

This girl might be interesting after all, Tom thought. That old feeling of living on the edge kicked in for him. It was familiar and felt good in a place where he had not had time to settle.

"You are feistier than I thought you were, little girl."

Laura smiled, taking his words as a compliment.

"Is that a bad thing?" she asked.

"There's nothin' bad about you," he replied.

Tom took her by the hand, and led her in the direction of the barn.

"Let's dance," he said, grinning. "Do you like to dance?"

Laura nodded. *Her dreams were really coming true*, she thought.

On the way to the barn, Laura and Tom laughed as they watched Calvin and Martha Cowles' arrival. The couple was making their way to the food tables. Calvin was carrying a sliced ham and Martha had two rhubarb pies. He was whirling her around, and she was trying to balance them as she turned.

"Come on, you good lookin' hunk 'a woman. We got some eatin' and drinkin' and dancin' to do."

"I'm comin', Calvin."

Martha turned to Betsy Scott and Martha Gilbert as she was being dragged to the food tables, trying to explain her husband's behavior.

"Once in a while he acts like this," she explained. "Acts like a crazy man; wants to dance and drink like he did when he was young."

Martha Gilbert had already enjoyed several mugs of hard cider by the time the Cowles arrived.

Giddy and holding on to Jonathan's arm she asked, "What else does he want to do that he did when he was young, Miz Cowles?"

Martha Cowles pretended to be shocked by the question. "Martha Gilbert, you better be in church come Sunday mornin'. Lucifer is workin' on you," she teased.

"Yes, he is, Miz Cowles. Praise God, yes, he is!" Jonathan yelled, raising his mug of hard cider.

Shocked, Martha Cowles turned to stare at Jonathan Gilbert. Plied with corn liquor, the Gilberts were clearly enjoying themselves.

Everyone laughed and clapped for Jonathan.

"What's gotten into those two?" Martha Cowles asked Calvin.

In all the time that she had known her, Miz Cowles had never seen Martha Gilbert so giddy.

Calvin looked at the happy couple. "Lots of hard cider, sweetheart, lots and lots of hard cider."

Martha lovingly laughed with her husband and pointed a warning finger at him as he pulled her towards the barn.

Jack Adkins finally found the girl he was looking for. Caroline Barnes was standing at the food table with some of her friends. Awkwardly, he rushed over to her. She was wearing a pretty blue dress. It wasn't fancy like some of the others, but that didn't matter to Jack. What did matter was that it was cut real low. That view to Jack Adkins was prettier than any bow or piece of lace could ever be. The poor boy was so smitten with Caroline and all her curls and curves—he could barely control himself. What was even funnier to his friends was that, for all his temper, Jack behaved like a lamb around Caroline.

"Wanna dance, Caroline?" Jack asked in his sweetest voice.

Caroline turned just in time to see the Melton wagon pull up by the barn. She grabbed Jack's arm and held on to him for dear life.

"I would love to dance with you, Jack," she said.

Caroline never took her eyes off the wagon. She pulled Jack quickly into the barn. The crowded barn was a good, safe place to get lost. Jack Adkins had not seen the Meltons arrive, so he had no idea what had caused all the excitement in his new sweetheart. He just knew that Caroline had never been so thrilled to see him and he was convinced that she had finally fallen for him in a big way. His heart swelled with pride.

At the same time Caroline Barnes spotted the Meltons, Laura did, too. She held on to Tom's arm and turned to see if he had noticed. By the look on his face he clearly had. Trying to hide his feelings he turned to Laura and smiled. Laura continued to watch the Meltons out of the corner of her eye as she talked to Tom.

James got down from the wagon and tied the horses to a hitching post. He walked over and helped Anne down. Laura noticed how gentle he was with his wife. As soon as Anne's feet hit the ground, she took off without so much as a word or a glance to her husband. She left James standing there staring after her. Laura's cheeks burned. She didn't know James well, but she felt ashamed for him.

Laura could tell Anne was clearly searching for Tom. He must have thought the same thing and quickly pulled Laura into the crowd. A pang of jealousy washed over Laura as she turned and watched her cousin. People stopped and stared when Anne walked by. No matter what people thought about her, she was an unusually beautiful woman. Men always gawked and women always turned green at the sight of her. James Melton's money, and Lotty's and Perline's abilities as seamstresses, made her one of the best dressed women in Elkville. Anne was wearing a scarlet dress, with black lace on the bodice and cuffs. *As beautiful as her cousin was, she looked like the devil's daughter in it*, Laura thought. The flames from the fires reflected in the shine of the scarlet cloth, as Anne flashed through the crowd of people and tables.

Perline got out of the wagon with no one to help. She noticed Tom right off, but decided not to tell Anne. Instead, she let her go off in the wrong direction looking for him. As soon as Anne was out of sight, Perline headed straight for the couple. She glared at Laura as she walked past them. On the porch of the big house, she spotted Lotty with the fiddlers. Her aunt was laughing and drinking and sizing up her next customer. *That shouldn't take long*, Perline thought. Lotty was good at getting men to come home with her. One fiddler in particular was patting Lotty on her backside. *Poor fool*, Perline laughed to herself; *his pockets would be empty by morning.*

She decided to get some cider and look for Jack Keaton. Approaching the cider table, she could hear Gwendolyn, Betsy, and Martha Gilbert gossiping. Martha Cowles was getting some cider for Calvin and herself. Perline decided to stand back and listen before she stepped any closer.

"Well, the excitement is sure gonna pick up now," she heard Betsy say, pointing to James at the wagon.

"Hush, Betsy. Anne's a married woman now. Things'll work out alright," Martha Cowles chided.

Ignoring Martha, Gwendolyn chimed in.

"Her mama is over there on the porch with them fiddle players. She wasn't invited to this dance, now was she? Just up and came with them fiddlers."

It was so like Gwen to make trouble for someone at a party, Martha Cowles thought.

"Then maybe you would like to go over there and tell her to leave?" she asked curtly.

Old Gwen ignored Martha. "I hear the minute Tom came home Anne stopped behaving like a married woman."

Martha did not wait to hear anymore. She put her hands on her hips and walked over to Gwen.

109

"Gwen, you are headed straight for Hell," she answered, pointing her finger at the old gossip.

Betsy couldn't stand it any longer. Not living too far from the Meltons, she'd heard the gossip. Everyone on Gladys Fork Road was talking.

"But, it's true," she chimed in.

Perline decided this was the perfect time to give them something to really gossip about.

"What's true?" she asked.

Betsy was caught off guard. Perline worked for the Meltons and Betsy did not want her words repeated to Anne. The last thing she wanted was to be threatened by Anne Melton.

"Nothin'," she answered timidly.

"Well, it had to be somethin' or you wouldn't be talkin' about it. Course I can't imagine what it might be," Perline teased, grinning from ear to ear. "But if I was to pick a juicy subject to gossip about, my first choice would be James Melton's new wife, Anne—and her 'other man.'"

Betsy was shocked that Perline was actually talking to them like this. She clearly had juicy information. The temptation to find out what Perline knew far outweighed the danger for Betsy and she took Perline's bait, letting her curiosity get the best of her.

Her large brown eyes sparkled with excitement. "Is it true?"

This pleased Perline to no end. She had their full attention.

"Yes, Ma'am. I seen it with my own eyes."

"That's enough, Perline," Martha interrupted. "Let's have fun tonight and forget all of this sinful gossiping."

Jack Keaton came up behind Perline and slid his arm around her waist. Perline was glad to see him. She turned and kissed him in front of the women. Embarrassed, the ladies cast their eyes to the ground.

"Oh, I intend to have fun tonight, Miz Cowles. Don't you worry about me. I'm ready for a good time."

Perline picked up two cups of cider, took Jack Keaton's hand, and the two headed in the direction of the barn. When they were gone, Betsy clapped her hands and whirled around to her friends. She had good gossip, hard cider, and her favorite skirt on.

"Well, I intend to have some fun tonight, too—devil or no devil," Betsy declared. "Where's that hard cider Calvin was talkin' about? I'm gonna ask Hezekiah Kendall to dance."

Martha Cowles was just about to chastise Betsy but Calvin came up and grabbed her hand.

"All right, my turtle dove, let's dance. Let's get these folks to the barn."

Calvin pointed to Doc, "Doc Carter, find your missus and come on," he shouted. Whirling around he continued to point out friends in the crowd. He was clearly in a festive mood. "Will Foster, you get Mary Dooley and let's see some serious foot stompin'. Hezekiah! I believe somebody's lookin' for you! And somebody get Lotty Foster away from them fiddle players so's they can play them things."

Calvin started pulling his little wife towards the music.

"All right, Calvin, but don't you be jerkin' me around, and watch my toes," Martha fussed. "You had me limpin' for three days the last time we tried this."

Ignoring Martha, Calvin continued to yell. "Come on everybody, let's dance."

Gwendolyn Smith stood at the cider table alone. "Dancin' is the devil's work," she yelled.

"Then, what are you doin' here?" Martha snapped.

In a huff, Gwen ignored Martha and marched off to the barn.

Laughing, Tom and Laura made their way towards the music, too.

Tom turned Laura around, teasing her. "Well, Laura Foster, let's see if you are as feisty on the dance floor as you are at the cider table."

Tom winked at Laura, and she winked back before she had time to think about it. They both laughed again. *This one was fun to be with. Surprisingly, they were hitting it off,* Tom thought.

Anne Melton stood at the cider table and watched as Tom guided Laura into the barn. Jack Keaton and Perline stood behind her. Furious, Anne moved towards them, but Perline put her hand on Anne's shoulder.

"Now, how would it look for a respectable married woman like yourself to be chasing after another man at a dance?" Perline asked.

Anne turned to Perline. She was mad, and Perline was an easy target for her anger. She slid her hand up Perline's back to the nape of her neck and grabbed her hair, yanking it hard.

"You may think this is funny now, but it won't be when I get you home. You're just jealous and wantin' to make trouble for me and Tom," she whispered. "Well, you can look all you want, but he'll never look back." Anne laughed a cruel and fun-making laugh. "My God, take a look at yourself."

Anne tightened her grip and Perline winced in pain. For a minute she thought Anne would pull her hair out by the roots. "If I so much as even think you are runnin' your mouth here tonight, I will beat the livin' hell out of you when I get you home. Do you understand me?"

Perline knew it would do her no good to stand up to Anne. Jack Keaton would be no help. He was the kind that would enjoy seeing two women fight. James, of course, would side with Anne, no matter what was said or done. Out of the corner of her eye, Perline noticed that people were staring at them. Swallowing her pride, she nodded.

"I hear ya, Anne."

Anne turned and looked around the crowd. *She'd put a stop to this.* She saw Bob Cummings standing by the barn door. He looked like he'd just lost his best friend. It made him easy prey for Anne Melton. Jack Keaton knew right off what Anne was thinking and followed her as she made her way over to Bob. *Things were going to get interesting,* he thought to himself, laughing.

Perline started after Jack but stopped when she felt the firm grip of Lotty Foster's fingers on her shoulders.

Lotty turned Perline around to face her, "You better be careful, Perline. You better be real careful," she warned.

Lotty and her fiddler walked past Perline and went into the barn. Perline had no doubt that Lotty had seen and heard everything.

Anne reached Bob Cummings just as the fiddlers were tuning up for another round of dancing.

"Bob Cummings, you aren't gonna let Tom Dooley dance with your girl without a fight; are you?"

Bob didn't know what to say. He was hurt and embarrassed; but if she was suggesting that he dance with her, he wasn't sure that would be a good idea. Dancing with James Melton's wife didn't seem like the wisest solution to him. Helplessly, he looked to Anne and then to Jack Keaton. It was clear that his new buddy Jack agreed with her. The poor fellow didn't see any way out of the situation.

"I reckon not," he answered timidly.

Jack jumped right in to the conversation. He knew how upset Bob was. The two men had talked earlier about sweet little Miss Laura Foster. He slapped the timid schoolteacher on his back.

"Dance with her, Bob. Let's teach Laura a lesson. She's stabbed me in the back, and now you. That girl deserves whatever we decide to dish out. Get her where it hurts, Bob. Go for the heart."

The poor man allowed himself to be pushed into the middle of the strangest square dance anyone in those parts had ever seen.

He bowed to Anne and asked timidly, "Miz Melton, may I have the pleasure of this dance?"

Anne giggled and kissed him on the cheek. "Why Bob, I thought you'd never ask."

Jack Keaton let out a whoop and then yelled to the top of his lungs, "Go get her, boy!"

Perline turned to see James Melton's sister, Sarah, and her husband Benton, standing nearby. From the look on Sarah's face, she wasn't at all surprised by what she saw. Sarah still kept in touch with her brother, but she didn't come to the house to visit. Instead, she had James over for Sunday dinner every week after church. Anne did not attend church with her husband and was never invited to dinner. Sarah shook her head. This was not the first time her brother's wife had shamed him in public. Sarah had seen her behave like this many times, and she hated Anne for it. When she tried to tell James things she knew, he would ignore her. She would never understand why he was so taken with her. She couldn't even bring herself to think of Anne as a Melton. Beauty and sexual desire couldn't be all of it, surely. There had to be something more.

Amidst the hay and the barn wood, the music cranked up and the dance took off. The caller of the dance directed the men to walk in. Each man stepped forward and bowed to his partner. Laura was dancing with Tom, Perline with Jack Keaton, Anne with Bob Cummings, Lotty with her fiddler, Calvin and Martha, Jonathan and Martha Gilbert, Mary Dooley and Will Foster, Caroline Barnes and Jack Adkins. Each couple seemed to be happy to be there as they danced around the barn with spirit and enthusiasm. Old Gwendolyn Smith stood over to the side and pouted. Betsy Scott had not been able to find Hezekiah Kendall. Gwendolyn had seen him run off with one of those wild girls from up near Buffalo Cove, but she didn't have the heart to tell Betsy any of that. She blamed the hard cider for Hezekiah's behavior. *No one was in his right mind tonight,* Gwen thought—*no one but her.*

As soon as the dance took off and everyone was whirling around, Anne pushed Laura out of the way and took Tom's hand. Forced to be aggressive, Bob grabbed Laura's hand and pulled her into the line with him. The dance took on a life of its own after that. Tom quickly retaliated. As Jack Adkins came around with Caroline, Tom played Anne's game, and grabbed Caroline, leaving Anne with Jack. He knew that Anne would have a fit . . . and she did. Anne yelled at Tom, but he ignored her. Jack Adkins's face turned beet red, and poor Caroline Barnes looked into the eyes of Tom Dooley with a face frozen in fear. Tom couldn't help but laugh. Caroline would be afraid to go anywhere for days. She'd be scared to death Anne would come looking for her.

"Hello, Caroline. It's been awhile," he teased.

Tom almost felt sorry for the poor girl. She was shaking like a leaf. In all the commotion, Perline, watched with glee. She saw her chance as soon as they did the next sachet around the dance floor. When Caroline came around, Perline yanked her by the arm and swung her around to Jack Keaton—putting herself with Tom. Anne screamed at Perline as they whirled around. Tom ignored them both, watching for his next chance to grab Laura when she came back around with Bob Cummings. He liked dancing with a girl that so many men wanted to dance with, and so many women were jealous of. He forgot his woes and began to enjoy himself. Interestingly enough, it made him think of a night long ago in Wilmington when another pretty woman had the same effect on him. He grabbed Laura during the next sachet. As Anne whirled around, she caught a glimpse of Tom leading Laura to the cider table. She watched them grab two glasses of cider and a lantern from the table and run out of the barn. Anne left Jack Adkins standing and ran to the barn door. Poor Caroline ran to Jack Adkins and hugged him tight. Walking out into the cool night air, Anne caught sight of the two just as they cleared the edge of the pines on Colonel Horton's property.

She started to follow, but James Melton stopped her.

"Here," James smiled. "I brought you some barbecue and cornbread."

For a minute, she wasn't quite sure about James. Was he protecting the couple? *No*, she thought, *he's not bright enough for that. Or was he?* Sarah stood at the barn door watching Anne and her brother with a triumphant smile.

When Anne turned back to the pines, the two were gone. Looking around, she saw Jack Keaton coming out of the barn. She nodded in the direction that she had seen Tom and Laura leave. Jack tipped his hat to her and disappeared into the pine trees. Perline watched everything from the barn door.

Lotty stood behind them all, and in the glow of the campfire, watched and remembered her dream.

CHAPTER TWENTY-THREE

Deep in the midst of a pine forest is a world in and of itself—insulated and peaceful. The thick aroma of the trees surrounds its visitors and footsteps fall silent on its pine needle floor. It is a place where animals roam free in safety, hidden from view.

As a child, Laura used to love playing there. She would bring apples and pears for the deer and was delighted when they were bold enough to take the fruit from her hand.

In the heart of the forest, the quiet was music to Laura's ears. The privacy the pines provided was perfect. She finally had Tom all to herself. In the soft glow of lantern light they made their way to a clearing in the forest's center.

Laura felt lightheaded and tugged on Tom's arm.

"Slow down!" she laughed. "My legs aren't as long as yours."

Tom laughed, pointing to her mug.

"Drink up, Laura."

Laura took a sip of the hard cider.

"No," Tom grinned, "drink it straight down."

Laura was so smitten with Tom that she desperately wanted to please him. Wanting to prove that she could be just as adventurous as Anne, she did what he asked. The hard cider was strong, filling her nostrils and burning her throat. Coughing, she made her way to a stump and sat down. Tom set the lantern on the ground and squatted beside her.

Tom threw his head back and drained his mug. Smiling, he reached up and kissed her playfully on the mouth. Laura looked into Tom's eyes, believing she saw all her hopes and dreams waiting there. He surprised her by pulling her to him and kissing her again, this time rough and hard.

"Slow down, Tom. I just met you yesterday," she said, trying to pull away.

"And, isn't this exactly what you were dreaming of just yesterday?" he asked, still holding her to him. "I saw the way you looked at me, girl. This is what you wanted."

Laura had noticed all evening that Tom was bold in everything he said and did. It was something that she was fascinated by and fearful of. She didn't know how to handle herself around someone like him.

Timidly, Laura spoke, "I thought I was somethin' special."

Tom's demeanor immediately changed.

"Laura," he flattered, "you are something special . . . but you have to remember, I have been away to war. I was a prisoner for the last part of it. That does somethin' to ya. It made me see life different than I used to." He snapped his fingers. "One day you're here and the next you're gone. You have to grab life while you can and enjoy it."

He put his face close to hers and she could smell the liquor on his breath. "Knowing what I know now, I'm not willing to let one precious second get away from me . . . or you."

Laura tried to look away, but Tom put his finger under her chin tilting her head towards his.

"Do you believe in love at first sight?"

He let his finger trail down her neck to the swell of her breasts as he waited for her answer.

"I do," she whispered, "but you scare me a little. You don't seem to answer to nothin' or nobody. You got your own set of rules."

Tom grinned at her. Clearly, he'd taken what she had said as a compliment.

"You're right. I do. You should stand up for yourself more, be your own woman. Girl, you need to do what you want to do for once in your life. Not what your daddy or your brother or anybody else wants. Just what you want."

Tom spoke to Laura as if he could read her mind, and she hung on his every word. He said the things that she had wished so many times to hear from a man—the right man; but when the words were actually spoken, she found herself unsure. Struggling with herself as she listened, Laura chose to take his words to heart.

"I love you, Tom," she blurted out. "I know that sounds crazy, but I do."

Tom's fingers found the ribbon that held her hair back and gently loosened it. Her chestnut hair fell down around her shoulders.

Stroking her hair, he whispered, "I know, I know."

It all seemed like a dream to Laura. She needed to tell him things—things that were important to her—things that were in her heart.

"I've been looking for you for a long time. I dreamed about you before I ever saw ya. I even told my daddy before breakfast one day. My grandma says if you tell your dreams before breakfast they'll come true." She looked in his eyes and touched his cheek. "When I saw you at the store yesterday, I knew it was you, right off—from the first minute."

Tom found the buttons at the back of her dress and slowly unbuttoned each one. He was careful and deliberate as he kissed her.

"I know, I know, love at first sight," he murmured between kisses.

"It was . . . for me," she answered.

Laura pushed him away and stood up. This was the man she'd been waiting for and her one chance to make her dreams come true. She did not intend to let this moment pass. There would be no regrets. In the safety of the pines she made her choice. Shyly, she stepped away from Tom and pushed the unbuttoned dress from her shoulders. It fell to the ground without a sound.

Tom stood up and pulled off his shirt. As he moved towards her, he realized that there was something different about this one; and he found himself surprised. She was kind and gentle, and believed in him. Everything he told her, she accepted without question. Tom decided someone like Laura was just what he needed. He didn't have to act with her. Tom laid his shirt on the ground and gently guided Laura to it. Laura gave herself to him with her whole heart, and Tom was grateful for her warmth. He made love to her slowly and with a kindness he did not always show. Laura was surprised at how gentle he could be. *It was all right*, she thought. *Things were moving fast, but it was all right.* She knew they were meant to be together. Afterwards, Tom held her close. Laura was like a rope thrown to a drowning man. *She made the pain go away,* he thought—*at least for a little while.*

Jack Keaton stood in the darkness and watched them. Hot anger coursed through his veins. Jack turned away from the sight. The scorned lover hated them both.

CHAPTER TWENTY-FOUR

When the Meltons arrived home, Anne went straight to bed. She had not spoken a single word on the way back.

Perline was ready to go to bed herself, but James had other things on his mind. When he motioned for her to help him get the wagon to the barn it had seemed odd to her. He usually did things like that himself. After the horses were put up, James put his hand on Perline's shoulder and turned her to him. Her relationship with James had never bothered her before; but tonight, she was surprised to find that she did not want him to touch her. James did touch her, though. His hands were all over her, and she could smell liquor on his breath. Disgusted, she tried to pull away. He stopped for a minute and looked at her. Perline had never refused James before, and her behavior surprised him. When she tried to pull away again, he turned her face to his and forced her to kiss him. She let out a gasp as James angrily pushed her up against the barn and lifted her skirts. Perline saw a different side of James that night. She also came to know full well where she stood. She was nothing more to him than the hired help. Whatever she had tried to pretend to herself was a lie—her feelings meant nothing to him. No matter how hard she tried to get away, he held her there and pushed himself against her. Finally, Perline relaxed and let him have his way. There was no use struggling, she knew she couldn't stop him. Men had treated her this way all her life—and now she knew James was no different. He ripped her pantaloons off and parted her legs with his knee, taking her there by the barn. Perline closed her eyes tight as he pressed her up against the wall, taking her mind to another place—*a place with Tom Dooley.*

CHAPTER TWENTY-FIVE

Laura woke the next morning to the sound of her papa's axe outside her window. He was chopping wood with James. Will had not been happy with her on the way home. He and James had been looking for her for awhile when she finally came back down the hill to the party. Will had given Tom the hardest look he could muster when he spotted them returning to the party. It was very plain to Will what Tom and his daughter had been doing. Laura's hair was mussed and her dress was wrinkled with stains of pine rosin. Tom looked just as disheveled. Laura couldn't look her papa directly in the eye when she first saw him. She was embarrassed and had obviously not given much thought to the consequences of her actions.

Later in the day, Laura heard someone on the porch talking to James. She looked out the window and saw Tom Dooley standing outside with her brother. He had come to ask Will's permission to call on Laura. After that morning, he came by almost every day. Over time, her papa and James seemed to enjoy his company. Tom spent many nights, over the next several months, at the Foster cabin. He charmed the whole family with his stories and his fiddle-playing. To his surprise, he found that Laura had a beautiful voice and so did her brother, James. They would sing together while Tom played, and it was a peaceful time for him. The Fosters provided a family feeling and filled a void in the lonesome soldier's life.

The two had fun together during those months. Laura would go with him to barn dances and talk to the ladies while he played his fiddle. They would sit up 'til all hours of the night and talk while she did her weaving and sewing. Laura made a shirt for Tom from some of the blue cloth left over from her dancing dress. She was proud when he wore it and complimented him on how good it looked with his dark eyes and hair. Tom seemed to enjoy having a girl to go out in public with, too. Being with someone that was unattached was much easier than being with someone who was married. Still, for all the trouble, he missed Anne.

Laura quickly learned to leave Tom alone when he was angry. His temper was quick and flared up over the silliest things. She soon learned never to argue with him or talk about things that she thought might upset him. As strange as it seemed to her, Tom was the kindest and the meanest man Laura had ever known, all at the same time. After awhile, Tom rarely got angry with her at all; and Laura felt pride, believing that she was good for him. What she didn't know was, Tom had simply become bored. Laura tried too hard to please, becoming whatever she thought Tom wanted whenever he wanted it. Soon, there were no surprises left. The newness and thrill of her was gone.

Completely unaware of Tom's feelings, Will Foster's daughter fell deeper in love each day. She wanted to marry Tom; and one night, she found enough courage to tell him.

One night as they lay in her bed she whispered softly to him, "Tom, I think we should make a match. I want to be your wife."

Tom was quiet for a minute. At first, Laura thought he hadn't heard her.

Finally, he turned to her and kissed her gently on the forehead. "Ssshhh, go on to sleep, and we'll talk about it in the mornin'."

Laura kissed him on his chin. "I love you, Tom," she whispered.

"I love you too, girl," he said.

Tom held Laura and stroked her hair until she fell asleep. Closing her eyes she drifted off in the arms of the man she loved, happier than she had ever been and looking forward to the future. The next morning when Laura woke up, Tom was gone.

CHAPTER TWENTY-SIX

Tom slipped out of bed as soon as he was sure Laura was sound asleep. He quietly put on his clothes and left by the front door. Laura had been good to him. She'd taken him in and loved him at a time when he was sure he would die of a broken heart. Feelings of guilt crept in as he walked down the road towards home. Laura would be hurt—he knew that—but he was convinced she would be hurt a lot more if he stayed any longer. Marriage was the last thing on his mind. Anne and Elizabeth had not been happy. Their vows certainly meant nothing to them. Why would he need to get married? Tom did care about Laura, but he still loved Anne. The truth was, she consumed him. He knew he could never be the salt of the earth, dependable husband someone like Laura would need. *Yep, he was doing her a favor*, he convinced himself.

Tom's mind wandered to Mary Beth as he walked. She was such a beautiful little thing—fair skin and dark hair like her mama's. The last time he had seen Anne was about a month after he started seeing Laura. The meeting had not gone well, so he didn't go back. The only good thing about that day was that he brought Mary Beth a little black kitten. His Mama's cat had given birth to a new litter a few weeks before. The little girl was so excited she'd talked to him more that day than she ever had. She even let him help her name it. They named the kitten Shadow. Tom smiled, thinking of the little girl holding the soft little kitten to her face.

No, to marry Laura would be a mistake. Still, he knew he would miss her. She was fun to be with at times, and she was the only woman he had met in a long time that he truly trusted.

Just as Tom reached the path to home, the air started to change. It was a snow air. He took a deep breath smelling the unmistakably crisp, clean smell. From the looks of the gray sky he knew it would start falling soon. Tom quickened his steps and walked in the dark light that comes just before dawn.

With the break of day, soft and silent flakes began to fall. By the time he reached his mama's cabin, the roof was turning white. Smoke from the fire inside circled low around the chimney.

Tom opened the front door and felt the warm welcome of his mama's hearth. He took off his wet clothes and boots and left them by the fire. Once inside his room, he crawled under the heavy quilts on his bed. Tomorrow, after a long sleep, he would pay Anne a visit. Tom buried himself under his bed quilts, sinking into the softness of his feather tick mattress. His nose and feet felt like ice. Drifting off to sleep, his last thoughts were of Anne and Mary Beth. He intended to start over with Anne and make things right between them. They had both made more than their fair share of mistakes, but maybe they could leave together—make a fresh start somewhere else.

Outside, the snow continued to fall silently in the little valley. It covered Tom's world in a blanket of white, making his plans and everything around him feel fresh and new.

CHAPTER TWENTY-SEVEN

Perline was outside on the porch stacking firewood when she saw Tom coming up the road. Her first impulse was to run to him, but she knew better. Anne had beaten her good the morning after the molassy boiling. Remembering the beating, she did what Anne would expect of her and ran into the cabin to let her know.

"Anne!" she yelled, "Get up. He's back."

Anne sat up from her nap. She'd been sleeping a lot since that night at Colonel Horton's.

"Who's coming, Perline?" Anne asked.

"Tom Dooley's comin' up the road towards the house; get up."

Anne jumped out of the bed.

"You go and talk to Tom while I freshen up. Go on now; I'll be out in a minute."

Perline walked out of the cabin and made her way to the woodpile. Standing there, she knew Tom would have to walk right by her. Clutching her shawl, she could feel the temperature dropping. James had given her strict orders to keep the fire blazing all day. He said he didn't want Anne and Mary Beth to catch cold. Mary Beth had the sniffles already. *All of this snow will be as slick as a baby's butt by morning*, Perline thought.

Several months had passed since Tom first danced with Laura Foster. Anne and Perline hadn't seen Tom but once in all that time. After a few months, Anne confided to Perline that she was afraid she'd had lost him for good. Perline refused to believe it at first; but after awhile, she began to think Anne might be right.

As Tom neared the woodpile, he smiled at Perline.

"Is Anne here?" he asked.

"Now where else would she be in this kind of weather?" Perline snapped, trying to act irritated. Then she shrugged, "She's inside," Perline answered.

"I reckon I'm not one of her favorite people right now; am I, Perline?" he asked.

"I reckon not. Anne's been real angry these past few months, Tom. I don't know if she'll see you or not."

Tom laughed. No matter how many times the two of them fought and broke up, he was still sure enough of himself to know that Anne would take him back.

"I'll make it up to her. I always do."

Perline was amazed at his confidence. He was big feeling and that was one thing Perline didn't like about Tom.

He continued, "This time, I had every right to do what I did. I come home from war and find her married to another man. How do you think that made me feel?"

Perline glared at Tom. She loved the way he laughed and the way he looked. She loved the sound of his voice and she had relived the kiss that night in the woods many times; but again, she was struck by how cocky he was.

"The way I see it, the two of you are about the most selfish, spoiled people I've ever known. You're both good lookin'. Your mama would die for you, and Anne's had men fallin' all over her since the day she was born."

Angry now, the words flew from Perline's lips. She was fed up with both of them. Being at the Meltons had kept her comfortable, but living with Anne had been pure Hell.

"It's not that easy for some of us," she continued, "but people like you never take the time to see that. You take your looks and your charm for granted, and you never have a thought for the rest of us. You stand there and whine about whether or not Anne is gonna take you back, and you never give a thought to all the people you've used and left behind."

Perline shook her finger at Tom.

"I hear people talk. Don't you think I don't know about that married woman in Wilmington. You just had to brag about it, didn't you? Well, that's nothin' to be braggin' about if'n you ask me. Caroline Barnes ain't much, but you've done about ruined her reputation. James Melton is a nice man . . . and even me . . . when you kissed me . . . "

Without thinking, Tom turned on Perline. He had not planned for a confrontation, but he'd heard enough from her. "That was a mistake, and you know it. It didn't mean nothin'."

Perline was shocked by the coldness of his tone. In her mind, that day had come to be far more than it was. His dismissal of what had happened between them hurt as much as if he'd slapped her in the face.

"How would you like to be somebody else's mistake, Tom?" Perline snapped. "You better watch your back, Tom Dooley," she threatened.

Perline turned to see Anne walking towards them. She looked beautiful in her new green hooded cape that Lotty had sewn for her a few weeks before. Mary Beth had one, too. James had paid Lotty well to make the matching capes. He told her he wanted his wife and daughter to be warm for the winter. Lotty had lined the capes with soft rabbit fur. Perline looked down at her plain brown skirt and muslin blouse, and the old feelings crept back in. She felt ugly and plain. Tom watched her and felt a pang of guilt for what he'd said. Without another word, Perline broke into a run, almost knocking Anne down as she passed her. She didn't stop until she was back inside the cabin door. Once she was safely on the other side she leaned up against it, barricading herself from the selfish pair. *They were porcelain*, she thought. *They were porcelain and they could be broken.*

Outside Tom and Anne stood, each one sizing up the other.

"What can I do for ya, Mr. Dooley?" Anne finally asked.

Tom laughed at her icy tone.

"Come on, girl. I need to talk to you." Tom motioned her towards the path that followed Reedy Branch, but Anne stayed where she was.

The two immediately started playing their game — a game they always played after they were finished with the people who got in their way.

"What makes you think I'll go with you?"

"Because you love me, and deep down you know I love you. That's about the only thing either one of us has ever known for sure."

Anne's eyes teared up just the tiniest bit, but she didn't cry. Instead, she walked over to Tom and took his arm.

"I expect you to have some pretty important things to say if I go walkin' with you in this snow," Anne said.

Tom nodded, and the started down the path by Reedy Branch.

Tom and Anne walked and talked for more than an hour. Their differences melted away, and soon it was like they had never been apart. He asked her to forgive him, saying that he'd acted out of anger. Almost childlike, he confessed to her. Anne listened, forgiving him as he talked. He told her all about Laura — saying she was a sweet girl — but he knew he could never love her the way he loved Anne. His words seemed to satisfy her, and they started their relationship back that day in an old abandoned barn. Perline had followed them after she collected herself. She knew where to find them. Standing outside the barn she listened and peered through cracks in the wood. The sound of their lovemaking made her sick to her stomach. When she could take it no longer, Perline headed home to cook supper and get her mind off the two of them.

After Tom and Anne made up, Perline became the blind she was hired to be. Strange things were done in the Melton household. Sometimes at night Anne would go to sleep with a string around her wrist. The string ran between the bars of her headboard and through a tiny hole she'd made in the wall of the cabin. She tied a nail on the end of the string outside. Sometimes at night, Tom would come to the side of the house next to her bedroom and find the nail. Then, he'd tug on it until the string pulled Anne's wrist enough to wake her. If James ever noticed, he never acknowledged it. He seemed willing to put up with whatever Anne dished out. Tom would often visit the Melton home and spend the night, too. Sometimes he would pretend to go off and sleep with Perline until James fell asleep. It was those nights that Perline lived for. Tom would lay in bed with her and they would whisper and laugh. They came close to being friends during that time. This new twist to their relationship made her try and push Tom's cruel words far back in her mind. He was beginning to warm up to her and that meant the world to Perline. She even tried to believe that someday she would come to have her moment with Tom.

Anne seemed to sense the change between them and deliberately started doing things to hurt Perline. She piled more work on her than ever before and started complaining to James about most everything Perline did. Without fail, James always bowed to Anne, and this made Perline hate Anne even more. Anne had James Melton's ear and Tom's heart. Perline had neither.

When Perline got angry, she would go down the road to Lotty's and ask to help with her *friends*. At Lotty's, Perline was appreciated. At least there she could drink herself into a drunken stupor with a wild night of men and music—and for a short time nothing else mattered or could hurt her.

Lotty didn't mind having Perline come over once in awhile. It was a small price to pay for what the girl did for her daughter. Men and whiskey could help you forget all of your problems, for a short time.

Then again, sometimes it made the problems worse.

CHAPTER TWENTY-EIGHT

Perline's fingers were so cold they itched and burned as she wrung out the last of the bedsheets and put them in her laundry basket. On most cold days she usually heated up a big tub of water and washed on the porch, but she'd wanted to get out of the house; so she'd stripped the beds and headed for the creek. Things had been tense at the Meltons since the molassy boiling. James made her feel uncomfortable at times, and even with Tom back in the picture, Anne was cruel to Perline most of the time. Picking up the reed basket full of laundry, she balanced it on her hip and started for home. The rustle of leaves stopped her.

Turning around, she saw Tom storming out of the woods. He was mumbling to himself and his eye was red and swollen.

"What got hold of you?" Perline yelled to him.

"None of your damn business!" Tom shouted back.

Perline was used to having people yelling at her. Even Tom Dooley's hateful tone didn't phase her. Ignoring him, she turned to leave.

"Where ya goin', Perline?" Tom yelled after her.

"Where do you think? I got more important things to do than stand around and let you cuss at me."

"Aw, come back!" he called to her. "Come back and talk to me."

Perline cautiously made her way back to the creek and set down her basket. She looked at him for a second or two, but he just stood there. Finally Perline broke the silence.

"Tom, I don't have all day. If you got somethin' to say—then say it."

Tom staggered a little and laughed.

"Look what the little bitch did to me!" he said, pointing to his eye. "You and me got somethin' in common now, Perline," he said giving her a wink. "Anne's been all buddy buddy with Jack Keaton, lately. Did you know that? Hezekiah Kendall saw 'em walking down by the creek together the other day." Tom tried to look indifferent, but Perline knew he was mad. "When I asked her about it, she slapped me."

Perline was hurt by the news. Deep down she'd always known that Tom was out of her reach, but Jack was her fella—or so she thought.

"What did you do to her?" she asked.

"She's a married woman, Perline. My hands are tied and she knows it. I can't very well leave my mark on a married woman, now can I?"

"Well then what do you want me to do about it?" Perline snapped.

"Oh, Perline, I know somethin' you can do about it," Tom flirted.

Perline had waited for a moment like this since the day Tom came home, but now that it was here she found it to be nothing like she had imagined. She'd always attached romance to her desire for Tom—nothing like this —some drunken fool with revenge on his mind. Still, Perline knew her chance had come, and she decided to take it.

Tom pushed Perline up against and tree and lifted her skirts. He kissed her, and she sighed. Tom stopped for a moment, laughing.

"I should warn you, girl, I'm a little drunk and a lot mad. This don't mean nothin', Perline. You understand me? It don't mean nothin'."

Tom was rough and fast with Perline, and she found herself crying out in a mixture of pleasure and pain. When it was over, Tom casually buttoned his pants, awkwardly patted her on the butt and left her there by the tree, without a word.

Perline collected herself and picked up the laundry basket, marveling at how her most intimate wishes had presented themselves. Before she reached the cabin, the encounter had grown to be far more important than it was in Perline's mind. She told herself, *it did mean somethin', 'cause it meant somethin' to me.*

CHAPTER TWENTY-NINE

The smell of bacon frying had turned her stomach again. Laura stood on the porch and wretched over the rail.

Inside her brother, James, grabbed the pan of sizzling bacon from the stove and set it away from the heat. He didn't aim to eat burned bacon for the fifth morning in a row.

Will Foster sat at the table and shook his head, puzzled. "The coneflower and goldenseal ain't workin'," he said, with a worried look on his face.

James nodded. He wanted to tell his papa about his conversation with Laura the night before, but he had sworn to his sister he would not. Instead he moved forward with their plan.

"Maybe I can take Laura with me tomorrow when I go to Calvin's for supplies. Calvin might know something to give her."

"That'd be good, James. She's actin' poorly, and I don't know what to do for her," Will answered.

James felt put in the middle and he didn't like it. He knew now that his sister's malady was nothing that nine months couldn't cure. Still, he and Laura agreed that it needed to be verified by Doc Carter. They would stop in to see him on the way to the store.

Tom Dooley had left his sister in a terrible mess. He'd just taken off one night and never come back. At first, when Laura started acting different, he'd just thought it was from a broken heart, but the sickness and crying had continued on. Last night Laura had asked him to meet her on the porch after their papa was in bed so that they could talk. That's when she told him what she believed was the cause of her frailty.

Laura felt bad about putting so much on her young brother's shoulders, but with no mama and a father that could be quick tempered at times, she had no one else to turn to. When the sickness passed, Laura went back in and cleared away the breakfast dishes. She spent the rest of the day cleaning house and thinking about how she should handle the situation when her suspicions were confirmed.

The next morning, Laura woke up early and started breakfast. Again, the smell of frying bacon proved too much for her, and James walked into a smoke filled room with burning meat once again. After setting the frying pan aside he reached in and pulled out the biscuits baking in the woodstove. The bottoms of the biscuits were a little too brown but they would still be good. He left the stove door open, taking advantage of its warmth and took some apple butter from the shelf above the stove. This would be enough to get his papa started when he came in from the barn. James stepped outside and found his sister on the porch leaning up against a rail.

You gonna be ready soon?" he asked.

"It won't take me long," Laura answered, wiping her mouth.

After breakfast, James and Laura told their papa goodbye and started down the road to Cowles' store. James had a bag of ginseng root to barter when they got there. Calvin told Will the last time they were there that the Foresters down in Wilkesboro would pay high dollars for it.

About halfway to the store, James turned on the Grandin Road and headed towards Doc Carter's house. Laura dreaded the visit, but she had to know for sure.

When they arrived at the Carter house, James hitched the mare and left Laura sitting in the wagon while he went to the back porch. Doc Carter's office was in the back of the house. In a minute, he returned with the doctor. The old man always wore a starched white shirt with a black tie at his throat. He was dressed in a dark suit and wore wire spectacles. His white hair stuck out on the sides and blew in the breeze. The kindly old man extended his hand to Laura and helped her down. He was known for his patience with the people in and around Elkville. Since the war, very few people could pay him for his services, so he'd begun to barter with them. There was an extra bag of creesies in the cart for him with a small slab of fat back. James took out the bag, and they all walked to the porch of his office.

"James, you best wait out here," Doc Carter said. "I'll need to examine Laura in private."

James nodded. Laura almost laughed when she saw the look of relief on his face. *Bless his heart*, she thought. He clearly hadn't wanted to, but he'd been prepared to walk in with her if he needed to. Doc Carter's office smelled like alcohol. It was a tiny room with a big examining table in the middle. He helped her up on the table and brought the lantern over.

As Doc Carter examined Laura he asked her some important questions. "When was the last time you bled?"

Laura thought for a minute. "The middle of February, I think."

Doc Carter shook his head as he poked around on her belly.

"That would be about right, by my calculations," he said, peering over his spectacles. "You're gonna have a baby, Laura. I estimate you to be about three months gone, maybe a little more. Who's the lucky man?"

Laura blushed at the question.

"I haven't told him yet."

Doc Carter hesitated when he heard her answer. He shook his head as if he understood.

"Well, my dear, good luck to you both. You just send your papa or your brother, James, 'round when the time comes, and I'll come straight away."

Then Doc Carter added in a serious tone, "I'm sworn to an oath, darlin', so please know that nothin' will be discussed by me. You talk when you're ready."

Grateful for his words, Laura shook her head and thanked Doc Carter for his time. The last thing they talked about was what she should be eating and drinking over the next few months—molasses, greens, and liver if she could get it. These things would give her the iron she needed, he told her. A baby will take a lot out of your body, he said. It would be up to her to eat for the both of them. She'd need plenty of milk and water, too. Apples and meat would be especially good. James gave the doctor the poke of creesie greens and thanked him.

As they drove away, Laura looked back and waved to the kindly old man. *Doc Carter was good people*, she thought. James turned the cart right leaving Grandin Road and headed for the store. Laura told James everything about her visit. James listened to his sister, promising to help her in any way he could. That promise gave Laura the opportunity she needed to ask James an important favor. She reached over and firmly grasped her brother's arm.

"James, I need your help. I need to get word to Tom. When we get to the store, I want you to drop me off. I'll do our barterin' and maybe rest awhile on one of the benches on the porch 'til you get back."

The look James gave his sister was answer enough. Laura knew she would have to beg him, but she also knew she could sway him. Her brother was all bark and no bite. He was kind hearted and loved her.

131

"James, please, this is his child, and he needs to know it. What if this were happening to you? Wouldn't you want to know?"

James thought about that for a minute. He was young, but he understood the pain of losing a parent and wanted to do the right thing for her baby.

"I always get caught in the middle of things that I shouldn't with you, Laura. My biggest problem is lovin' you too much. I can't turn you down."

"Then, you'll do it?"

"Yeah, I'll do it," James said reluctantly. "But, of all the things I have ever done for you, this feels the worst. I'm worried about you, Laura. Tom Dooley ain't like most folks, and he's got a girlfriend that's mean as a snake. Everyone says her mama is a witch, and you know how Anne is. You've fallen into bad company, and I don't know what people like that might do to you if you keep getting in their way."

Laura answered her brother, laughing, "Tom Dooley would never do one thing that would harm one of his own, James. I may not know much, but I do know that. I've heard him talk too many times about wantin' sons someday. He'll come around; you'll see."

"It ain't Tom I'm worried about," James answered.

Ignoring her brother's fears, Laura put her arms around James and hugged him tight.

"By this time next year, you'll be bouncing your little nephew on your knee. I gotta strong feeling it's a boy."

James just shook his head. Laura was doing it again. She had him where she wanted him, and she knew it.

"What about Anne Melton?" he asked protectively.

"Tom'll handle her," Laura said. "She may have his heart right now, but I have his child, and he won't let anything happen to this baby."

"Don't it bother you that he loves Anne?"

Laura stiffened at his question.

"He loved me—I know it—but she put a spell on Tom that took him away from me. Just as sure as day, that's exactly what she did. Anne and her mama and that Perline Foster are bad, and I know that. I'm not as trustin' as you think. That's why I sprinkled a little salt around the house yesterday. It'll keep the bad things away. Don't tell Papa. It wasn't much, just a tiny bit. Don't you worry, James. No harm is gonna come to any of us. I know what I'm doin'."

"God, I hope so, Laura. I just think it'll take a lot more than a little salt to keep you safe from the likes of those three." James replied.

As they approached the store, Laura gave James his instructions. "Drop me off and go straight over to Tom's cabin. Today's Saturday. Tell him to come to the house tomorrow afternoon. Tell him it's real important. Tell him that I have somethin' to tell him, and he needs to know it right away."

James pulled up to the hitching post at the store and tied the reins to it. He gave Laura his hand and helped her from the wagon. James carried their goods inside so she could do the trading while he was gone. James loved the smell of that old store. He slowly breathed in the earthy aromas of herbs, wood smoke, sweet tobacco, and gamey furs. The place was full of people, and there was always a group of men telling stories and either chewing or smoking tobacco. He always enjoyed his trips there and wished he could stay; but instead, James hugged his sister and reluctantly left her there. He would make his trip a fast one. The sight of her standing on the porch, alone, made his heart ache. She looked so pale and thin to him. His big sister needed to be home in bed.

James unhitched the horse and left the wagon at the store. He ran the mare at a trot all the way to the Dooley cabin. He'd give the horse extra oats and take special care to brush her down when they got her home.

CHAPTER THIRTY

Laura sat by the window watching for him. She had practiced her speech a hundred times. Once again, James had helped his sister by convincing Will to go fishing with him. Laura wanted time alone with Tom to talk.

It was a beautiful Sunday afternoon. Laura had stayed home from preaching because her stomach felt queasy, and she was nervous. Sitting through a sermon was the last thing she thought she could handle. Besides, she was too anxious. Looking out the window, Laura noticed the greening of the grass and the budding of the trees. The red buds and yellow bells were more beautiful than she'd ever seen them. Gently touching her belly she realized that everything was alive and growing, just like the baby inside her. Although her pregnancy was not yet noticeable to others, she could tell a difference in the way her clothes fit. Her waist had thickened and her breasts were swollen, making her dress tight around the middle and chest. She was going to have Tom's child, and she'd do everything she could to have a healthy baby. Laura was determined to give Tom a son. She believed a son would win his favor, and she wanted that more than anything in the world. Once the baby was born, Laura knew that Tom would realize how important she was to him and forget about Anne. This child would break Anne Melton's spell. Love and family would prove to be worth more to Tom in the long run.

In the distance Laura saw Tom. He was walking at a fast pace towards the cabin with his hands in the pockets of his jacket. She fought the urge to run and meet him. Instead, she stayed by the window and waited. Being too clingy would scare him away again. She now realized her mistake on the night he left. Pushing Tom for marriage had been the wrong thing to do and she'd lost him because of it. Laura would have to choose her words carefully or he would leave again — this time for good — baby or no baby. This would not be an easy conversation for her. Her cousin, Anne, was cunning; and Laura was not. Laura Foster was just who she was.

When the knock on the door finally came, Laura made herself wait a moment before answering. When she did, she tried not to show how excited she was to see him again. By the look on his face, she could tell that he felt put upon and there was an awkward silence between them. Finally, Laura collected herself and invited Tom in, offering him a chair.

"Can I pour you a glass of water?" she asked.

"Thank ya," he answered. The sound of his voice was cool, but polite.

Laura tried to make small talk while he drank the water. She talked about starting their garden and the mild winter. She laughed and told him that James had gotten himself kicked by Granville Dooley's mule several days before. Tom actually laughed about that. Encouraged, she got around to talking about how sick she'd been. Tom's face darkened as he sat quietly and listened and Laura quickly noticed the change. She'd seen that look many times and knew she needed to be cautious. In an effort to lighten the mood, she tried to change the conversation to happier times. Looking out the window she started telling him about a little chipmunk that was living in a hole by their front step, but the story fell on deaf ears.

"So why did you ask me here today, girl?" he interrupted. "What's so important?"

His harsh tone startled her. She blurted out the news before she had time to think.

"I'm carryin' your child, Tom." Laura lowered her eyes to the floor. She had not planned to be so abrupt and was afraid of the commotion she may have caused by doing so.

Tom set his jaw and stared at her. He seemed stunned by the news and did not speak right away. When he did, his tone was sharp.

"Are you sure?" he stormed.

"Yes, I'm sure, Tom. I went to see Doc Carter yesterday. I wanted to be sure before I told you. He reckons I'm about three months gone."

Tom stood up, agitated. He'd never hit Laura, but she'd always known he was capable of it. She watched him carefully.

"Can't you do somethin'? Ain't there doctors that would . . . "

"Doc Carter is the only doctor I know, and he would never do such a thing. Even if he would, I wouldn't do it. I'm gonna have this baby. It's startin' to grow . . . just the tiniest little bit . . . here . . . " she reached for Tom's hand but he pulled away from her.

The cold hard truth hit him with full force. Accusingly, he glared at her.

"How do I know it's mine?" he asked.

"That's mean. I haven't been with anybody since you left. I was so hurt when I realized you weren't comin' back around. I didn't want to see anybody else. There's no one but you for me; don't you know that? How could you say somethin' like that to me?"

Tom made his way to the door and walked outside on the porch. Laura followed behind him.

"Don't walk away from me, Tom. You can't deny this child. And you can't deny your part in this. Everything you told me, I believed, and everything I have ever told you has been the truth. Deep down you know that."

Tom nodded his head. As upset as he was, he knew Laura was right. He knew Laura didn't have it in her to lie. It was one of the things that had drawn him to her in the first place. His mood softened. She had been kind to him at a time when he needed her. His anger quickly faded into frustration.

"I gotta have time to think, Laura. Just let me have some time to think. Listen, I'll be back here on Wednesday; and we'll talk, all right? You just gotta give me a few days."

Laura knew what that really meant.

"You have to talk to her first; don't ya?"

Tom turned away.

"You're crazy, girl. I don't know what you're talkin' about."

Laura walked over to him.

"Everything in your life has always centered around her. You wouldn't have looked twice at me if you hadn't made up your mind to pay her back for marryin' James Melton. Was that all I was to you?"

It was Tom's turn to be uneasy. The words she spoke hit him hard.

"No, Laura, that ain't so," he answered.

Laura shook her head. "I wish I could believe you. But I'd say there's been a lot more than just me. I don't know all their names but I'd say we've all spent time in Anne Melton's shadow. It's been a hard lesson for me, but I've learned it."

Laura paused for a moment. She had been so hopeful, but nothing was going right for her and the baby. Anger washed over her.

"Well just because I'm easier goin' than she is — make no mistake, Tom — I hate her as much as she hates me!"

Tom stood up, trying to defend himself. He knew she was partly right, and he needed to explain.

"You don't understand, Laura. I reckon there is some truth to what you say. Girl, when I first met ya — I was mad, and I was hurt, and you know that. Then, there you were — looking at me with those eyes and that smile. There you stood at one of the worst times in my life and yeah, I took advantage of that . . . at first. But then, I got to know ya — the real Laura Foster — and she was pretty and kind and knew how to love a man with her whole heart."

Laura wiped the tears from her cheeks as he spoke.

Tom smiled at her. "You know what's funny? That night in the woods, you told me I scared you a little. Well, Laura, you scare me a whole lot. When I look into your eyes, I see myself settlin' down and growin' older. I've never seen that in a woman's eyes before — not even Anne's."

"Is that why you left me?" she asked.

Tom nodded. "I went back to what I know best. Before I met you — I thought love was all fire and fury; but now I know it's not. I'm torn between what's good in my life and a darker side of me that's wild — and it's not at all what a girl like you needs. I don't want that dark side to spill over and hurt you."

Tom sat back down. "God help me Laura, I'm just torn."

Laura walked over to him and kissed him on the cheek.

"Tom, listen to me! You don't have to run anymore. Please know that this baby has nothin' to do with any of this — no matter how much you love Anne Melton or me."

Laura saw her papa and James coming up the path from the river. Tom saw them, too. He was relieved to be finished with the conversation. Tom nodded to Laura and stepped off the porch.

"I need to think. I'll be back on Wednesday mornin'. We'll talk then."

With that he disappeared down an old path opposite the one Will and James were traveling. He was angry and confused. A part of him truly loved Laura — or at least the good person she was. Another part of him wanted nothing to do with a baby and wished the girl was dead.

CHAPTER THIRTY-ONE

In the days that followed Tom's visit with Laura, he didn't see Anne. He spent his time working for his mama and playing his fiddle. He had a lot of thinking to do. By Wednesday morning, he came to a decision. He woke up early and saddled his family's only workhorse. He would need to ride to save time. He had several places to go and a lot to do.

The little cabin at the bottom of German Hill was his first stop. Tom needed to talk to Laura first, or he would change his mind. As he approached Laura saw him coming and ran out on the porch to meet him. Tom was shocked at the sight of her. She looked frail. The dark circles under her eyes told Tom she hadn't slept much. Tom hadn't either. Will was standing in the doorway watching. He didn't look too happy to see Tom. Laura quickly left the porch and met him in the yard. She pointed to him towards her favorite walking path. It was awhile before either one of them spoke. Tom stopped at the bottom of German Hill and looked up at the little mountain. He let out a heavy sigh and nodded to Laura.

"All right, girl, you need to get some things together. Friday mornin' before dawn, you get up and get ready. You'll need to bring your mare and we'll meet at the old Bates place off of Reedy Branch. You know where I'm talkin' about?"

Laura nodded.

"It's on the way to Tennessee. We'll travel through Darby and Triplette and then on through Watauga to get there. We'll get married in Tennessee and come back in a few days when your papa's had time to cool down."

"I'll be there, Tom; don't you worry," Laura answered.

She put her arm on his shoulder.

"I love you, Tom, with all my heart."

Tom nodded, "I love you, too, girl."

"I've thought about what you said, and I do aim to do right by this child. I gotta get on now. I got things to do so, I'll see you bright and early Friday mornin'."

He kissed Laura tenderly on the forehead and left for the store.

CHAPTER THIRTY-TWO

Tom stopped by the store and visited with some of the men until mid afternoon. Talking and laughing with the boys helped him forget about his predicament for awhile. He convinced himself that marrying Laura would be all right and that she would be good for him. Besides, he enjoyed her company. *In a way, he did love her.* More than anything he wanted his child to have a daddy.

By mid-afternoon, Tom headed home. The older men at the store were predicting rain that evening, so he quickened his steps to beat the showers. As he walked, he talked to himself, practicing how he would tell Anne what he planned to do. She would be furious, but he would make her understand. It was sunset when he reached his mother's cabin. Golden light shined in Tom's face making him squint as he made his way across the yard. His mama had supper on the table waiting for him. He ate and turned in early. The next morning, he woke before the sun came up. Tom dressed and grabbed a cold biscuit from a pan on the stove. Although the biscuit was a day old — it was still soft and good. He quietly made his way outside being careful not to wake his mama or Eliza. Taking another bite of the biscuit he headed towards the Melton cabin.

The first person Tom saw as he neared the place was Perline. She was hauling water to the cabin from the creek just as she had been on the day they ended up in the barn. He couldn't help but notice that she was soaking wet. He hadn't looked forward to seeing her, but he knew he needed her help to get Anne outside, so he forced himself to be nice.

"What happened to you?" he asked.

"The foot log we been usin' to get over to the rocks was loose. The rain washed away most of the dirt that was holdin' it. When I got to the middle of the log, the dirt gave way and I fell in. Anything else you wanna know?"

Tom tried not to laugh. *At least maybe Perline would have to wash her hair now,* he thought.

Dealing with Perline had become difficult. She followed him around more since the afternoon in the barn. She was always trying to touch him, or make suggestions about the places that they could go and the things that they could do. Having sex with her had been a big mistake. Perline wasn't like other women. She wouldn't take no for an answer. Tom was convinced there was something about her that just wasn't right in the head. He made quick small talk with Perline and asked her to go and get Anne for him.

Anne came outside to meet him in an unusually good mood. He could tell she'd missed him.

"It's good to see you," she said. Surprisingly Anne didn't even question where he'd been the past few days.

Tom took a minute to really look at her in the doorway. She was smiling, and her dark eyes were sparkling. He loved her so much it hurt. Tom reached out and touched one of her long dark curls. He'd gotten lost in those curls many times.

Anne's eyes met Tom's, and her smile faded.

"What's wrong?" she asked.

Tom Dooley's resolve broke into a million pieces. He grabbed Anne and held her so tight he almost hurt her.

"Tom, tell me; what's happened?" she asked, backing away.

Tom could see Perline out of the corner of his eye, watching them.

"Not here. Let's go for a walk down by the creek."

This was not information he wanted to share with Perline. Anne nodded, this was important, she could tell. The two started down the path to the creek where they'd met so many times before. Perline watched, knowing where they would go. She would give Tom and Anne a head start and then follow, hiding in the trees. It was obvious something was wrong, and she intended to find out exactly what it was.

When Tom and Anne reached the creek bank, they took off their shoes and jumped from rock to rock as if it was the most natural thing in the world—and to Tom and Anne, it was. They knew every nook and cranny there. It was their special place and the biggest rock in the middle was theirs. When they reached it, Tom took Anne's hand and pulled her down beside him. Nervously, she remembered the night Tom had told her he was leaving for the war.

"Somethin' bad has happened, Anne and I want you to know, it's my fault. I take full responsibility for it so don't go blamin' anybody else."

Anne listened, anxiously.

"Tom, please, tell me what's wrong," she pleaded.

"Laura Foster sent word that she needed to talk. She asked me to come by last Sunday," he started. "I went by as a courtesy to her and nothin' more. You know as well as I do, I hurt her real bad."

Anne waited for him to continue.

"She's with child," he blurted out. "Laura's carryin' my child."

Anne sat stock still, staring at Tom. Tom could not look her in the eye. He waited for her to speak putting his head in his hands.

When Anne finally found her voice, she asked, "What do you plan to do about it?"

Tom sighed a heavy sigh. "I went back to see her yesterday mornin' to tell her my decision. I plan to meet up with her tomorrow and leave for Tennessee. Anne, we're getting' married."

"How could you do this to me" she asked, her voice barely above a whisper. "Tom, you can't do this."

Tom remained silent.

Without warning Anne lunged for Tom, kicking and screaming. Tom used every bit of strength and balance he had left to calm her down. She was hard to handle when she lost her temper, and he grabbed her shoulders trying to pin her to him. Furious, Anne slapped him hard across the face.

"I won't let you do this!" she yelled.

"Anne, you can't stop me!" Tom yelled back.

"The Hell I can't!" she shrieked.

"Anne, stop your yellin'. Everybody in Elkville's gonna hear you."

Anne struggled to get free of Tom and bit his upper right arm. He pulled away from her, looking at the blood on his shirt.

"Do you think I give a damn!" she shrieked. "I hate you for this. I hate you for what you've done!"

Tom grabbed her again and held her to him, forcing her to listen.

"Anne, settle down. I didn't mean for this to happen. You, of all people, know that I'm not the marryin' kind—but, that girl is three months gone, at least. I've watched my mama try to raise three boys and two girls after my daddy passed away. It was hard on her, and it was hard on us. I don't aim to let no child of mine go without a daddy."

Anne broke free and jumped to the next large rock, letting the water divide them.

"How do you know you really are the daddy? It could be Jack Keaton's or Bob Cummings'. Laura Foster ain't no angel, Tom, no matter what you think."

Tom found himself surprised at how defensive he felt when she said that.

"Anne, I love you, but Laura don't deserve that kinda talk. I know that baby is mine."

His defense of Laura was like a slap in the face to Anne. Tom saw the pain his words caused her and immediately wished he could take them back. Words were powerful and sometimes they could do greater damage than actual deeds. Anne turned her attention to the sound of the water and tried to drown out Tom's cruel words.

"Anne!" Tom yelled to her. "I didn't mean for this to happen."

"You've only known her for a couple of months," Anne yelled back. "You've known me your whole life."

"This baby is gonna know me its whole life, too," he answered.

"I won't let you do this," Anne screamed. "I've kept you away from Caroline Barnes . . . I've kept you away from my mama . . . Perline knows I'll kill her if she ever lays one finger on you. What makes you think for one minute that I'll let this happen?"

Tom jumped across the water, and landed on the wet edges of the flat boulder where Anne stood. He stood resolutely beside her. They had been through so much together and he knew he'd hurt her many times—but, this was different—it was not a game between two foolish young people. It was a serious mistake. He clasped her hands in his and held them tight.

"We've both made mistakes; but, Anne, you're the love of my life, girl. You are the heart 'a my heart. Marryin' Laura is just for the baby's sake. I could never stop lovin' you. Listen to me, I can be a good father; but it don't mean I have to be a good husband. I can still sleep in your bed."

He held her close and kissed her tenderly. "I've forgiven you for James. Now, you forgive me for this. Anne, please, this was an accident. I didn't want this; but it's here; and I gotta deal with it."

Anne sat down on the rock, pulling Tom down beside her.

"What are you gonna do? If Will Foster finds out, he's gonna come lookin' for you with a gun."

Tom shook his head. "We'll be married by the time Will Foster finds out. When we come back, he'll have a new son-in-law and a grandbaby on the way. We're gonna meet up in the mornin' early. We'll be gone a few days, and when we get back, I'll come see you first thing."

Anne leaned over and kissed Tom fully on the mouth. She parted his lips with her tongue and heard him sigh. He needed her and she knew it. *Sometimes when things are at their worst, lovemaking is at its best*, she thought.

"I guess there's nothin' I can do, then," Anne said in her most innocent voice. Will you come back and see me later tonight, at least? We can go over and see mama and toast your new life. We'll pop some corn and drink some shine."

Anne whispered in his ear and nibbled on it.

"Then, if you're a good boy, we'll come back down here for a little while. I know what you like, Tom. Laura Foster will never be able to do the things for you that I can, and you know it."

Tom knew she was right. He truly loved Anne, but he craved her in a way he could not explain. The one thing he did know was that when he was with her everything felt right. Looking at her, he knew he wanted her as much as he had ever wanted a woman. Tom kissed Anne with a desperate, hungry kiss.

He slid his hand down the front of her dress and whispered into her black curls, "I'll be there."

With that, he quickly made his way across the rocks, leaving Anne in the middle of the creek. Once he was on the bank, he turned and waved to her.

Tom never saw Perline in the shadows as he headed up the path for home. She stepped to the edge of the creek bank and called to Anne. Still reeling from what Tom had told her, Anne made her way across the rocks. She never thought to question why Perline was there—she was too upset. Perline was shaken, too. She couldn't hear much of the conversation, but she had been able to make out enough from their yelling to know that Tom was leaving. Worried, Perline spoke without thinking.

"He's gonna leave us, Anne."

Anne shot Perline an accusing look.

"What do you mean *us*, Perline?"

Perline twisted her words to appease Anne.

"I just meant things was workin' out real nice here. I have a roof over my head and good food, and a man to sleep with when he wants it . . . and you have Tom. It'd sure be a shame to lose all of that, a real shame."

Perline stopped for a moment and decided to appeal to Anne's vanity.

"Of course, you could stop it. You've always been able to make Tom do whatever you want him to."

Tears sprang to Anne's eyes.

"I'm gonna try, Perline, but I don't know . . . he's different this time. She's trapped him good."

Perline smiled at Anne.

"Sometimes us women gotta take things into our own hands."

Anne wasn't sure what she meant by that, but she had a good idea.

"Sometimes, we do. I'm goin' over to Mama's for a little while, Perline. Mama knows how to deal with men better than anybody I know and right now I need her advice."

Perline laughed at that. "She sure dealt with Mr. Triplette; didn't she?"

Anne grabbed Perline by the arm. Her fingers bore down hard on her skin. They would leave more bruises, Perline knew.

"I swore to Mama that I'd never speak about Mr. Triplette again. If you know what's good for you, you'll swear the same," Anne warned.

Perline shook her head in agreement. She did not want to be on Lotty Foster's bad side.

"Then, I won't speak on it," Perline promised.

Anne's mind was spinning as she tried to decide what to do next. "Have you seen Jack Keaton today? Do you know where he is?"

Perline nodded. As mean as Anne was to her—she loved to be needed. She also delighted in trouble.

"Yes, I do. Do you want me to go and get him?"

Anne shook her head. "Not now. You wait at the cabin for Tom to come back. He promised to meet me after dark. You and him go get Jack and come on over to Mama's. He lives right on the way. We'll have some corn popped and some shine waitin' when you get there. Tom needs a proper party before his weddin' day. Now you go on and get James and Mary Beth fed and tucked in for the night."

Perline pulled a little bottle from her apron pocket. Aunt Lotty had taught her many things on her visits there.

"I've got a little nightshade here. I'll put it in James' stew. It'll calm him right down and make him sleep like a baby."

Anne hugged her. Although it shocked Perline she wasn't taken in by it. Anne had treated her like a dog since the day she came to Elkville. The only reason she was being nice to her now was because she needed her. *Perline would do whatever was best for Perline from now on,* she thought. *To Hell with Anne.*

"I'm countin' on you, Perline," Anne said as she reached over and hugged her again.

"Don't you worry, Anne," Perline said hugging her back, "right now, this very second, I feel like we're really kin. No cousin, don't you worry about a thing."

Anne kissed Perline on the cheek and disappeared into the woods towards her mama's cabin.

Perline stared after her in disgust, wiping the kiss from her face.

That evening, she fed Mary Beth and James a big supper and had them in their beds just after dark. When she was certain the nightshade had done its work, she put on a shawl and made her way outside to stand in the trees and wait for Tom. An owl hooted in the distance. She stood in the dark and listened to the sounds of the creek. The water was talking to *her* tonight. Annoyed with the old bird, Perline took a stick and beat it against the nearby tree branches to scare it. The owl screeched at her as he flew away.

"No use tryin' to warn anybody, Mister Owl," she whispered. "I'm gonna show 'em all. You can hoot all night, but it won't make any difference."

Perline laughed and giggled to nothing and no one but herself in the darkness . . . and it felt good. It felt right. Filled with years of venom, she'd been waiting for this moment for a long time.

"Yes, siree, you and Tom can count on me . . . Miz Anne."

Reaching the front porch of the cabin, she stepped up and leaned against rail posts. In the darkness she could just make out the outline of Tom Dooley walking towards the cabin.

The moonlight made him an easy target, she thought.

CHAPTER THIRTY-THREE

Anne stood on her mama's porch and laughed at Jack Keaton. Jack was a willing cohort and open to any and all suggestions. When she ran into him on her way to her mama's house, he'd jumped at the chance to come along with her. Perline would be angry, Anne knew, but she'd get over it. Jack's eagerness faded as he reacted to Anne's laughter.

"Are you laughing at me, girl?" he asked, unsure of himself.

"No, Jack, you're just fun to be with, that's all," Anne answered.

Anne's answer seemed to please him.

"I like your company, too," he flirted. "Matter of fact, I'd like to spend a lot of time with you."

Anne deliberately brushed up against Jack; and he eagerly grabbed her around the waist, holding her to him.

Anne tried to laugh it off and pulled away. She did not intend to have sex with Jack Keaton—she just wanted to make him think she did.

"Let's go inside and get some shine to warm us up," she whispered.

"I don't need to be warmed up," Jack answered.

Ignoring him, Anne took him by the arm and led him inside.

Once they entered the cabin, Anne looked upon a familiar scene that had always been home to her. A couple of musicians sat near the fire. One played the fiddle and the other a guitar. Several men sat at the table near the stove. They were drinking shine and eating from a loaf of bread in the center. Lotty was serving them beef stew and potatoes. One of the men patted her on the behind as she leaned over to spoon the stew into his bowl. Anne turned away from the familiar sight. Looking around, she recognized a girl named Emma from Buffalo Cove. She was known to be a wild girl and would go off with two or three men at a time. Anne had heard the stories. Emma was sitting beside the fiddler. There were lanterns on the large rough hewn beam over the fireplace and candles lit throughout the room giving everything and everyone a warm glow. Jugs of shine were being passed around. Anne took

146

one of the jugs from Emma and handed it to Jack. He grinned at her and took a big swig.

Wiping his mouth, he handed the jug back to Anne. Turning her head so that Jack couldn't see, Anne pretended to take a big drink. She wiped her mouth and winked at him.

"I need you to do me a favor," she whispered, as she ran her tongue along the edge of his ear.

She could feel him shiver against her. Slowly, she eased him down into a rocker and sat in his lap.

"And if you help me, I'll make it worth your while."

If she didn't before, Anne now had Jack's full attention. The two talked for a long while. Jack had always wanted her and she knew it. Anne also knew that he would do anything to get what he wanted, and she intended to promise him whatever he asked for.

Lotty ended their conversation abruptly. She clapped her hands to get Anne's attention and pointed outside. Anne stood up quickly and ran to the window. She saw Perline and Tom headed towards the cabin.

"You two can finish your talk later," Lotty said. "Come on, Jack, let's go get us somethin' to eat. Perline's comin' and she'll pitch a fit if she sees you sitting here with Anne in your lap."

Jack started to protest; but Anne kissed him before he could; and Lotty took his hand and led him to the table. On the way Anne's mama turned to her daughter and pointed to a jug by the washbasin. Anne nodded and went over to it. She took a mug from the shelf above the basin and poured a full mug of shine from the jug.

Tom and Perline walked across Lotty Foster's yard and stopped to warm their hands by the big bonfire that crackled and blazed near the porch. Tom could hear the familiar fiddle music that Lotty loved so much coming from inside. As his hands began to warm, he looked up and saw Anne standing in the doorway smiling at him. She looked beautiful. Pangs of regret knotted in his stomach when he thought about having to leave her. She was wearing the scarlet dress she wore at Colonel Horton's just a few months before. *So much had changed for both of them since then*, he thought. Anne was holding a mug of shine and motioning for him to come and take it, but he didn't go right away. He let himself stand there and enjoy the view a minute longer. Anne's dress was cut low and was shorter at the bottom, exposing bare ankles underneath. *Knowing her the way he did*, Tom thought, *everything under that dress was bare.* Tom left Perline at the fire and eagerly ran to his girl, greeting her with a kiss. Anne kissed him back and took his hand, leading him inside.

Tom was greeted by the smell of corn being popped and another unfamiliar scent. Was it sage or ginger root? He couldn't tell what it was, but it was bold—even with the strong smell of fresh popped corn.

Anne took a sip of shine and kissed Tom again, letting the shine run from her mouth into his. The two laughed, and she handed him the mug. Tom was grateful for it and took a big drink.

Watching the two, Perline turned away in disgust. She spied Jack in the corner of the room and made her way to him. She was angry that he'd come with Anne and not her and planned to give him a piece of her mind. Before she could get out the first word, Jack grabbed her and hugged her so tight her feet left the ground. Perline's anger quickly faded after such a big welcome. Jack was clearly feeling the effects of the shine, and she liked him that way. Still, she couldn't help but notice that he kept glancing at Tom and Anne. What she didn't know was that Jack was undressing her pretty cousin over and over with his eyes. Perline mistook his excitement, not realizing that it was in anticipation of a promise Anne had made to him before she arrived.

Perline sidled up to Jack

"I went to your house lookin' for ya. Your mama told me you done took off."

"Aw, now Perline, I ran into Anne on the road and she invited me on up," he told her. "I didn't have nothin' to do. Anne said you was busy getting James and Mary Beth to bed and I'm used to waitin' on you while you're doing that."

Jack leaned over and kissed her neck.

"Besides, I know you'll make it worth my wait, won't ya?"

Perline grinned at him. His flirtatious words seemed to ease her mind. She was clearly jealous and Jack liked that.

Anne curled up in Tom's lap and fed him the popped corn. They laughed and drank and teased each other. Tom was surprised to find that he was enjoying himself more than he had in a long time. The shine had relaxed him and made him feel like he didn't have a care in the world. The liquor was strong and burned his throat, but he didn't mind. After a time, things started getting fuzzy and everything around Tom started moving at a slower pace. His eyes began to burn and blur. He remembered dancing and drinking and at some point making love. Was it to Anne? He thought so, but he kept seeing Perline and Jack, too. Sometimes he saw Lotty and the girl from Buffalo Cove . . . and the fiddler . . . or was he the fiddler? The man he'd seen playing earlier looked different somehow — with dark hair and eyes like his own. He remembered seeing the man reach his hand out to him and for some strange reason Tom took it. Then somewhere far away he heard a baby crying. He was barely able to hear it, but it was there. It was far off in the distance . . . crying and crying and crying . . .

Whatever happened that night felt too good to stop. All Tom's worries faded as he surrendered — letting his mind and body have their way.

Tom let himself drift off into a haze of whiskey and women . . . two of his favorite pastimes.

CHAPTER THIRTY-FOUR

It was still dark when Laura woke up. Easing out of bed, she knelt down and pulled a small bundle out from under the mattress. James had been his sister's confidant once again and knew all about her plans to leave with Tom. He didn't like it, but he agreed to keep her secret. Having a father would be important for his little neice or nephew. James would tell their papa where Laura was and what she was doing after the couple had traveled a few days — putting some distance between them and Will Foster. Will would be mad, but after the baby came, Laura was convinced everything would be all right. James prayed she was right.

Taking the pretty blue dancing frock from a peg on the wall, Laura slid it over her head and buttoned it up. Then, she took her old homespun day dress and slid it on over the frock. This would be the easiest way to carry them and also the easiest way to keep the nicer dress protected. The blue frock was the dress she planned to wear on her wedding day. Gathering up everything she intended to take along, Laura stepped outside in the cold morning air and made her way to the barn. The morning was crisp, as spring mornings often are. In May, there was always a cold-snap during blackberry winter. It was the season's last cool breath before things started heating up for the summer. Laura rubbed her hands together and looked up at the sky. The moon was still out with just a thumbnail of bright light showing on its surface. Will had always called a moon like that, a dry moon, because it looked like someone had tipped it over and emptied it of its golden liquid. Watching the thin sliver in the sky, the young bride to be worried about her papa. He would be upset that she ran off without telling him. Of course, he would have been upset even if she had told him. Taking the mare would make him even madder, even though he'd always told her that it was hers. He used it a lot on the farm. But there was no way she and Tom could walk all the way to Tennessee. Besides, they were only borrowing the horse. Laura would bring it back when they returned in a few weeks. Laura bridled the mare and placed a heavy blanket across its back. There would be no saddle, but that wasn't a problem. The girl had ridden bareback many times. Carefully, not wanting to take any chances with the baby, she used a bench to mount the horse. She confidently took the reins and steered the horse out of the small corral where she was kept. As she rode away from her home, Laura looked back and saw her brother James in the kitchen window. Although he had vowed the night before that we wouldn't, the boy had gotten up to see her off. Laura blew James a kiss and turned the mare towards the old Bates' place.

The sliver of moon and the bright stars lit her way. *Everything would be all right*, she told herself. This was a turning point in her life. She'd made a womanly decision. It was only normal for a girl of her age to leave her family and start a new life when the time was right—and the time was right for her to be with the father of her child.

By the time she turned on to the creek path towards Gladys Fork, day was breaking. It was a cool day, and the two dresses she wore with her shawl felt good. The closer she got to the Bates' place the lighter her heart became. Laura intended to put her worries behind her and allow herself to feel the excitement any woman should feel before her wedding day. Nothing would go wrong now, unless he got cold feet. Laura thought about that for a minute and dismissed it. Tom wouldn't do that. He was too serious about being the father he needed to be to their baby. He'd be there, and she would be a good wife to him; he'd see. Tom would come to realize that he needed her. He was getting on in years, just like her. Twenty was old to still be out gallivanting around and single. They both needed to settle down. Her papa would even be pleased when he got used to the idea.

Up ahead, she saw Betsy Scott coming towards her. Betsy was carrying a lantern and a big basket of food. *It must be a sick neighbor or a death for her to be out this early*, Laura thought.

"Mornin', Miz Scott," Laura called out.

"Well, Laura Foster, what brings you out this early? Why girl, you had to get up at the crack of dawn to be in these parts this time 'a day."

"I got important business today, Miz Scott," Laura blurted out. She was so excited she was beaming.

"Ooooh, tell me, child! What are you doing out here?" Betsy asked.

Laura leaned towards Betsy. "I'm not supposed to tell anybody, Miz Scott, but I'm too excited. I just can't help it. I'm meetin' up with Tom Dooley at the old Bates' place. We're goin' off to Tennessee to get married."

Betsy Scott's eyes lit up.

"Well, bless my soul," Betsy said, more than a little shocked. "Best wishes to you, darlin'. Why, this is special news, sure 'nuf."

Laura suddenly felt she'd done something she shouldn't have.

"Miz Scott, I'd sure appreciate it if you would keep this a secret. I want to tell my papa in my own way. He doesn't know anything yet."

The little gossip smiled at Laura. "Why, darlin', you don't have to worry about me. I won't tell a soul. Besides, I got food to deliver to Miz White from our church. She's been real sick. I don't have time for no small talk today. You just go on now. Sounds like you got a big day ahead of ya."

"Goodbye Miz Scott. I can't be late — not today."

Laura waved goodbye to Betsy and continued on her way. Betsy Scott didn't even take the time to let Laura clear her sight before she took off to Martha Gilbert's house. She practically ran all the way to tell her the news. *Poor Miz White would just have to wait*, she thought.

When Laura arrived at the old Bates' place on the ridge, Tom was nowhere in sight. She tied her mare to the sturdiest post on the rickety old porch of the old abandoned house. Waiting for Tom, she walked around the yard and examined what was left of it. The place had been deserted for as long as anyone could remember. Her grandpa had known the Bates before they moved away, but that was when even he was a young boy. The morning was breezy, making the old boards creak and moan in the wind. Laura stopped walking — thinking she heard something or someone moving inside the house. Trying not to let her imagination run away with her, the frightened girl convinced herself that she was being silly — *it was just the wind*. Then, a door slammed on the back porch. Laura walked in the direction of the sound. This time it was coming from the woods behind the house.

"Tom Dooley, is that you?" she called out. "This is no time for you to be teasin' me."

Tom was always playing pranks. His sense of humor was different from most folks. In the months they had spent together, she quickly found out that he enjoyed scaring people. He thought it was great fun to catch people unaware and watch their expressions. It was just like him to want to tease her this morning. Trying to relax, she examined the old house again. Most of the glass was missing from the windows. The porch rails were broken in places. An old shutter banged occasionally in the wind. The back door of the house was just a few yards from the woods and Laura still clearly heard someone walking around in the leaves. Laughing, she suddenly knew what Tom was up to. He wanted a little fun before they started out for Tennessee. She made up her mind to play along. Tom could have his fun and the day would start out with laughter, just as she wanted it to. With reckless abandon she ran towards the edge of the woods, stumbling over an old broken-down piece of chair laying in the yard. The commotion stirred a crow perched on the roof of the old house. The sudden flapping of its wings startled Laura. Rubbing her ankle she rose to her feet and watched the black bird disappear into the woods. Laura took a deep breath and resolutely followed. *The sooner this game ended the better*, she thought.

"Tom, I know what you want. I'm comin' in, but don't you be scarin' me anymore. It's bad for the baby, do you hear?"

Laura moved into the trees and looked around. "Tom?"

Sometimes when things get too quiet, it sets off a warning signal to the senses. Once Laura entered the woods, the silence around her became louder than any noise possibly could. The excitement felt just minutes before had vanished and the nervous young girl found herself wanting to be out of those woods as fast as her legs could carry her.

"Tom," she called once again. "This ain't funny no more, now stop it or I'm leavin'. I ain't playing this game no more."

A twig snapped behind her. Laura wanted to turn around but stood frozen with fear. Before she could gather her courage to run, a hand cupped over her mouth and another wrapped around her waist. Laura Foster fought with all her might to break free but could not. Something struck her head and her vision blurred. Knowing now that whoever this was, meant to do her harm, the young girl fought for her life and somehow managed to break free, whirling around to face her attacker. Blood ran down Laura's face from the sharp blow to the head. Through warm ooze and blur, she could just make out a form standing before her. Her head was spinning and it was hard to focus. She struggled to see her attacker but everything was whirling around and happening so fast. A sharp pain shot through her left breast. It was so fast she wasn't sure it was real at first. Laura's knees gave way and she fell to the ground, hands fumbling to find the source of pain coming from her chest. To her horror she found the handle of a knife. Another pain shot through her as the sharp weapon that had pierced her was yanked out. Looking down at her fingers, she could see they were covered with her own blood.

Looking around in disbelief, she called out, "Stop, please! You're killin' me."

No one answered.

A commotion of leaves and footsteps followed. Were there whispers, too? Or was it the wind in the trees? Just as suddenly as the commotion began, it stopped. The deafening sound of silence fell all around her. Laura was alone now. She had been left to die. She tried to scream for help. The scream rose in her throat, but no sound came out. Struggling for control, she tried to prop herself up but could not, falling into a mound of leaves. Lying there in the midst of the trees, she looked around her. People rarely came to this lonely place—it was off the beaten path with heavy undergrowth. It could be days or even weeks before she was found. James was sworn to secrecy and would be the loyal brother he had always been. Betsy Scott . . . Laura rolled over and tried to brace herself with one arm—the other clutching her chest, but she could not support her body. The trembling fingers of her right hand pressed down hard on the open wound. Weariness fell over her and a deep, icy cold.

Laura knew she was dying, and there was nothing she could do to stop it. She was all alone in the woods save for the child inside her. She cradled her belly and gently rocked the baby that would never be born. Her beautiful baby would die along with her. In the last seconds of her life, a sweet and peaceful release fell over her. Laura Foster let herself and the tiny soul she carried float upward, leaving everything she had ever loved behind.

Her killer had robbed her of even the simplest of goodbyes.

CHAPTER THIRTY-FIVE

A large crowd had gathered at Calvin Cowles' store to see a medicine man and his squaw. He was selling snake oil tonic, and people were coming out of the woodwork to buy it. Everyone needed a good spring tonic to get them through a long hot summer. Even if a person didn't buy the tonic, the medicine man's traveling show was fun to watch.

The traveling salesman played his harmonica while the squaw beat her drum to draw a crowd. Once a good crowd had gathered the medicine man jumped up on an old apple cart and began his sales pitch while his Cherokee wife sold bottles of snake oil. He was dressed like a dandy in a fancy red suit and sported a handlebar mustache and thick sideburns. The man's hair was so plastered down with grease that every hair stayed in place as he moved through the crowd. Calvin hugged Martha as they stood on the porch and watched. Martha knew these days were some of his favorites. Calvin always made more money on days like this. People bought things because they were already there. Traveling shows were always a welcome sight. When the squaw started to dance to the music, Martha thought Calvin was a little too enthusiastic. Reaching up, she popped the top of his head with her hand and started pulling him back into the store. That's when they heard the commotion. They turned to see Will Foster running towards them.

He seemed completely out of sorts, grabbing different people in the crowd and asking them questions. Each time, Martha saw that the people were shaking their heads no. Something was terribly wrong.

"What's the matter, Will?" she called to him.

"Has anyone seen my Laura? Miz Cowles, have you seen my girl?"

"No, Will. I don't think she's here. When did you see her last?"

Will didn't answer.

He turned to the crowd and screamed, "Has anyone seen my girl?"

The crowd fell silent at the tone of his voice. Even the medicine man stopped to listen. Calvin nodded for Will to continue. Will frantically tried to explain.

"Laura wasn't home when I woke up yesterday mornin'. When I went outside to look for her, I noticed her mare was gone. I just figured she was off somewhere at first, you know, daydreamin' or maybe she'd found a new beau—but, she didn't come home all day. Come dark, I was getting' real worried so I went out lookin' for her. Nobody'd seen her. It got so late that when I got to Francis Melton's, he let me spend the night with him. When I got back the next mornin', James still hadn't seen her."

The crowd began to murmur and Will held up his hand to silence them.

"I went to her room and looked around. Both of her dresses is missin'. That made me think she'd run off, but this mornin' her mare came home without her. Even if she had run off, she wouldn't turn her mare loose like that. The horse still had a lead rope tied on it. It was broke in two."

The ladies in the crowd gasped. The crowd had gathered around Will now.

"That's when I knew somethin' was wrong for sure. I come straight down here. Thought maybe one of y'all might know somethin'."

Will was overwrought. His hands shook as he wiped his forehead with his handkerchief.

"Has anyone seen my girl?" he pleaded.

Now, Betsy Scott loved having information. She and Martha Gilbert looked at each other and Martha nudged her to tell Will what she knew.

Proudly, Betsy approached Will.

"I saw Laura early yesterday mornin' on the road, Will. She was ridin' her mare bareback and carryin' a bundle of clothes in her lap. Said she was goin' off to meet someone up near the Bates' place. Said they were gonna meet up and get married."

Betsy was thrilled at being the center of attention. All eyes were on her, and she was beaming.

"She seemed awful happy, Will."

Will came to the edge of the porch and looked at Betsy. The reaction she got was not at all what she expected. Will was angry.

"Who was she gonna meet?"

Betsy didn't know what to say. She was suddenly embarrassed.

"Well, I . . . I . . . I can't think with you yellin' at me, Will . . . I . . . "

Will came off the porch and stormed over to Betsy, grabbing her arm.

"Betsy Scott, you tell me who she was gonna meet right now!"

Startled, Betsy moved away from the porch. She had never seen Will Foster behave that way. In all the years she had known him, this was the

156

first time she could ever remember being frightened of him. He seemed like a stranger to her. Martha Gilbert pulled Betsy away.

Reluctantly, James Foster approached his papa. He knew he needed to speak now. It had been hard for him to see Will leave yesterday and go out looking for his sister. Seeing his papa in so much pain, Laura's brother could no longer keep his promise to his sister. His papa deserved to know the truth.

"Leave Miz Scott alone, Papa. I know who she was gonna meet. She told me on Wednesday."

Silence fell over the crowd.

"She was gonna meet up with Tom Dooley. They was gonna go off and get married."

The crowd began to murmer. Will's panic turned to anger; and before he took the time to think, he slapped his son hard across the face.

"Damn you, boy! Why didn't you tell me this before I came down here and made a fool of myself in front of all of these people?"

James hung his head down.

"I promised Laura," James answered. "She asked me not to tell. I love my sister as much as you do . . . and she asked me not to tell. She made me swear."

Will Foster looked into the shocked faces of the crowd that had gathered around them, and felt shame for what he had done. His son was clearly torn.

Gwendolyn Smith spoke up.

"She's in trouble, like as not. You get down with dogs, you get up with fleas."

Will had listened to Gwendolyn tear down just about everyone in the community, but he was not about to stand there and let her do it to his own daughter.

He started towards Gwen just as Perline Foster stepped out of the crowd. "Tom Dooley ain't with Laura Foster," she announced. "Tom was visitin' with Anne Melton just yesterday. I saw 'em whisperin' and lookin' all solemn-like outside the house."

Perline always looked unkempt, but today, she looked worse than usual. Her clothes were filthy and her eyes were swollen and puffy with dark circles. She looked like she hadn't slept in days. James Foster approached her. He could smell whiskey on her breath, and her hair was full of sweat and oil.

"That can't be. Are you sure it was Tom?" James asked.

The question seemed to please Perline.

"I know Tom Dooley. There's no mistakin' that man."

James turned to his father. "Somethin's wrong, somethin's bad wrong. I know what Laura told me and that's a fact."

Will Foster let out a heavy sigh. He put his hand on his son's shoulder.

"We gotta go look for your sister, son."

Bob Cummings quietly made his way to them.

"I'll help you, Will," he said.

Jack Adkins was ready for anything that might cause trouble for Tom Dooley. "You can count me in," he yelled.

Ben Ferguson patted Will on the back. "We'll find Laura; don't you worry."

Hezekiah Kendall joined the men. "I'm in . . . as long as it takes."

Men started raising their hands and yelling their support. One by one, they stepped forward to help in the search for Laura.

Calvin pulled Will aside as the men started collecting their things. He pulled out the pocket watch Will had traded for the cloth for Laura's dress. He had fully intended to sell it, but in the end he didn't have the heart to. He had planned to hold on to the pocket watch for a little while, and then trade it back to Will the next time he came to the store to barter. He placed it in Will's hand.

"She looked beautiful at the molassy boiling, Will. She's too pretty to lose. You take this so's you can keep up with the time while you're out there."

Calvin turned to the crowd. "You've got about three more hours before twilight. Better get movin'. I'll set up headquarters here for information and supplies. Now get your dogs! Get your horses!"

James saw the watch in his papa's hand. He had not known, until then, what his father had traded for that cloth. It was Will's grandfather's watch. James stared in amazement. Will saw the look on James' face. Tears filled his eyes as he put the watch back in its proper place inside his worn vest.

"It was worth it, son."

James didn't argue. The two nodded and left with the others to begin the search.

Martha Cowles went straight to work, organizing food for the men with the ladies at the store. Calvin went in search of lamp oil and canteens.

Jack Keaton and Perline watched the crowd leave to search for Laura. Jack was grinning, as usual.

"Where is old Tom Dooley, Perline?"

Perline laughed. Jack could be funny sometimes.

"Why, I don't know, Jack, but I'd swear a lie for Tom Dooley any day; wouldn't you?"

Jack reached down and kissed her. "I'm gonna go on a little trip; wanna come?"

Perline thought about that for a minute.

"I just might need to go visitin' in Watauga soon, Jack. But, not today. I wouldn't miss all the goin's on here for the world. No sir, not for the world."

Jack kissed Perline again and whispered to her. "Well then, I guess I'll see ya when I see ya."

Jack Keaton turned and left in the direction of his family's cabin. The next morning, he struck out for Tennessee.

CHAPTER THIRTY-SIX

Weeks passed and still no sign of Laura Foster. The men refused to give up, but after a time, they did not search as often. They all had work to do and families to feed. As time passed, people became convinced that she was dead.

Will became a different man—he didn't sleep, didn't eat. He looked thin and unkempt. His neighbors and friends began to worry about him. They all wanted to find his girl—and soon. No matter what, they wanted the poor man to have some peace. The not knowing was killing Will. His mind was tormented by *what ifs* and *hows*. Many feared without a quick resolution the poor fella would lose his mind.

By the end of June, Laura had been missing for a month. People were looking around and starting to cast doubt or blame on several of the men in the community. No one had seen Jack Keaton in awhile, and several other men who had courted Laura were missing as well. There was suspicion on all of these men, but the name that came up most of the time in conversation was Tom Dooley. With the information that Betsy Scott and James Foster had given at the store the guilt clearly pointed to him.

By the first of July, Tom was feeling the tension from the people around Elkville. He kept hearing bits and pieces of neighborhood gossip through family members. Anna and Cajah were worried about what people might do if they got stirred up enough.

Tom spent most of his time at home after Laura's disappearance. The only person he did visit was Anne and those visits did not go unnoticed by the Meltons' neighbors. People did not look favorably on his involvement with a married woman. It only added to their suspicions.

By mid-July, Tom made a decision to leave Elkville for awhile until things calmed down. He would leave for Tennessee to wait things out. He packed a bundle of clothes, kissed his mama and sisters goodbye, and took off. On the way, he stopped to tell Anne goodbye.

CHAPTER THIRTY-SEVEN

The last person in the world Tom wanted to see as he walked up to the Melton cabin was Perline Foster; but there she was. When she saw the bundle over his shoulder, Perline knew right away he was leaving. Before he could say a word, the sneaky little snake was telling Tom everything she'd seen and heard.

"They know it was you she was gonna meet. Your name keeps comin' up everywhere I go. Ain't nobody in Elkville that don't think you're the one that done it, Tom."

Several men had left right after Laura disappeared, but Tom deliberately stayed to try and prove to people that he was innocent. It was hard to believe what Perline was telling him, but still, he knew it was true. Anna and Cajah had heard all the speculation and warned him that there was even talk of a lynching.

Perline could see that Tom believed her.

"You know I'm tellin' you the truth, don't ya? I watch and I listen . . . you know that. That's what I been doin' all my life. When I was younger, I was always on the lookout for Yankees. My family would hide the livestock in the hills so's they wouldn't be found by the bushwhackers and mama would say, *'Perline, you go on up the ridge and be my lookout while I milk these cows.'* Then, Lotty sent word for me to come to Elkville and be Anne's blind. She said, *'You come down off those Blue Ridge Mountains before you starve to death, and I'll give you a job. All you have to do is keep your mouth shut and do as you're told. You be the blind for Anne and Tom and take care of the wifely duties with James.'* So's I did. Now, I'm watchin' and listenin' again . . . for you . . . I know what I heard, Tom."

Tom shook his head, accepting Perline's words.

Anne heard voices in the yard. From her bedroom window she could see Perline talking to Tom. With all the gossip and rumors going around, Anne could only imagine what Perline was telling him.

161

Anne grabbed her shawl and stormed out of the cabin.

"Perline, get on in the house. You got things to do. Stop wastin' Tom's time with your lies. Go on."

Tom nodded for Perline to go on, but she just stood there. Perline was angry and tired of being brushed aside by the two of them.

"Y'all need to be careful out here. There's a lot of angry people walkin' about. Jack Keaton knows it. He's already left for Tennessee. Said he wouldn't be hangin' around to find out who some mob might turn on. Tom, you need to think on that."

She shook her finger at the two.

"Last night, I dreamt of snow. That's a sign, Tom. Dreamin' of snow out of season means trouble without reason. My grandma taught me that and it's always held true. Then, here you come walkin' up in the yard today, and I thought of that dream. You need to take heed. It's a warnin'.'"

Anne started across the yard to her.

"Get in the house, Perline! Now! Tom, don't listen to her. She's crazy. You know that. She enjoys scarin' people."

Tom ignored them both and sat down on a log near the woodpile.

Anne shooed Perline into the cabin and hurried back to Tom. When he finally spoke it was in a low monotone voice.

"I told Jack Keaton after Laura turned up missin', I said, '*Jack, any man that wants to accuse me can come on. They might just get the beatin' of their life, but they can come on.*' Me and Jack had a good laugh. Then, that night he left. Can you believe that? He just up and left."

His mind seemed miles away to Anne. When he finally turned and looked at her it was like he was almost surprised to see her.

"I've been plannin' to leave even before I talked to Perline tonight. I got a few things packed. I wanted to see you first, though, before I go."

Anne sat down on the ground beside him. She put her head in his lap and hugged his legs close to her.

"Tom, no. You can't leave. Where would you go? What would you do?

The two sat quietly for a minute, both lost in thought.

Finally Anne spoke. "Let me get my things and I'll go with you. We can leave right now and never come back."

Tom pulled her to him and held her tight.

"Anne, they can track two better than one. I'm goin' to Tennessee . . . Mountain City. I can travel through Darby and Triplette. If I make good time,

I can be in Watauga in about five days and Mountain City in another three or four. They can't touch me there. When I get settled and things die down, I'll come back for you and my mama. We'll start a new life in Tennessee."

Anne touched his face. "You promise to come back for me?"

Tom nodded. "If you'll leave James Melton's money, I'll be back."

Anne took his hand and pressed it to her cheek.

"I would do anything for you, Tom. Surely, you know that. I . . . I'm so sorry for everything. I should've waited for you. I never should 'a married James."

There was no pretend with Anne that evening. Tom could see it. She was telling the truth.

"We both have things to be sorry for, Anne. But I love you; and you love me; and nothin's ever gonna change that. I swear on my life, I love you . . . and you have to know I'd do anything to protect you. If you left with me now and they caught up with us, they might hang you right alongside me. They're angry and they want blood for blood. I can't risk takin' you with me. It's not safe."

Anne knew Tom was telling the truth. Perline delighted in telling her how her name was always coming up with Tom's. She never missed an opportunity to tell Anne how much she was hated.

"No one is gonna put a noose around this pretty white neck. Don't you worry about me. I'll be right here waitin' when you come back."

Tom smiled at Anne's brave words. The little cat was always ready for a fight and he loved that about her. He leaned over and kissed her tenderly on the forehead.

"You best go while you can, Tom. You need the dark to protect ya," Perline yelled from the porch.

Tom and Anne turned to see Perline leaning against a rail on the porch. She had been watching the whole time, Tom felt sure of that. He touched Anne's cheek and gave her a knowing look. Glancing back at Perline, Tom leaned in and whispered in Anne's ear.

"Don't trust anybody, Anne, especially her."

With that, he turned and headed towards Darby.

CHAPTER THIRTY-EIGHT

The men in the community formed search parties and looked for Laura all summer. It was an unusually hot season. After several weeks, they began to take turns in their searches. Some lost interest altogether, or had to go back to a regular routine out of necessity. Not everybody could take care of a farm and spend so much time looking for the missing girl.

Luckily, Colonel James Horton and Colonel James Isbell could afford to. The two old Confederates, were steadfast in their search, recruiting and organizing volunteers. They vowed to the community and promised Will Foster that they would find the missing girl.

One evening in late July, their dedication paid off. The sun was setting and only a few beams of light remained. The search party had been out since noon. They had formed a battle line and were walking down Reedy Branch from the Melton cabin. Colonel Isbell was getting ready to dismiss the men for the evening when Colonel Horton met them leading his horse. About an hour before, Horton had left the branch and rode up the hill to the main path. The men had seen him cross the path and go up a holler on his horse. When he returned, the men knew he had found something. The old man's face was ashen, and his voice shook when he spoke.

"Get your lanterns oiled and your shovels out. I need you to follow me," he told them.

No one said a word. They just did what they were told. From the look on the colonel's face, they all expected the worst.

As they walked up the holler, Colonel Horton had Colonel Isbell count the two hundred steps it would take to get back to the spot. He talked to the men as they made their way.

"If I'm right, it makes perfect sense. Reedy Branch runs right alongside this holler. The branch is shallow. Someone could have carried the body down the branch to throw off the scent and then crossed over and walked up here. That's why our huntin' dogs couldn't pick up the trail. It's got to be the reason why it's taken us so long to find her. The water threw off the scent."

He stepped over to the right of the holler and walked up on a small knoll.

"Over here," he motioned. "This is where my horse was spooked."

What Colonel Horton did not tell them was that it had scared him to death. The stallion had reared up and was almost impossible to reign in. The woods had taken on a funny golden color after that—the kind of light that comes just before sunset—but this light had given off an eerie glow. The colonel could not find words to describe it. Looking around the woods, a strange feeling had fallen over him. The noises a person would normally hear in the forest were gone, and it was deathly quiet. It all happened at once. His horse reared, the light changed, and the woods seemed to stand still. He remembered thinking as he looked around that time had stopped.

Colonel Horton was not a superstitious man, but it felt to him as if he had actually been led to the place where he found Laura. At the spot where his horse had reared, he saw a strange discolored spot in the dirt. Cautiously, he dismounted his horse and walked over to it. A few strands of hair stuck out from the dirt. The strands glistened in the beams of sunlight streaming down through the trees. For some odd reason, the colonel felt compelled to bend down and touch them. The copper in the auburn tresses danced like fire as the light reflected there. Horton reached out his hand, but a foul odor stopped him. With the stench came such a feeling of dread and doom; a cold shiver crept up his back and neck. He quickly withdrew his hand and backed away from the hateful place. Turning towards his horse, Colonel Horton all but leapt into his saddle and headed for the others as fast as he could. He did not look back.

The Colonel was grateful that he had found the presence of mind to count his steps on the way back down the trail. He secretly hoped he was wrong, but in his heart he knew those copper tresses were Laura Foster's. When they reached the spot, James Isbell pulled out his handkerchief and placed it over his nose and mouth. He was the first to speak.

"Somethin' foul is here, that's for sure," he said.

James Melton seemed uneasy. He looked to the sky.

"Let's commence diggin'. It's getting' late," James told them. "I don't want to be out too late. There's a blue moon tonight."

Bob Cummings smiled at his superstitious friend.

"That's nothin' to be afraid of, James. A blue moon's just a freak 'a nature. Something that comes around every seven years."

This did not convince Hezekiah.

"James is right, Bob. Your books can't explain everything. It's a sign. Don't take it lightly."

Colonel Horton pointed out a stained spot on the ground and the men immediately started to dig. It didn't take long. They hit something within a matter of minutes. J.W. Winkler got down on his hands and knees and gently brushed away the dirt from their discovery. Once he got a good look, he stopped and bowed his head.

"I know that dress. It's made from her own homespun cloth. Boys, it's Laura."

Bob Cummings bent down and finished brushing the dirt away. He could see that an apron had been folded and placed over her face. He gently pulled the apron away and was horrified to find how little was left. Being out in the elements had taken its toll on the body. The woman staring back at him bore very little resemblance to the pretty young girl he had pinned so many hopes and dreams on. Clearly shaken by the sight of her, Bob put his head in his hands and wept.

"Oh, my God," he whispered. The face was nearly gone. The high cheek-bones and slight gap in her front teeth — the coppery auburn hair — were all that was left of Laura that was recognizable.

J.W. helped Bob up and turned to Doc Carter. "Can I help you, Doc?"

"Hold my bag for me, J.W and get a lantern."

Darkness had fallen in the little holler. The old doctor handed J.W. his bag and knelt down beside the body. Hezekiah Kendall stepped forward holding his lantern near the grave. As Doc Carter opened his medical bag he thought about the vivacious young girl that had come to his office just a few days before she turned up missing. He remembered her smile when he had told her the news. She had been so full of hope. Laura had listened to his every word as he told her what to eat and how to care for herself and the baby. He reached down and removed a small bundle that had been placed under her folded arms and handed it to Colonel Isbell.

Doc Carter could tell immediately that there had been foul play. He saw a tear in the cloth of her dress, near her heart. A great deal of blood stained the front of the dress. When he looked under the fabric, he could see that something, a knife by the looks of the wound, had pierced the body between what appeared to be the third and fourth ribs. The knife had entered with such force that there were knife marks on the rib bones. Doc Carter knew that the person responsible for this had to be filled with rage to use such force. This was personal. The body's tissue was so decomposed he could not tell if the weapon had pierced the heart or not. He spoke aloud to the men during his examination of the body. The grave, he noted, was shallow and short. Doc Carter shook his head. This made him think whoever did this was in an awful hurry. He shuddered at his next finding. He saw with disgust that the murderer had broken Laura's legs and folded them up under the body to make them fit into the grave. He did not tell the men what he already knew about the baby. Will should know before anyone else.

Bob watched through hot, salty tears as Doc Carter finished his examination.

"Merciful God, why?" Bob asked.

Hezekiah stepped over and put his hand on Bob's shoulder.

"We'll find the person that did this. Don't you worry, Bob."

Jack Adkins slammed his shovel into the ground.

"James told us at the store weeks ago that she was supposed to meet up with Tom Dooley that morning," he accused.

Colonel Isbell raised a hand to Jack.

"Now, boys, don't jump to conclusions. Is there anyone else that coulda done this?"

Bob Cummings turned to Isbell, remembering the molassy boiling.

"At the molassy boilin' back in the fall, Jack Keaton was making threats. He told me she deserved anything we wanted to dish out to her. Jack had been drinking and was still mad because Laura had stopped seeing him. He even said she would pay for it someday. That's just what he said."

"Well, you ain't gonna find Jack Keaton around. I heard he done packed up and left," Hezekiah said, remembering the conversation.

"I ain't seen Tom Dooley around in a week or so neither," Jack Adkins added.

Doc Carter was too sad and weary to listen to any more accusations. The men would have plenty of time for that tomorrow.

"We can talk about this later, boys. Right now, we need to get Laura home. She's been out here alone long enough."

Hezekiah helped Bob to his feet.

"Let's take a moment to bow our heads in prayer," he said.

The men took off their hats and lowered their heads.

"Dear Lord, we place our Laura into your hands. Bless her and keep her that she may walk with you in your glorious home. Amen."

Amens were heard all around.

"Now, come on; help me carry her to the horse," Doc continued, "this child needs to go home."

Solemnly and silently the men took a blanket from the roll on Colonel Horton's horse and put it under the body. They lifted her up and put her lifeless form over the horse. The animal fidgeted as they secured the body on his back. Hezekiah held on to hold the reins until the men were finished.

A silent trail of lanterns lit the way down the holler in the fog. Colonel Horton listened to the sounds of the crickets and the tree frogs. No matter what anyone could possibly say, he knew that these sounds had stopped when he first came upon that shallow grave. Chill bumps rose on his forearms at the thought.

J.W. didn't follow right away. Sadness filled his heart as he watched them carry his little niece home. He dreaded telling his wife, Mary. She had always loved Laura so. Looking up to the heavens for an answer, the only thing that came to mind was an old, old expression — *Once in a blue moon*.

How true, he thought, *how true*.

Turning, he followed his friends down the holler towards home.

CHAPTER THIRTY-NINE

It was the first of August when Laura Foster's body was laid to rest. All of Elkville turned out for the service.

Her coffin was kept in the Foster cabin until the funeral. It remained closed because of the decomposed condition of the body. The strong smell of camphor filled the house, covering the stench of death. Food and flowers filled the Foster home. Martha Cowles watched Will and James closely. Will wept openly at times. James did not. The boy's face was full of torment. Martha knew he blamed himself for what happened. What a burden of guilt for one so young to carry, she thought. It was not James' fault. People do what they want to do. When they set their mind to something, it almost never mattered what anyone else said or did. She tried to tell him that, but he wouldn't listen. Martha worried, too, that Will and James wouldn't take care of themselves now that Laura was gone. They looked so lost. Laura stepped in and filled her mama's shoes after she died several years before. The young girl had cooked and cleaned and cared for them.

Now, Laura was gone.

People came from miles around to the funeral of Laura Foster. Tension was thick in the crowd. A murderer was still on the loose, and everyone had his own theory as to who it might be. They all were convinced they knew what really happened on the morning Laura Foster turned up missing. Tom Dooley and Anne Melton were the two names on most people's lips. Tom was involved with both Laura and Anne, and it was well known that he had plans to meet Laura. Betsy Scott was the last known person to see her alive, and Laura had told her so.

At the gravesite, Will and James placed a wreath of daisies on the fresh mound of dirt. Aunt Mary and Emily covered the grave with fresh picked roses. The two would come back later and plant flowers.

Amazing Grace how sweet the sound,
That saved a wretch like me.
I once was lost,
But now I'm found.
Was blind,
But now
I see . . .

The voices of the little community rose up past German Hill and drifted in the wind above Laura's final resting place.

After the service, Aunt Mary and the other women went back to the house to store the food and clean up for Will and James. They each had memories of Laura growing up and shared them with one another as they worked. Sometimes, the conversation would turn to more normal things. Betsy Scott had been counting the foggy mornings for the month. The number of fogs in August told folks how many snows they would have during the coming winter. Betsy figured there would be at least four big ones. Talk moved to husbands and children and funny songs. The ladies found comfort in each other's company.

Most of the men stayed at the cemetary and talked after the funeral. Some were there to help shovel dirt into the grave and some were there to simply watch. The names of Tom Dooley and Jack Keaton came up again and again. It was common knowledge that both men had taken off for Tennessee. By the time the men broke up to go home, they swore to each other to bring the two back for questioning.

Colonel Horton and Colonel Isbell made it clear to everyone there they wanted answers, and they would have them. These two men had the money and the means to do it. The community seemed relieved to have them in charge and rallied behind them.

After the funeral, the search for Jack and Tom began.

CHAPTER FORTY

Calvin Cowles's store became the place to go for news and the latest theories about the murder. Betsy Scott was the last person known to see Laura before she disappeared. According to Betsy's story, Laura was on her way that morning to meet Tom at the old Bates' Place. So it wasn't long until the community forgot about the Bates family that had deserted their home so long ago, and the area was referred to as Laura's Ridge. News of the details of Doc Carter's examination of the body spread like wildfire and soon everyone knew the gruesome details of the stabbing and how the killer broke her legs to bury her in the shallow grave. They also learned she was with child. Everyone became convinced that the father of Laura's baby was the killer, but there was nothing solid to support that theory until the day Perline Foster came back to Elkville. Until that time, no one had even realized she was missing—even though she had not attended the funeral. Most people tried to avoid Perline on a regular basis making her the kind of person that would not be missed.

Perline showed up on one of those busy days when everyone was sharing stories and offering their ideas on what might have happened to Laura. Martha Cowles and some of the other ladies noticed right away that she had been doing some serious drinking. Her words were slurred when she spoke and she staggered when she walked. Noticing their stares, Perline stopped before she entered the store and stared back at the women. The girl was used to their disapproval; but now, plied with corn liquor, she was not tolerant of it. The women saw the anger on the drunken woman's face and quickly turned away. They did not want a confrontation with her. She smirked at them and walked into the store.

Calvin could tell immediately that Perline was in bad shape. He quickly approached her and began to gather the things on her list. The last thing he needed was trouble at the store. Once they had settled up he guided her to the front door. The sooner she left the better.

As Perline made her way outside, she noticed that the women had moved away from the porch. *Good,* she thought. *They needed to know that she wouldn't stand for their insults.* She started to leave, but a voice yelled to her from the group of men by the shed. It was Ben Ferguson

"Where you been, Perline? I heard you done run off like the rest, after Laura disappeared. Why, I wouldn't be a bit surprised if you're the one that killed her."

Silence fell over the crowd. *Perline should have known better than to come to the store,* Miz Cowles thought. Her name had come up with Jack Keaton's many times since the funeral.

A long moment passed until Ben and Jack Adkins laughter broke the silence, and that was all it took for Perline. Storming over to the checker table she threw her sack down beside Ben's chair and reaced over to him, grabbing a shine jug from his hands. Deliberately she brushed up against him as she raised up and took a slow drink of it. Jack and Ben stopped laughing and stared at Perline. She smiled at them, enjoying the shocked look on their faces. Slowly and with great deliberation Perline wiped the liquor from her mouth.

"Sure, Ben! Me and Tom done away with Laura Foster, and then we run off to Tennessee."

The two sat speechless at the checker table. Triumphantly, she began to laugh at them. It was a loud, drunken laugh. She was so out of sorts that she cackled until her face hurt. The murmers of the crowd silenced Perline. Whirling around, she saw angry stares and accusing eyes. Her laughter quickly turned to fear as she realized the trouble she had just brought to herself.

Sobered by the mess she had made, she turned back to Ben and Jack. "You boys don't know how to take a joke, I reckon."

She set the jug back on the table in front of Ben. Gathering her courage she tried to shock the crowd and rubbed herself against him again. Ben recoiled from her touch.

"It's your loss," she bragged a little too loud to be real.

Ben shot Perline a challenging stare and picked up the jug. He poured what little was left of the shine on the ground.

"I don't think so," he said.

The crowd began to murmer again—this time louder than before and there were snickers mixed in. Snatching up her sack she stalked off towards the Melton cabin.

The shocked crowd was left to ponder her words.

With that, she laughed. It was a loud, drunken laugh. She turned to the men to get their reaction but nobody else thought her words were amusing. Ben and Jack stared angrily at Perline. They both knew her connections to Tom Dooley, Jack Keaton, and Anne Melton.

Perline grabbed her sack and stalked off towards the Melton cabin. She could hear Ben and Jack laughing at her.

One day they'd be sorry, she thought.

CHAPTER FORTY-ONE

Tom arrived in Trade, Tennessee, by late July and found work at the farm of Colonel James Grayson. He'd heard from the locals that Colonel Grayson was looking for a good farm hand to work in the fields. It was harvest time and although most of the crops were in, there was still plenty of hay to put up for the winter. Practically barefoot by the time he reached Grayson's farm, Tom had tied the soles of his shoes onto his feet with old rags. Now, even the rags were mostly gone. Tom needed a pair of boots to get to Mountain City. His feet were stone bruised and blistered. The work at Grayson's farm would give him time to recuperate and earn money for at least a pair of used boots.

About a week after Laura was buried, the news reached Trade. Tom overheard men talking about it at the local store. The Foster murder had become big news in several states. Now that a body had been found Tom knew there would be renewed interest—and with that—renewed anger. Outrage grew with the news that the murdered girl was pregnant. Someone would need to pay for the crime—and soon. News of the baby would cast more doubt on him, thanks to Betsy Scott and her big mouth. Tom stayed away from the local store after that. He knew he needed to keep a low profile and leave as soon as he possibly could. He had no intention of facing an angry mob.

With all the talk, Tom was grateful that he had been cautious and told Colonel Grayson his name was Tom Hall. Grayson had been good to him and allowed Tom to sleep in the bunkhouse near the fields. He liked the fact that his quarters were in such a secluded area of the farm and he could come and go easily should he need to make a quick escape. During his stay on the Grayson farm he felt safe. The food was some of the best he'd ever eaten and there was plenty of it. Colonel Grayson's wife, Julia kept help. An old black woman they called Aunt Lizzie ran the house for her and cooked. Surprisingly, her cornbread was every bit as good as his mama's. Aunt Lizzie carried food to the workers in the fields every day, always in what she called *lunch pails*. Tom's favorite meal from Aunt Lizzie was green beans cooked in fat back with a slice of cantaloupe and a big cake of cornbread. He actually put on a little weight while he was at the Grayson's farm.

Watching the colonel and his pretty wife, Tom often wondered what it would have been like to be born into a different family. This didn't mean he would change his own family for anything in the world, but to be a man of means seemed so much easier. Would a man be able to make better decisions if the decisions put before him were not so tough? How hard would it be to decide which shoes to wear or which horse to ride? Tom's decisions had never been that easy. His decisions were always based on surviving day to day. He worried about basic things like food, clothes and shelter.

Each night before he fell asleep, he allowed himself to think of Anne. The life she had chosen while he'd been away to war was about surviving, too. For the first time since he came home, he felt no blame towards her for marrying James. She had made hard decisions the same as he had. Anne had done what she needed to do to keep her family fed and clothed. He loved her and always would . . . and he loved Mary Beth, too. Tom was glad they were taken care of.

CHAPTER FORTY-TWO

Perline laid low after her little conversation with Ben Ferguson and Jack Adkins. *They were both jackasses,* she thought—always having something smart to say. She should never have said what she did, but they'd made her mad and she was tired of being run over by people.

Having stayed home for days, when Perline got word from Celia Scott that she needed some help, she was glad to go. The two women would be stringing beans and preparing them to dry. Celia's husband loved leather britchey beans, and she intended to hang several bushels in the attic. Perline needed the extra money. She was seriously thinking about going back to Watauga. She wanted to get out of Elkville for good and get away from Anne Melton.

As Perline started to leave for Celia's, she noticed that Anne was getting ready to leave, too. Anne told Perline she was stir-crazy and needed to get out of the house. She said she needed to get away and was going to the store to buy more salt. James wanted Perline to pickle some beets. The two went their separate ways.

When Perline arrived at Miz Scott's, she saw Celia on the porch with her pipe. As she balanced herself on the foot log that crossed the creek to the house, Perline waved to Celia. The old woman smiled and waved back. Perline liked her. She was a spunky little woman who smoked if she wanted to and always spoke her mind.

Making her way up the creek bank, Perline saw that Celia was not having any success getting the pipe lit.

Perline called to her, "I'm comin' Miz Scott, just wait and I'll help ya."

Perline ran up to the porch. Celia had some iron tongs in her hand from the cook stove, and a red-hot coal between them. Perline eagerly took the tongs from Celia's hand. In her overzealousness, she dropped the hot coal into Celia's lap.

Celia sprang from her chair and threw the coal off her apron into the yard.

176

"Lord, help me, girl; you're gonna burn me alive!"

Both looked down to see a big hole in Celia's apron. The two women looked at each other for a moment and then broke into laughter. They stood on the porch pointing to each other and laughing hysterically. When they were finally able to collect themselves, Celia motioned for Perline to sit down.

"If I'd 'a known you were gonna be this much help, I'd 'a gotten you over here sooner."

They both started laughing again.

Finally, Celia took the two bushels of beans and put one in front of Perline's chair and one in front of hers. Then she handed Perline a big darning needle and some thread. She got one for herself, too; and they sat down to work.

Celia and Perline commenced stringing. When they finished getting the strings out of the beans, they started stringing them up with a needle and thread. After Celia and Perline were finished, they would take them to the attic to dry. They didn't talk much—just enjoyed the day and each other's company. It was a pleasant fall day, so they stayed on the porch in the shade. Once in awhile, a welcome breeze passed through.

It was one of the most relaxed days Perline could remember, and she let her guard down. Laughing and enjoying the breeze she didn't notice Anne Melton coming towards her. When Anne reached the porch, she leapt up and charged Perline. Caught completely unaware, Perline tried to flee from her chair, but she never had a chance. Anne grabbed her by the hair and pulled her off the porch. Poor Celia was barely able to clear Perline's chair as it came flying towards her. The little woman watched in horror as Perline was dragged to the front yard, kicking and screaming.

"You ignorant, sorry, piece of white trash! What have you done?" Anne screamed.

"Let me go! Let me go," Perline whimpered.

"When I got to the store, I heard how you told Ben Ferguson and Jack Adkins that you and Tom killed Laura Foster!"

Anne threw Perline to the ground, keeping a few pieces of hair between her fingers. She hit Perline hard with the stick. Perline screamed in pain. Jumping on top of Perline, Anne started choking her. Frantic now, Perline managed to push her off, convinced that she was there to kill her. Clutching her throat, Perline gasped for air and tried to roll away, but Anne's stick came down hard on her shoulder. The pain was so fierce Perline feared it was broken. She tried to stand, but Anne grabbed her by the blouse and kicked her in the ribs. Perline heaved in pain and struggled to breathe. She clawed at the ground, trying to crawl away, but Anne still had a handful of Perline's hair. Knowing there was nothing else she could do, she drew herself into a protective ball and stayed there. If she didn't fight back and stayed still, maybe Anne would say what she needed to say and stop the beating. She had to have time to get to her feet.

Anne leaned in to her. "Don't you know this puts you in an awful mess . . . and brings attention on me? I could kill you for this," she shrieked.

Perline continued to lay there, stock still.

"But, maybe I won't have to . . . maybe they'll hang you for runnin' your drunk, stupid mouth!"

Anne let go. As far as she was concerned, it was over and it was time to go home.

Anne was wrong. This time it was not over.

With her head bowed, Perline murmured to herself, *"No more!"*

Shocked, Anne turned to see Perline Foster, hands clenched, and rising to her feet. Her face was swollen, her knees were bloody, and her left shoulder was numb with pain. The shooting pain in Perline's ribs was so sharp she found it hard to breathe. Yet, she had never been more alive than she was at that moment. She moved towards Anne.

"If I hang," she yelled, "you will too, Anne Melton. You are as deep in the mud as I am in the mire!"

Perline lifted her right hand and slapped her china doll cousin across the mouth with all her might. Anne staggered from the blow. Bright red blood trickled from the corner of Anne's mouth onto her porcelain skin. The two women eyed each other in disbelief. Anne's voice was barely above a whisper when she finally found her voice.

"Liar! You get on home Perline before I kill you right here."

Celia Scott stood frozen on the porch witnessing it all.

Perline turned and ran into the woods as fast as she could.

Anne started off in Perline's direction—not giving Celia a second thought—until Celia, in all her panic, let out a gasp. As soon as it slipped out, Anne turned to her. Remembering the one witness to their fight, Anne walked to the porch, still carrying the stick in her hand. Celia backed against the outside wall of the cabin as Anne approached her.

"You seem like a smart woman, Miz Scott, so you let this be your dyin' secret. If you tell one word of this, I'll know it was you; and there is no place you could hide that I wouldn't find you. You remember what I'm tellin' ya. If you speak to anyone about this I'll be back for ya, and I will follow you straight to hell if I have to!"

Anne threw the stick down at Celia's feet, challenging her. Celia did not move. Without another word, she whirled around and took off after Perline.

That evening when Celia's husband came home, she told him what had happened and the things that were said. It took Mr. Scott a long time to calm her down. Before they went to bed, every shutter was closed and latched, and the bolts in both the front and back doors of the cabin were put in place. The poor woman was so terrified she jerked and moaned all night in her sleep.

First thing the next morning Celia's husband hitched his horse to his wagon and took his wife straight to the Wilkes County jail. Celia told the sheriff everything. Mr. Scott told his wife in front of the sheriff that he'd be damned if they'd live in fear from white trash the likes of Anne Melton.

Perline ran deep into the woods after the fight. When the battered little troublemaker was far enough away, she stopped and leaned up against a big pine to catch her breath. The girl's eyes and lips were bruised and bleeding. Her knees were skinned, and her head ached. Each time she took a breath, sharp pains stabbed her side, convincing her that her ribs were definitely broken. Yet no matter how severe the injuries, Perline knew she couldn't go back to the Meltons'. She stayed in the woods until the sun went down and she could made her way to the creek to wash the blood from her face and hands. The cold water felt good. She splashed her face and felt her left eye. It was almost swollen shut. Bone tired, Perline followed the creek to the Gilbert farm and spent the night in their hayloft. Despite her injuries she slept like the dead. The next morning she immediately began making plans for herself. There would be no turning back now.

CHAPTER FORTY-THREE

Perline hid in the woods for two days before she resurfaced. The first day she stole a throw blanket from a chair on the Hendrix' front porch, and a knife that Mr. Hendrix had left on a bench. Perline was on her own again and knew she'd have to make do with nothing. On the second day, she found a mud turtle sunning itself on the creek bank and taking a big rock, cracked open its shell and clubbed the slow creature with a large branch. After washing the turtle in the creek, she built a fire in the woods and roasted the big lizard. Perline had eaten turtle before. It was like eating fish and chicken at the same time. The taste wasn't so bad. Especially if a person was starving.

By the third day, Perline headed for Granville Dooley's house. The man had befriended her during her many visits to Lotty's cabin and she knew he lived alone. Granville was glad to let her stay with him. He didn't like a lot of people; but, for some reason, he liked her. On this particular day he was ranting and raving about Will Foster. Perline learned from Granville that on the day Will had reported Laura missing, he had included Granville as a possible suspect along with the likes of Jack Keaton, Anne Melton, Tom Dooley and Perline. Granville told her it was no secret that he and Laura's papa hadn't gotten along, but that was no reason for him to be accusing Granville of something like that. Pickins Carter, who was justice of the peace in Elkville, had questioned Granville about it. Pickens was a small man with a big title. He used his authority to intimidate people. This of course, made Granville even madder. Perline listened to Granville and tried to look interested. The truth was she wasn't really interested in anything but the fact that she could stay there. Granville could talk all day if he wanted to—as long as she had a bed to sleep in and food to fill her belly.

Unfortunately, this comfortable new situation did not last long. Four days later, Pickins came to Granville's house with Ben Ferguson and Jack Adkins to arrest Perline. Pickins had deputized Ben and Jack after he questioned them about her bold statement at the store. With their statements and the statement from Celia Scott about the fight at her house, the sheriff felt he had more than enough cause to arrest her. Granville yelled at the men and cursed them as they tied her hands and put her in the wagon. *He was sick and tired of the whole mess,* he told them. Pickins sat in the back with Perline and kept his shotgun ready in case Granville decided to give them any trouble. Ben drove the wagon, and Jack followed alongside on his horse. Perline didn't say a word on the way. She kept quiet and thought about what she would tell them when she got to the jail.

The men took Perline to the Wilkes County jail and turned her over to Sheriff Watson. Watson was waiting for them when they arrived. Perline was led into the old stone building and taken directly to the sheriff's office. They started asking her questions right away. Perline told them everything they wanted to hear. The little blind had an answer for every question.

Watson, a rugged man with piercing eyes, a square jaw and a thick brown mustache, turned a critical eye to Perline. She sat before him, tired and dirty with a bruised face and brown bloodstains on her blouse. Finally, he spoke to her in a slow, matter of fact tone.

"Now, Perline, we all know about the fight you and Anne had over at Celia Scott's the other day. Miz Scott was pretty upset when her husband brought her here."

Perline shook her head yes.

"A lot was said that day; don't you agree, Perline?"

Again, Perline shook her head yes.

"Why don't you start by tellin' us why you left for Watauga."

"I just got homesick, that's all. I just wanted to go back and visit with my aunt and uncle."

Watson looked at Ben and Jack standing by the window.

"Well, Ben and Jack here tell me a different story. They tell me you told them at the store that you and Tom done away with Laura Foster, and that the two of you run off to Tennessee. Did you tell 'em that, Perline?"

Perline squirmed in her chair.

"I'd been drinkin' all day that day. I was upset about somethin' and real blue. I'd just been drinkin'. When they asked me that, I thought they were bein' all smart and actin' suspicious of me, so I made a little joke; that's all. Sometimes I get smart-mouthed when people make me mad."

Watson looked at Ben and Jack; they nodded for him to continue.

"Tell us about your fight with Anne Melton the next day."

181

Perline told her version of what happened in great detail. She showed them the bruises, cuts, and skinned places on her body with much relish.

"Y'all accused each other, didn't you, Perline? Why do you think Anne would come over there and accuse you like that?"

"The only accusin' that was done, was by me. Anne came over to scare me and shut me up. She knows I know too much. I told her she was guilty; and she knew it; and that's when she proceeded to beat the tar outta me."

Watson leaned in to Perline across his desk and asked, "What do you know, Perline?"

That was the moment Perline Foster had been waiting for. She was ready to tell her story. Perline asked for a glass of water, and Ben got it for her. All eyes were on her, and she loved it.

"I been stayin' with the Meltons for awhile now. I was hired to do the chores around the house and be a blind for Tom and Anne whenever he got back from the war.

"What do you mean by blind, Perline?" Watson asked.

"Tom was supposed to make it look like he was callin' on me; but, ya see, he was really there to see Anne. I was there to help hide the truth, you know, make people blind to what was really goin' on."

"So you are saying that you covered for Tom and Anne to hide their relationship."

"Yeah, that's what I'm saying," Perline shook her head impatiently. "Tom and Anne started seeing each other again as soon as he came home. He stopped seein' Anne for awhile when he met Laura Foster, and that made Anne mad. She is not someone you want to be around when she's mad, believe you me! I had an awful time while he was seein' Laura. Anne took it out on me."

Perline leaned towards the sheriff. "If you think these bruises are bad, you should have seen me durin' that time. She slapped me windin' every time I turned around for somethin' or another. I'm telling y'all, Anne is a violent, dangerous woman."

"Why didn't you just leave?" Sheriff Watson asked.

"Now just where would I go? The Meltons paid me a little and fed me and gave me a bed. Just where else would I find that? Where else would somebody like me go, Sheriff?"

The sheriff shrugged. Seeing him shrug satisfied Perline. She knew she was on the right track and continued.

"I was happy for little Laura. She seemed so sweet. I thought she would be good for Tom. But several months later, there he was—back again. He spent a lot of time at the Melton's after he stopped seein' Laura."

She shook her head in disgust and added, "Anne was bad for Tom, but he couldn't see it. I tried to be a friend and tell him, but he wouldn't listen. He kept comin' to call. It was like he was possessed by her—just couldn't leave her alone. Then one night, the night before Laura was murdered, he came by and talked to Anne for a long time. I could hear yellin' and screamin'. Sometimes I would hear Anne cryin'. I couldn't really hear anything that was said, but I did hear Laura's name mentioned a couple a times.

"What do you think all the fuss was about, Perline?" the sheriff asked.

"I know what it was about 'cause Anne told me later. After Tom left, Anne got a canteen of liquor from the house and told me she was gonna meet up with Tom at her mama's. She told me to go and get James to bed. Anne even gave me some nightshade and asked me to drug him good. That's just what she said! She was cryin' because she said Tom was gonna meet up with Laura Foster the next mornin' and run off and get married. She started carryin' on about herself and Mary Beth. It was pitiful really. She was in bad shape when she left the cabin. When she didn't come home all night, I was real worried. Somehow I managed to lay down and sleep, though. Just before daybreak, I heard the front door open. It was Anne. She took off her dress and shoes and just left 'em in the floor. Then she come and got in bed with me. I could feel her shiverin'. About an hour later, I got up and got ready to do my chores like I usually do. Anne stayed in the bed. I noticed that her dress and shoes were all wet and muddy. She stayed in bed for most of the day while I went out and worked in the fields. When I come back to cook the midday meal, Tom Dooley was there standin' over Anne's bed. They was talkin' and whisperin' all solemn-like, and I could see that they had both been cryin'. Later that day, I saw Anne hide a knife behind her headboard. I didn't dare go near it, and I ain't seen it since, but it looked like the Bowie knife Tom always carries. Two things Tom Dooley always carries, his Bowie knife and his fiddle . . . I can remember . . . "

"Just stick with the story, Perline," Sheriff Watson reminded her.

Perline nodded, trying to be as polite as she could, and continued, "A couple of days after that, I heard that poor little Laura was missin'. It just about broke my heart. Everybody was so worried. Anyways, a couple a weeks later, I went to see my family in Watauga. My aunt and uncle still live up there. I had no idea that Tom Dooley and Jack Keaton left Elkville around the same time. When I come back, that's when Jack Adkins and Ben Ferguson over there was so mean to me. But I forgive 'em."

Perline took a moment to look at Sheriff Watson and Ben and Jack. She smiled a syrupy sweet smile at each of her captors. Jack and Ben could not bring themselves to smile at her and cast their eyes downward, but the sheriff smiled back and encouraged her to continue.

"I know everybody's been real tense these last couple 'a months and I really do want to help you. So let me tell you about what happened when I first got back to the Melton cabin from Watauga. I come in to find Anne cryin', and she told me all about Tom leavin' and how sad and upset she was. She said people were searchin' high and low for the body 'cause they believed there had been foul play. Then she hugged me and asked me if I was really her friend. I told her, "sure I was." I wasn't about to tell her no. Anne asked me to come with her, said there was unfinished business to take care of, and she needed some help. Said it would bother her until it was taken care of."

Perline leaned over to the sheriff to tell her secret. *Perline was a piece of work*, Watson thought.

"She took me out with her after dark. Took me down Reedy Branch a ways and up a holler. That's when I saw it."

"Saw what, Perline?"

"The body! That's when I saw an arm barely stickin' out of the grave. Anne said she . . . ," Perline stopped and corrected herself, "*they* hadn't had time to cover the body up real good, and she was worried someone would find it. Now, let me tell you boys right now, I wouldn't go near it. I told Anne I didn't want no part of somethin' like that, and that I wished she had never showed me. She covered it up with twigs and leaves herself, and we left. Anne was plenty mad that I didn't help her."

"Are you sayin' you actually saw where Laura was buried?"

"I did."

"Then why didn't you come forward and save these men and the others long hours of searchin', Perline?"

Perline almost came out of her chair. Agitated, she shrieked at the sheriff. "Look at me! Do you not think I was afraid for my life?"

She pulled her blouse off her shoulder and showed Watson, Ben, and Jack a nasty bruise. It was still black and full of blood.

"I got this for makin' a bad joke with Ben and Jack over there. What do you think she would have done to me if I had told?"

Perline was questioned a little while longer and then taken to her cell. Sheriff Watson had heard enough from Perline Foster.

For her own protection the sheriff kept Perline in custody for several days. Her statement made a lot of strong accusations and considering her previous injuries, Watson decided it would be best to keep her there until the others were arrested. Perline didn't mind. She had Alfred Dula and Nimrod Triplette to talk to. When she walked past them on the cellblock, she laughed to herself. *Those boys were always in jail for fighting and drinking*, she thought. They'd have some interesting stories to tell. Besides, she planned to eat and sleep while she had the chance.

A warrant was taken out for the arrest of Angeline Pauline Foster Melton. Ben and Jack were deputized and instructed to leave the jail and head directly for the Melton cabin.

CHAPTER FORTY-FOUR

Lotty Foster was on the porch when she saw them. With Perline locked up, she had known it would only be a matter of time before the sheriff came for her girl. Without even taking the time to put on her shoes she broke into a run towards Anne's cabin. Mary Beth would need her Grandma.

When Ben and Jack reached the Melton's, they hitched their wagon and went straight for the front door. Before they could knock, James opened it and motioned them in. *James must have seen them coming*, Ben thought. He didn't ask any questions. He just nodded to them and pointed in the direction of Anne's bedroom. The house smelled stale, as if no air had been stirring inside for days. Old food sat on the table. The wash pan was full of dirty dishes. James looked bad. His eyes were puffy with dark circles underneath. Ben wondered when he last slept. Ben and Jack found Anne lying on the bed turned towards the wall. Her shallow breathing told the two men she was sleeping. Mary Beth was sitting on the bed beside her holding a cat. Old wooden thread spools were lying across the bed, connected by string. It was clear the little girl had been stringing a spool necklace.

"Sssshhh!" she said, putting a little chubby finger to her lips. "Mama's sleepin'!"

Ben and Jack looked at each other, not knowing what to do next. They had not anticipated the child and did not want to arrest her mama in front of her.

It was James that spoke to Mary Beth, gently and truthfully. He had moved to the bedroom door behind them.

"Your mama has to go with Ben and Jack here on a little trip. She'll be back soon."

Mary Beth studied their faces for a long time. She was sizing up the situation, and they could all tell it. Children were always smarter than grown-ups gave them credit to be.

Firm now and protective, she said, "I told you my mama's sleepin'."

This was going to be much harder than they had first thought, Jack realized. For all his outbursts and hot temper, he had never been mean to a woman or child. He didn't want to upset this little girl if he could help it. Cautiously, the two men moved in. Anne sat up in time to see them walking into the room. Mary Beth was hovered over her mama, protecting her. They both knew why the two men had come. Perline's arrest was big news and Anne had been expecting them. She had even tried to prepare Mary Beth for it as best she could. Putting her fingers gently into the little girl's soft, shiny, dark curls, Anne pulled her close.

"Mary Beth, Mama loves you. You know I do. But you have to do what I tell you and move away. I need to go with Ben and Jack for a little while."

Mary Beth's eyes were wide and full of distrust. She started to protest, but James made his way towards her and scooped her into his arms.

Anne Melton turned away from her daughter. She knew what she had to do. To say anymore would only make it worse. Stone faced, she stood up abruptly and put on her shoes. Ben and Jack led Anne Melton out of the cabin to the wagon. They would tie her hands when they were out of the child's sight. James walked behind them to the door, holding on to Mary Beth. He watched frozen in the doorway as the wagon started down the dirt road. The wagon passed by Lotty, leaving her in a cloud of dust.

"No!" Lotty screamed. "You bring her back! You bring her back; do you hear me?"

When Mary Beth heard her grandma's voice, she wriggled free from James. As soon as her feet hit the floor she broke into a run moving in Lotty's direction. When she reached her grandma, instead of stopping, she ran past her chasing the wagon and screaming for her mama. A few yards down the road, the little girl stumbled and fell. Lotty ran to Mary Beth, dropping to her knees beside her. Lotty held her close watching the wagon carry Anne over the hill and out of sight. James got his cane and made his way to the fence to try and comfort his mother-in-law and his baby girl. For all that had happened, it was that moment when James Melton's heart began to break. He loved his little girl. Mary Beth looked up at him.

"I want my mama," was all she said.

James took his handkerchief from his pocket and wiped the dust and tears from her delicate face and brushed the dirt from her skinned knees and hands. Gently, he put his finger under her chin and tilted it up to him. She stared back at him — the spitting image of her mama.

"I swear to you darlin', we'll get her back. No matter what it takes, I'll bring your mama home."

Lotty stood up and helped James' to his feet. Silently, he leaned down and picked up his little daughter.

The three started back to the cabin. There was much to do.

CHAPTER FORTY-FIVE

The sheriff questioned Anne for hours but she gave him nothing he wanted to hear. Through it all, she stayed calm and quiet. The only thing she did say over and over was, "She lies. Perline Foster lies."

Before they took her to her cell she turned to Sheriff Watson and said, "You've put my life in the hands of a jealous, connivin' liar, and you're lettin' her get away with it! You have believed every word she's told you!"

She maintained her innocence and the innocence of Tom Dooley, without one weak moment.

Perline was released shortly after Anne was arrested. As Perline made her way down the hall leaving the jailhouse, she passed by Anne's cell. Ben Ferguson was troubled when he turned and saw the look Perline gave Anne. *She was taunting Anne and enjoying it*, he thought. Furious, he wanted to take Perline back to her cell, lock her up, and throw away the key. Ben believed the look in Perline's eyes was the look of a dangerously crazy person. He had never trusted Perline, and he never would. She lied and drank at every available opportunity and was shameless with men.

Several weeks later, a young man arrived in Elkville on the mail pony. He told the men at the store he knew Tom Dooley's whereabouts. He said he'd been to Colonel Grayson's farm in Trade, Tennessee, and he'd seen Tom Dooley working there.

"Do you think he recognized you?" Ben Ferguson asked.

"He didn't appear to, but I can tell you boys right now, that was Tom Dooley for sure. I didn't let on, though. I told one of the workers I thought he looked a lot like one of my cousins, and asked the man his name. The field hand told me his name was Tom Hall. He told me Tom was a good ole boy. Said he played a mean fiddle, and they had some good times singing and dancing in the evenings. That was enough for me. I knew that man was Tom Dooley."

The men around the store, with the help of Colonel Horton and Colonel Isbell, formed a posse to ride to Trade, Tennessee and talk with Colonel Grayson.

Horton and Isbell would lead them. Both had been involved in the search for Laura's body from the beginning and were now even more committed to finding her killer. They also knew that Colonel Grayson would have no allegiance to a Confederate soldier. It was a known fact that he had attended several East Tennessee conventions where he had unsuccessfully fought to stave off Tennessee's entry into the Confederacy. When those attempts failed he'd crossed into Louisville, Kentucky to fight for the Union Army with the 4th Tennessee regiment. Grayson fought for what he believed was right and the posse felt confident he would help them when they told him what had happened.

It took a couple of days, but they arrived in Trade with surprising speed. Traveling through Darby and Triplette was easy enough. They reached Watauga by nightfall and camped in an open field. Local farmers were more than happy to help them once they heard their reason for passing through. That evening, some of the farmers delivered stew and bread and sat with the posse to listen to the sad tale of Laura Foster. The next morning, the men crossed over the mountain into Tennessee. They reached the Grayson farm at sunset. As they approached the house, they could see Colonel Grayson sitting on his porch with his pretty wife. He was sharpening his knife, and she was sewing. Grayson stood up when he saw the men approaching. His wife looked uneasy.

"It's all right, Colonel Grayson," Colonel Horton announced as they approached the house. "We are all friends here."

Colonel James Grayson stepped from the porch to greet the men. He stood six feet tall at least, with dark hair and a full dark mustache. He offered his hand and introduced himself, then turned and introduced his wife, Julia. The men in turn did the same, tipping their hats to the lady of the house. Julia politely excused herself and went in. She could tell from the dust and lathered horses that the men had ridden for hours. Quickly, she went to the kitchen to get some lemonade and glasses.

"We need a word with you, Colonel," Colonel Horton explained. "We've traveled here from Wilkes County to ask for your help."

Grayson nodded, knowing it must be pretty important. They'd come a long way. He offered them the few rockers and benches on the porch.

After he saw to it that everyone had a place to sit, he leaned up against one of the porch rails and asked, "Now, what brings you here, gentlemen?"

Colonel Horton spoke for the men.

"We are in search of a murderer, Colonel. Several months ago, a young girl by the name of Laura Foster was brutally stabbed to death. It was a most heinous crime. She was buried in a shallow grave in a holler off Reedy Branch in Elkville. The grave was not long enough for the body. Her legs were broken and folded under her to fit. She was with child. We have reason to believe that the father of the child is the murderer, and we have a serving girl's sworn testimony to corroborate that fact. There are also several accounts from members of the community as to what they have seen and heard since Laura's murder. It all points to Tom Dooley and his married lover, Anne Melton. Miz Melton is already in custody."

Colonel Grayson looked puzzled. "I've heard about this. The crime sounds most heinous indeed, Colonel Horton; and I will gladly help you any way that I can; but I'm not sure why you think I am the man you need to talk to."

"A young man that rides the mail pony through these parts came to Calvin Cowles' store the other day. He told about an interesting visit to your farm. He feels certain that the man we are looking for is working here. He spoke to one of your field hands about the man. The worker told him the man's name was Tom Hall."

Colonel Grayson reacted to the name.

"Tell me what this Tom Dooley looks like, Colonel Horton."

Horton continued, "He's of medium build, dark curly hair, dark eyes and skin. Tom can be quite popular when he sets his mind to it. He'd have a fiddle with him — takes it wherever he goes. It's been said that he took it with him when he left. He's an accomplished fiddle player and always glad to play for people when asked."

Colonel Grayson nodded.

"I do believe I know the man. He came here lookin' for work about two weeks ago. Said he wanted to earn enough money to buy a pair of used boots. Tom said he needed them to finish his trip. Said he was travelin' to Mountain City, Tennessee, to be with his girlfriend. Tom Hall fits your description and plays a fiddle. The hired hands have enjoyed his fiddle music at suppertime."

Julia came out on the porch with a pitcher of lemonade and some cups. The men were grateful. They were hot and tired from their long trip.

Colonel Isbell spoke next, "Is he still here, Colonel Grayson?"

Colonel Grayson shook his head.

"I'm afraid not. Tom left yesterday afternoon traveling on foot. I believe I know the path he'll be takin' to Mountain City. I would suggest that we go and get the sheriff here to go with you, but unfortunately he's out with another posse. A local man killed his neighbor in a land dispute and is on the run. I'll be glad to help you in his absence. With fresh horses, we should be able to locate him, in say, half a day at the most. Bein' on foot, he'll be easy to catch up with." Colonel Grayson looked lovingly at his pretty wife. "Now, if you noble men are very nice and polite, Julia just might see fit to feed you somethin'. I'll get some of the help to make up ticks in the barn so you can turn in early, right after supper. We'll leave before daybreak tomorrow, while Tom Dooley is still sleepin'."

Julia eyed the six dusty men scattered around on her porch. She had overheard why they were there and what the man that called himself Tom Hall had done to that poor girl.

"You boys go out back to the well and get cleaned up," she said. "James, you get some sawhorses and planks and make a table outside for these fellas. I'll go get Aunt Lizzie, and we'll warm up some leftovers from lunch. Aunt Lizzie always cooks plenty for us and the field hands. You men look like you could use a good hot meal. You have to be tired and hungry—and you are doing a fine thing. I don't know what I would do if that was my daughter."

Julia turned and left to find Aunt Lizzie. The men relaxed for the first time in four days. With Grayson's help, they felt confident they would find their man.

The posse turned in early and rallied before dawn. Before they could get to the horses, Aunt Lizzie brought ham and biscuits to them. It was still dark as they struck out in search of the man calling himself Tom Hall. Grayson kissed his wife goodbye, put his pistol in its holster, and climbed on his horse to join the group. The posse knew every minute counted if they were going to capture Laura Foster's killer. Ben Ferguson and Colonel Isbell were the only ones that had doubts. One way or another, Ben thought, Tom needs to be questioned like the others. The truth needed to be found.

Grayson seemed very comfortable riding alongside the men. He enjoyed talking with the posse about the war. Colonel Horton and Colonel Isbell shared war stories with him along the way. It was cooler in Tennessee. The men enjoyed the stories and the change in weather. September and October were still warm down in the foothills.

The path to Mountain City was heavily traveled. Grayson was quick to question travelers they met along the way. The Colonel had an important air about him that made people want to readily share information. A few recognized the description Grayson gave them and remembered seeing Tom on the path. The information they collected confirmed they were on the right track, and that Tom was indeed following the directions that Colonel Grayson had given him. This was encouraging to the group. After months of searching for Laura and now trying to find her killer, they were all anxious to see justice done and move on.

Several hours into their ride, Grayson stopped at a familiar farm. He knew the farmer who lived there. He rode up to the man's house and knocked on his door. The man answered the door, recognizing the colonel immediately. He and Grayson stood on the front porch for a few minutes and talked. When Grayson returned to the posse he was in a hurry. His friend had given him the answer he was looking for. Tom Hall had stopped by the man's house the evening before and asked if he could spend the night in his barn. The farmer found him so polite and friendly, that he agreed to let him stay there for the night. The man went on to say that Hall had just been by to thank him before he left. It had not been more than a half-hour since Tom left in the direction of the creek. Grayson had explained the situation to his friend and asked him if they could hitch their horses and walk down to the creek for a look. Grayson's friend was clearly disturbed to know that a murderer had been so close to his family. He agreed and immediately started helping the men with their animals.

"I don't want no murderer on my property," he said. "I got a wife and two daughters to protect. If you find him, it don't matter to me if you kill him right there."

Grayson winced at the remark. It was not the best thing his friend could have said to such an overzealous posse. Grayson could tell that the men were fired up enough. He reminded the small group of what they had come to do. He intended to deliver Tom safely back to Wilkes County to face his accusers. The men reluctantly agreed and Grayson led them in the direction of the creek. The farmer went back in the house and bolted his door.

The posse walked softly down the trail to the creek. When Grayson spotted Tom sitting on the bank's edge, he raised his hand motioning for the men to halt. The colonel stepped quietly out of the thicket to get a better look. Tom was skipping rocks in the water. He seemed to be lost in thought. His boots were off, and his feet were in the water. Grayson laughed to himself. *Those new boots were not a perfect fit afterall*, he thought. Tom seemed to think they were when Grayson sold them to him. Even though they were a little snug, he believed the leather would give after he wore them for awhile. The truth was, Tom had never had a good fitting pair of shoes in his life. To have anything on his feet was an improvement.

Sizing up the situation, Grayson motioned for the men to ease forward. They carried their rifles, in case Tom turned on them, not knowing if he was armed. Slowly, Grayson moved towards the man he had known as Tom Hall. Noticing a big rock lying on the ground, he picked it up and stood directly behind Tom, ready to use it if he needed to. His father had always told him to never to draw his weapon unless he intended to use it. *For now, the rock would do*, he thought, *unless the situation changed drastically*. Grayson did not intend to kill this boy. Tom was a young man and he deserved a fair chance to tell his side of the story. The truth was all James Grayson was after. It was clear to the colonel that most of this posse had already decided that Tom was guilty and wanted to see him hang. Grayson had also noticed that the little schoolteacher was carrying a noose around his saddle horn. *No*, he thought, *this rock would do*. If guns came out, he was afraid things would turn ugly fast.

"Tom Dooley," he proclaimed, "put your hands up over your head and stand up real slow. You are under arrest for the murder of Laura Foster."

Tom did as he was told. Very slowly, he stood up, coming face to face with Colonel Grayson.

"I won't give you no trouble, Colonel," Tom said. "I'll go peacefully."

He was so complacent that Grayson wondered if Tom had heard them as they approached. Acting as if he had expected to see them, Tom nodded to Grayson with an understanding smile. He eyed the rock and then the pistol in Grayson's holster. Grayson threw the rock down.

"Just so's you know, that pistol holds a little more weight with me than that rock, Colonel. I've watched you clean that thing many times, and I have no doubt it works."

Grayson fought the urge to smile. Tom had always been a likeable fellow at the farm. He turned and yelled to the men, knowing he had a job to do.

"Ben! Jack! Tie him up!"

Bob Cummings pulled out a noose he'd been carrying since the beginning of the trip. He stepped forward so that Tom could get a good look at him.

"I loved Laura Foster, and you need to know it. I wanted to marry her. You took that away from me," Bob said. Then he turned to his friends. "I say we hang him right here for what he's done. Let's hang him now and be done with it!"

"Bob, hangin' me 'cause Laura didn't love ya don't hardly seem right. If it's jealousy that brought you here, then you need to let me go," Tom answered in a calm voice.

Jack Adkins spoke next, "You killed that girl. You took that Bowie knife of yours and you stabbed her to death!" he yelled.

As soon as Grayson heard mention of a knife, he quickly frisked Tom, but found nothing.

Tom looked at Jack and grinned. "And you, you're courtin' Caroline Barnes these days, ain't ya, Jack?"

Jack Adkins didn't answer.

"Is Laura's murder the real reason you want to see me hang? Or are you like Bob here. Is this really about Laura Foster or the fact that I crawled in bed with your precious Caroline Barnes?"

Tom flashed a sarcastic grin at Jack.

"By the way, Jack," Tom challenged, "there's somethin' else you need to know—she liked it."

Jack Adkins lunged for Tom.

"That's a lie!" he screamed.

It took Hezekiah, J.W., and Bob to pull Jack off Tom. Grayson and Calvin grabbed Tom and held him.

The men collected themselves for a minute and then seemed to come to a silent agreement. Bob Cummings held up the noose, and the men started towards Tom with it.

That's when Colonel Grayson decided it was time to draw his pistol. He fired once in the air.

"I told you earlier, that I would help you bring this man to justice. I did not say, however, one thing about takin' part in any killing. You came to me and I agreed in good faith to help you. This man was captured with my help, in my territory, and I intend to personally see to it that he gets back to Wilkes County for a fair trial. Any man that wants to try to do otherwise will have to answer to me."

Jack Adkins laughed.

"We'll wait, Colonel. It might be more fun to see him hang with a big crowd watchin'. Besides, it'll be sweet to see Tom locked up with his little girlfriend."

Tom's eyes darted to Colonel Horton and Colonel Isbell.

"What's he talkin' about?"

Jack happily continued, "Anne Melton and Perline Foster got into a big fight at Celia Scott's house the other day. A lot was said. They were both arrested and questioned. Perline started talking her fool head off, and she's turned state's evidence against you and Anne Melton. Perline's been released, but Anne's still in jail. Oh, and Ben, what was it Perline told us to tell Tom when we found him?"

Ben shot a look at Jack. He was tired and confused and not sure what to think about Tom anymore. Tom looked to Ben for an answer.

Reluctantly, Ben repeated the venom Perline had spouted out. "She said to tell you she wasn't nobody's mistake."

Tom lunged for Jack again, but the butt of Grayson's gun stopped him. When he woke up he was on horseback with his hands tied to the saddle horn. Colonel Grayson was riding in front and pulling Tom's horse with a lead rope.

With Colonel Grayson's contacts and help, the posse was able to locate and arrest Jack Keaton before they left Tennessee. Jack had not been as clever as Tom. He was still using his own name and still up to his old tricks — too much liquor and too many women. People around Trade had noticed him and immediately been suspicious.

Grayson rode to Wilkes County with the posse. He did not feel comfortable sending Tom and Jack with these men. He feared Colonel Horton and Colonel Isbell would not be able to stop them by themselves if they got stirred up again. Grayson would not feel at ease until Tom Dooley and Jack Keaton were safely behind bars.

By the time the group reached Calvin Cowles' store, there was a trail of curious onlookers following the posse. A huge crowd stood waiting to catch a glimpse of the prisoners. The news of Tom's and Jack's capture spread like wildfire from the mountains of Tennessee down to the foothills of North Carolina. As soon as the posse reached one community someone would ride to the next to spread the word. Calvin and Martha Cowles stood nervously on the store porch. They were afraid for Tom and Jack. Calvin's biggest fear had been that things would get out of hand. The Cowles were relieved to see Colonel Grayson leading the way. Cheers for the posse and jeers for the prisoners started as soon as the group was in sight. Mary Dooley came out of the store and stood beside Calvin and Martha.

"Mary, please!" Martha begged. "Things could get ugly. You don't want to be here."

Mary Dooley turned to Martha. "I want to be here more than anything in the world, Martha. No matter what happens today, Tom is my son and I love him. He needs to see a lovin' face in the crowd. He needs to know I'm standing by him."

Martha shook her head. Mary's mind was made up and she knew there was nothing she could do. The posse rode up to the hitching posts and Mary ran to her son.

"Step away, ma'am; we have a prisoner here," Grayson said.

Mary Dooley looked up, and with a strong and steady voice she said, "That young man is my son."

Grayson was caught off guard.

"My apologies, ma'am," Grayson said, tipping his hat respectfully.

Mary Dooley approached the horse carrying her son. She touched Tom's leg.

"I love you, boy," she said, her eyes filled with tears.

"Don't cry, Mama," Tom said gently. "Everything will work out; you'll see."

Bravely, Mary nodded. Martha came down from the porch and put her arm around Mary. Tom smiled at her.

"Miz Cowles, would you take my mama inside and get her somethin' to drink?"

"If I can convince her to come, I'll be glad to, Tom," Martha answered.

The jeers and threats were getting louder now that the horses were hitched. Tom leaned towards his mama and looked at her.

"A lot is happenin' right now and I need to keep my wits about me. I can't do that if I'm worrying about you, Mama. Now, you go with Miz Cowles, please. Do this for me."

Reluctantly, Mary Dooley consented. She put her cheek to his leg, holding on for just a second, and then went with Martha into the store.

James Grayson saw Calvin Cowles approaching.

Calvin extended his hand to greet him and the two men shook.

"It's good to see you again, Calvin," Grayson said.

"You don't know how glad I am to see you!" Calvin answered. "Martha and I have been worried to death. We weren't sure how a crowd would react when this day came. I just pray you can get these boys to the jail all in one piece. Maybe you could say a few words before you head on down to Wilkesboro."

"That might be a good idea, Calvin."

With that, Grayson stepped on the porch, this time making sure his pistol was within reach. Calvin raised his hands to the crowd and asked everyone to settle down and listen. Colonel Horton and Colonel Isbell stood on either side of Grayson flanking him for support. The crowd knew the time and effort these two had put forth in the search for Laura and the capture of her murderer. The old colonels felt confident the crowd would be respectful to Grayson with them by his side.

"These two gentlemen brought a posse to my home several days ago, askin' for my help and I gladly gave it in the name of justice. I know from the accounts these men have given me how brutal this murder was. We all want to see someone punished for the untimely death of Laura Foster. But, ladies and gentlemen, her memory deserves nothin' less than justice. Without further investigation and a fair trial, we cannot guarantee that. If the wrong person is punished for this crime, then a murderer walks free; and we all deserve to know the truth."

The crowd stood silent.

Betsy Scott was the first to speak. She was swept away in the moment. Seeing the handsome colonel and knowing there would be a trial and testimony . . . some of it hers . . . was thrilling to her.

"I want to know the truth, Colonel Grayson. I want to know who really killed that child. It's important to all of us."

"Thank you, Ma'am," Grayson said. "We'll just be a minute here, folks. We'll just get a quick bite to eat and somethin' to drink and be on our way. We need to make Wilkesboro before dark. A wagon is being hitched; and as soon as it is ready, we will be leaving."

Some of the men in the crowd helped water the horses and get them ready to travel to Wilkesboro. It was a good thirty miles from Elkville. The posse went into the store to eat the food that Martha and some of the ladies in the community had prepared for them. When they were ready to go, Calvin thanked Grayson for his help. Mary Dooley and Martha Cowles walked back outside, and Mary quickly ran to her boy.

Calvin followed Mary and spoke to Tom. "Take care, boy," he yelled up to him. "Colonel Horton and I've been talkin'. He's gonna write a letter to Governor Zeb Vance. Zeb's a friend of ours. He's the past Governor of this state and a damn good lawyer. We're gonna ask him to consider representin' you. A Confederate war hero deserves nothin' less than that."

Tom shook his head and smiled at his old friend.

"I doubt if Governor Vance is gonna have time for the likes of me," Tom said laughing, "but I do thank ya. Y'all have been real good to me."

Martha Cowles stood on the edge of the porch. "Tom, if you see Anne, tell her I was askin' about her, will you?"

Tom nodded. "I'll give her your best, Miz Cowles."

With that, James Melton and Bob Cummings jumped on their horses and headed towards the Wilkes County jail. They flanked either side of the wagon carrying the prisoners.

They reached Wilkesboro just after dark. It had taken longer than Colonel Horton and Colonel Isbell had estimated. The droves of onlookers as they passed through Boone, Darby and Triplette slowed their progress. Sometimes the rowdier crowds would yell—sometimes they threw rocks. Ben Ferguson and Jack Adkins rode in the back on either side of the prisoners with their shotguns ready, in case there was any real trouble. Colonel Horton drove the wagon with Colonel Isbell riding shotgun. The passionate crowd could easily get out of hand. Onlookers shouted obsenities and approached the wagon many times along the way. Jack Keaton was clearly scared out of his wits. Tom Dooley, on the other hand, remained stoic throughout the entire trip. He set his jaw and stared straight ahead, trying not to look at anybody.

Deputy Jesse Ferguson was waiting for them at the jail as they pulled up. He and the other deputies helped Tom and Jack from the wagon and walked them quickly into the jail to avoid the mob that had gathered outside. They lined the street in front of the jail like sentinels, torches in hand, waiting to catch a glimpse of the accused men. Tom and Jack were led upstairs to their cells. The rock walls made the jail cool, even in the late summer months. Iron bars, damp rock, and prisoners, gave the jail a musty smell. As the men were taken down the hall to their cells they passed Anne's. She had been anxiously waiting to see Tom and reached through the bars to touch his arm as he passed. Tom stopped and turned. Their eyes met.

Before he was pushed on to his cell, he managed to tell her what he had told her so many times before.

"You are the love of my life, girl," he whispered. "You remember that."

Jack Keaton laughed to himself when he heard Tom talking. *It ain't gonna do him no good to tell her that now*, he thought. *Anne should have paid up while she had the chance.*

CHAPTER FORTY-SIX

Jack Keaton was questioned first thing the next morning.

Sheriff Watson looked at him and grinned. Jack reminded Watson of Tom, but he was scruffier. *It's funny,* the sheriff thought, *how two people can look so much alike; but one is better looking than the other.*

"Perline Foster speaks highly of you, Jack. She says you and her just got in with the wrong crowd."

Jack looked at Sheriff Watson and nodded.

"Perline's right about that. We seen and heard things we didn't want to. That's why me and her left town for awhile. We was scared."

Sheriff Watson noticed Jack looking off to the side as he spoke and casting his eyes to the floor. That boy had never been one to look people in the eye.

"Tell me what you were scared of, Jack."

Jack nervously looked to his left for the umpteenth time and started to speak, but Watson interrupted him.

"And, look me in the eye when you're talkin' to me. I need the truth, boy."

Jack tried to look up at the sheriff, but his eyes quickly dropped down and shifted off to the left somewhere. The sheriff didn't trust him—never had. Jack Keaton had been suspected of stealing and vandalizing for years; he'd just always been sneaky enough to avoid being caught.

"I was scared of turnin' up like Laura did, Sheriff. I loved that girl and I'd 'a never done her no harm. Perline knows that. She knows I loved Laura. Anne Melton and Tom Dooley are another story, though. Laura got in their way—and you don't ever want to get in the way of those two."

"Do you know what happened to Laura?"

"Not for sure, I don't. I just know how things changed after Laura turned up missin'."

With that, Jack proceeded to weave a tale so compelling, even Sheriff Watson forgot to doubt him. Between Jack Keaton's and Perline Foster's statements the local law officers believed they had enough to charge Tom Dooley and Anne Melton with Laura's murder. *Yep, Anne should have paid up,* Jack thought. He felt a twinge of anger as he remembered their conversation on the back porch that night at Lotty's. He knew now that Anne had never been interested in him. *Little miss high and mighty had always thought she was too good for him. And he had always been second best to his cousin, Tom.*

Well, maybe not anymore . . .

CHAPTER FORTY-SEVEN

Months passed, with many letters sent back and forth between Colonel Horton and Governor Vance. Colonel Horton finally managed to get his good friend to come and talk to Tom and consider representing him. Vance was practicing law in Charlotte since Holden defeated him and took office in the governor's mansion. Part of the appeal for Vance had been Colonel Horton's mention of the fact that Tom had served in Vance's beloved 26th Volunteers during the war. Zeb had a soft spot in his heart for his old regiment. This, coupled with the fact he hoped to run for governor again persuaded him.

Wilkes County had been divided in the war with many feeling it wasn't their fight. Vance lost many votes in the area because of his stand on the Confederacy. He needed to mend fences in the large county if he planned to seek re-election, and he did.

The courthouse lawn was packed with people socializing and enjoying picnics. There were pits set up selling barbecue and roasted cobs of corn to the crowd. Other little stands were set up with cakes, pies, and cider. The deputies were having a rough time trying to keep the children off the hanging tree. The old *Tory Oak* as it was called was used to hang war criminals during the revolutionary war and anytime there was talk of a hanging, for some reason, every child in Wilkes County thought they had to climb it.

Zeb Vance had come quietly into town the night before. He wanted to talk to Tom before he made a final decision. Zeb was furious when he learned the circumstances under which Tom was arrested. The old fire-eater was even more outraged when he learned that James Grayson, a southern man known for having left his home state of Tennessee to fight for the North, was involved. Tom had been captured by men clearly out of their jurisdiction and arrested by a man who had no authority to do so. He agreed to represent Tom and address the crowd at noon. Everyone was there. In the months that followed Tom's capture, a great many "witnesses" came forward with things they knew. Family members, friends, and people who saw or heard something they believed important to the case jumped into the fray. The number of possible witnesses grew to over two hundred.

Betsy Scott was thrilled with all of the activity. The bubbly little gossip thrived on it. She was the last known person to see Laura Foster alive and this elevated her importance in the community to an all time high. Betsy immediately spotted the reporter everyone was talking about. He was an Irishman and had come all the way down from New York City to cover the trial of Tom Dooley. The fact that such a well-known and controversial figure as Governor Zebulon Vance was rumored to be representing the accused had piqued a great deal of interest. Everyone wanted to be interviewed by him. Watching him standing there with his note pad and his camera, she decided to strike up a conversation first thing. There were things he needed to know and she was happy to fill him in on the details. To the young reporter's dismay, after Betsy started talking, she wouldn't stop. No matter how politely he tried, he couldn't get away from the woman, or get her to hush.

"Course some people say, if the truth be known, that boy is just too good lookin' for his own good . . . and I'm not so sure that's not true. Why, every time you turn around, Tom's gone and flirted . . . or worse . . . with some man's wife or girlfriend. He's made some powerful enemies in this community, I'll tell you that. Jack Keaton's just as wild really, but he don't have as many girlfriends or enemies as Tom. He talked himself right out of this mess, and they released him . . . said he had an alibi."

The Irishman politely stood and listened to Betsy, taking notes and eyeing the crowd. When Caroline Barnes walked by them looking for Jack Adkins, Betsy pointed her out to O'Hara.

"Ooooh, there's Caroline Barnes. Her boyfriend, Jack Adkins, just hates Tom 'cause Caroline used to be sweet on him. But, Jack's jealous ways ain't nothin' compared to Anne Melton. Lord, have mercy! I thought there was gonna be a murder long before the . . . "

O'Hara saw his chance and took it. Here was another woman that had been involved with Tom.

"Uh, excuse me, Miss Scott . . . and uh, thank you so much for your time."

He tipped his hat to her and took off after Caroline Barnes, leaving Betsy in mid sentence.

"Well, they! Wished I'm 'a never!" Betsy said.

Gwendolyn Smith had been watching Betsy curiously from one of the cider tables. When she saw the reporter walk away, she quickly made her way to Betsy and started questioning her about him.

O'Hara came up behind Caroline and gently tapped her on the shoulder.

"Miss Barnes, I'm Michael O'Hara, a reporter from the *New York Herald*. I understand you had a relationship with Tom Dooley, and I was wondering if . . ."

In an instant, Caroline whirled around and pointed her finger at the little reporter.

"You stop right there!" she scolded. "Tom Dooley called on me once . . . just one time . . . and I have suffered for it ever since." She yelled in Betsy's direction, "And, you! I've been gossiped about all I care to be!"

Betsy tried to look in another direction. Embarrassed, she wanted people to think Caroline was talking to someone else. It didn't work. Everyone knew exactly to whom Caroline was speaking.

"I've been threatened by a woman that's so dangerous she's in jail."

She stomped her foot and glared at O'Hara, nose to nose.

Her voice now shaking with anger, Caroline continued, "And now you want to finish me off by quotin' me in *The New York Herald* for the whole world to read! Well, unless you want me to go get Jack Adkins to thrash you good, you better move on, Mister . . . whatever your name is!" Caroline was shrieking now. "And leave . . . me . . . alone!"

Jack Adkins heard her and was at her side in a flash. O'Hara quickly saw the threat in Jack's eyes. The reporter lowered his hat so that he didn't have to face Jack. He nodded, and slowly made his way back to Betsy Scott. He would rather be talked to death than beaten to death, he decided.

Gwendolyn greeted him as he approached. "Don't let Caroline Barnes fool ya. She ain't no good neither. And she saw Tom Dooley more than once, I can tell ya. Why Hell's bells! Everybody knows she did more than just see him, too; no matter what she tries to let on."

Perline had been roaming around the crowd all morning. With Tom and Anne in jail she was clearly enjoying her new-found freedom, and being a star witness for the prosecution—her new celebrity. The traitor now stood listening to Caroline's rants with glee. She loved to see other people make fools of themselves. *This man needed to talk to her*, she thought.

"I'll be glad to talk to you, Mr. O'Hara," Perline announced. "I turned state's evidence on this whole mess."

Perline was thrilled to think about talking to a reporter. She loved all the attention she was getting. Everyone knew she was the prosecution's star witness. Before Perline could tell her story, O'Hara's attention turned to the murmers in the crowd. All eyes were now turned to the jailhouse. Someone was coming out. The reporter ran to the jail to get a better look.

Noon had finally come. The sheriff and his deputies were the first to step outside. They were making protective lines on either side as Zeb Vance exited the jailhouse. The group walked across the street and proceeded up the courthouse steps. Governor Vance stood beside the Dooley family. Mary Dooley was clearly scared to death. She'd heard all the talk about a lynching and her eyes were wide and fearful. Anna and Eliza held on to their mama's arms for fear she would faint. Colonels James Horton and James Isbell along with their wives, and Calvin and Martha Cowles stood off to the side in a show of support.

It was an impressive group that stood on the courthouse steps, but it was Governor Vance who quickly captured the crowd's attention. He was tall and slender, standing straight as an arrow. The past governor had an air of authority about him. His dark hair was touched with bits of silver at his temples and his thick dark mustache was groomed to perfection. Dressed like a gentleman, he wore a top hat and sported a silken vest under his topcoat. Vance held up his hand to quiet the crowd. The noise that had seemed so deafening just moments before, ceased. The only sound remaining was that of the barbecue sizzling on an open fire in the background.

The past governor of North Carolina cleared his throat. "Thank you, good friends of Wilkes. I've come here today to begin my defense of a war hero from my own regiment, the 26th Volunteers. I believe Tom Dooley to be a man of honor and courage, a true Confederate. He deserves a fair trial, as any of you in a situation like this would. I have talked with Tom Dooley and his family as well as many of you here today. Based on these conversations, I do not believe Tom Dooley to be guilty."

Vance could tell from the crowd's reaction that most did not share his view. The murmers and jeers were audible enough for the politician to take note of it.

He continued, "And because of the prejudice here in this community, and the passionate nature of this crime, I plan to request a change of venue asking that this trial be moved to Statesville. I do not believe that Tom can get a fair trial here in Wilkes County."

Bob Cummings, the meek schoolteacher, who had been so smitten with Laura Foster, shocked the crowd.

"Fair!" he shouted. "How about poor Laura Foster, Governor Vance? We can't bring Laura back to speak for herself, no matter what county you take this to! Don't you think the people in Wilkes deserve to see Tom Dooley hang for what he did? His knife went through her heart, and mine, too."

Bob turned to the crowd. "He's bound to die. I say let him die here!"

The crowd went wild with support for Cummings. Men shouted obscenities at Governor Vance and Tom Dooley. A few spectators fired pistols in support of Bob. Others screamed, "hang him"! Blevins flashed a photo of Vance and his supporters on the courthouse steps. Tension was clearly building among the passionate crowd.

Vance took one step down nearer the crowd and addressed Bob's remarks. "You cannot prove that Tom killed that girl!"

"We can, and we will, Governor Vance!" Bob yelled back.

"You are angry and hurt, and I understand that," Vance continued. "But anger and hurt can cloud good judgement. Swift judgement leaves room for error. I'm sorry to say that I think you have all reached a point where hanging this man would simply make each one of *you* feel better."

The crowd grew angrier with Vance's remarks. Mary Dooley shook with fear as her two daughters tried to comfort her.

"Well, justice is not swift, my friends. It takes time. Sometimes, the right way is not the easy way. We all know that deep down. I repeat—Tom Dooley deserves a fair trial, and I intend to see to it that he gets one."

The crowd began to chant *Hang him* and *Laura's* name. Vance knew his appeal to them had fallen on deaf ears.

Jesse Ferguson and the other deputies moved down to the edge of the steps near the crowd, trying to move them back from the steps and calm them.

Governor Vance was furious. The people of Wilkes had already done great damage to his political career. Now, they were ready to hang an innocent man. They wanted someone to pay for the murder of Laura Foster, and by now they didn't care who that someone was. Their narrow-mindedness infuriated the past Governor of North Carolina, and he allowed that fury to get the best of him. His temper flared and damning words flew from his lips before he could stop them.

"The life of this one Confederate soldier, is worth a thousand wenches the likes of Laura Foster!"

The crowd fell silent. They were shocked by his words. No one had spoken ill of Laura since her disappearance.

Calvin Cowles and Colonel Horton had been standing to the side as Vance addressed the crowd. Quickly they motioned for the deputies to get Vance back to the jail along with Tom and his family before people had a chance to recover. They followed behind the deputies, hearing the boos and jeers. At first, there were only a few, but by the time they reached the door to the jail, the sound was deafening.

Once safely behind the doors of the jail, Colonel James Horton spoke first. "That was not the smartest thing you could'a said, Zeb."

Calvin looked to his old friend. He and Colonel Horton had brought him here, and now Zeb was in a real predicament. Calvin was angry.

Calvin confessed to his friend, "Zeb, There's one thing I think you should know. Tom served in the 42nd Regiment, not your old 26th Volunteers."

Vance's head snapped around to Colonel Horton. "But James, you told me . . . "

Colonel Horton raised his hand to silence Vance.

"Well Zeb, it's too late to worry about the small details," Colonel Horton replied trying to smooth things over. "*The New York Herald* just took your picture out there. Tom Dooley is a Confederate soldier and deserves the best possible defense."

"You old goat! You did this on purpose!" Vance fumed.

Colonel Horton patted him on the back, rolled his eyes to the heavens, and stroked his beard. "Now, Zeb, I don't recall exactly what it was I said."

"Well, I do," Vance interrupted.

Calvin tried hard not to laugh at his two friends. This had become a bad situation, and he did not think the two would appreciate that he found humor in their disagreement.

"Let's get you to the boarding house, Zeb," Calvin said. "We'll see if Sheriff Watson can spare a guard for you tonight. Emotions are high. You've got a long day ahead of ya. You'll need your wits about ya tomorrow mornin'. You must know that no matter how you got here, you're where you need to be. James Horton's right. This Confederate soldier needs your help."

Vance left the room in a huff. He knew there was no turning back now.

Calvin Cowles and James Horton nodded to each other. With time, Vance would cool off. The two men still believed they had done the right thing. No matter how they painted the picture to Vance, Tom now had the help he so desperately needed.

Michael O'Hara had followed the group into the jail and listened with interest to their conversation. He made up his mind to follow this story to its end. The reporter felt he owed that much to the accused. He and Tom had clearly taken separate paths since that afternoon with the Bushwhackers just a few years before. O'Hara thought it a shame that Tom had survived that day in Virginia for this. It was a sordid tale. Even if O'Hara had not known Tom, he believed this story had all the makings of a headline—handsome war hero—two beautiful women—a lover's triangle—crime of passion. With all that, plus a past North Carolina governor to defend the accused, he believed it would peak the interest of his readers. The reporter would soon find out that his hunch was right. Michael O'Hara's story would not only peak the interest of his readers, it would grip an entire nation.

Tom Dooley would be his lucky charm—once again.

CHAPTER FORTY-EIGHT

Thomas C. Dooley, not having the fear of God before his eyes, but being moved and seduced by the instigations of the devil, did willfully, feloniously and of malice aforethought, make an assault upon one Laura Foster.

Anne Melton, late of the County of Wilkes, not having the fear of God before her eyes, but being moved and seduced by the instigations of the devil, did maliciously, feloniously, violently and in her malice aforethought stir up, move, abet and cause the said Thomas C. Dooley to do and commit the said felony and murder . . . and harbor, maintain, relieve, comfort and assist . . .

The words were harsh and damning but neither Tom nor Anne moved a muscle as they listened. Shackled, the two stood side by side as the indictments were read aloud.

To Anne, the words sounded like a condemnation to hell.

On Monday, October 1, Sheriff Watson brought Tom and Anne before Judge Ralph Buxton and a Wilkes County grand jury of eighteen. They both plead "not guilty" to the charges and were remanded to the Wilkes County jail until their trials began.

Based on his first meeting with the people of Wilkes on the courthouse steps, Zeb Vance had a good read on public opinion. It was not what he had hoped for. By Thursday, October 4, Vance presented an affidavit to the court requesting a change of venue. In the affidavit, Tom and Anne stated they did not believe that they could receive a fair and impartial trial in Wilkes County. Both Tom and Anne, along with Vance believed public opinion was so jaded and emotions so high that the jury would be prejudiced against them. They were convinced there was no way to select an unbiased jury in Wilkes County. Zeb also had ulterior motives for moving the trial to Statesville. In the last months of the Civil War while Vance was still serving as Governor of North Carolina, he set up temporary headquarters in Statesville.

The Union had taken over North Carolina's capitol of Raleigh. Because of this, Vance believed he still had a great many supporters in Statesville.

The court ordered the case be moved to Iredell County. Sheriff Watson was ordered to deliver the prisoners to the sheriff of Iredell before the following Thursday. The trial was set to begin Friday, October 19, 1866. Vance also requested Tom and Anne be tried separately. That request was also granted.

Tom's first trial began on October 19 and lasted for two days. Anne was present in the courtroom throughout the trial but was never called to witness. Lotty, James, and Mary Beth were there every day. Laura's family was also in the courtroom as was Tom's. Tom was called before the court on Sunday morning, October 21 at eight o'clock and sentenced to be hanged on November 9. Vance was shocked at how jaded the judge and jury seemed towards his client.

In tears, Mary Dooley was led from the courtroom. Her daughters, always by her side, guided her out. Tom did not allow himself to look at his family after the sentencing. He could not afford to let his emotions show. It would be too hard for them — especially his mama. Throughout the testimony and sentencing, Anne kept her composure. She showed no emotion. The only time anyone saw any tenderness from Anne was when she saw Mary Beth. Mary Beth had grown in the few months that Anne had been away. Anne could tell by the look in her little girl's eyes that she was shutting her mama out. Mary Beth felt abandoned by her mother, and Anne knew it. Her daughter's cold stare, hurt Anne Melton more than words could describe. She felt a part of her had been cut away.

After the first trial, Governor Vance immediately filed an appeal to the state Supreme Court. A new trial was granted, citing the evidence in the first one circumstantial. The new date was set for the spring term of 1867.

When the new date rolled around, three of Tom's witnesses failed to appear. Governor Vance asked for a continuance. The continuance was granted and a new date was set for the fall term of 1867. A whole year had passed since Tom and Anne were arrested. When the new date finally rolled around, three witnesses for the state failed to show. It was now the state's turn to ask for a continuance. A new date was set for Monday, January 20, 1868. This time, there were no delays.

CHAPTER FORTY-NINE

The night before the trial was to begin, Governor Vance sat in a cold Statesville jail cell with his client, covering the final details of his defense. Both he and Tom sat with blankets around them. Vance was weary. He had been questioning and coaching Tom for hours. Michael O'Hara sat in the corner as usual, quietly taking notes. Tom gave O'Hara permission to sit in on any and every conversation that interested him. Tom and Vance were so used to O'Hara they sometimes forgot he was there. Anne was asleep in the next cell. After hours of listening to them going over and over every detail, she had finally given up and gone to sleep. She had been fighting a cold for several days and was weary from it. Once in a while, they could hear her coughing.

"We were lucky to get an appeal from the first trial," Vance said. "At least we have one more chance. My only concern is that Judge Shipp has already made it clear that he plans to omit certain testimony that we desperately need. Rumor has it that Judge Buxton suggested it to him. He's still mad that we won an appeal. I will not be allowed to bring up the conditions of your arrest—illegal as it was—the judge will not allow it. The inner judicial circle is hard to fight. The cards seem to be stacked against us. We need to pray for a miracle. Well, that just about wraps it up. Are you forgetting anything?" Vance asked.

Tom shook his head. "No, sir. After almost two years of living like this, I believe I done told you just about everything that I know to tell you, and that's a fact."

Vance was tired and worried about what the morning would bring. With the omission of certain testimony and the constant change in the social climate in Statesville since the war, he had a bad feeling about the outcome. He did not have the support of the Confederacy that he once had in Iredell County. Carpetbaggers from the North had infiltrated the area and the South was under reconstruction. As the community struggled to recover from the ravages of war, they found themselves learning to deal with a united nation; and, like it or not, these Northerners became a part of their way of life. Zeb stood up to leave, but in a final act of frustration he turned around unexpectedly and crossed to Tom. He sat down beside him on the cot.

"Before we call it a night, I just have to ask you one more time, Tom. Did you kill that girl? Did you kill Laura Foster?"

Tom did not answer right away. Instead, he stood up and walked to the barred window of his small, dank cell and looked out. After a moment he turned to Vance.

"If God himself came down right now and told you the truth, you wouldn't believe it."

Vance lost all patience with Tom's answer. "Confound it, man, tell me!"

Tom took hold of the bars on the window and yelled at Vance in frustration.

"No! No! No! For the last time, I never touched her. Governor Vance, you gotta believe me. I was plannin' to marry Laura, not kill her. But she never came. I waited half the mornin' for her to show up. I was late — I've told you that. I've already admitted to you that I'd been out all night drinkin' at Lotty Foster's house. I woke up sometime after daybreak. My mind was foggy from the night before and I couldn't remember much of anything. All I did know was that I needed to get going. When I finally got to the old Bates' place I expected to find her there all mad and aggravated like women get. But, she was nowhere in sight. Finally, I figured she got mad and left or maybe she'd got cold feet and stood me up. She had every right to. I even thought that maybe her daddy caught her sneakin' out to meet me."

Tom turned to Vance, who was now sitting on the cot listening. He sat down beside him.

"I was gonna take her to Tennessee and marry her; don't you understand? I wasn't plannin' for no baby of mine to grow up without a daddy. Think about it. It don't make sense. Killin' her would be like killin' a part of me. It wasn't just Laura Foster that died that day. My unborn child died with her."

Tom's mood changed. He began to pace around the room. His footsteps echoed on the stone floor.

"All I hear is how that poor little girl died. Well, what about the baby, my baby? Not one livin' soul has ever stopped to think that maybe, just maybe, I'm a human bein', too. That just maybe I loved that girl or just maybe I would have laid down my life for that child."

Tom stopped, realizing that he was shouting. When he spoke again, it was softer and more controlled.

"That's all I got to say about it."

Governor Vance stood up and nodded to Tom. In the almost two years Vance had known Tom, his story never wavered. Sometimes, like tonight, Vance saw Tom as more than a client. Older now than his twenty-two years with so much trouble heaped upon him, Vance found himself feeling fatherly towards him. Vance felt ashamed for his doubts and put his hand on Tom's shoulder.

"I plan to defend you to the best of my ability. I aim to do right by you."

Tom shook his head. "I thank ya. Not just for myself, but for my mama too. This has been real hard on her. She's a good woman and don't deserve all this worry."

Vance nodded. "You try and get some sleep. You'll need your wits about you tomorrow mornin'."

Tom defeatedly shrugged his shoulders.

Vance turned to the reporter who was still writing in the corner. "You coming, O'Hara?"

Tom turned to him. "Stay for a few minutes, friend. I'm not sleepy."

Nodding, O'Hara stayed seated on his stool in the corner of the cell. Tom sat down on his cot. Vance said his goodnights to the two and left.

"Bet you never thought you'd see me again, did ya?"

O'Hara smiled. "No, I can't say that I did, but I might not have been here to see anything if it hadn't been for you."

"A reporter for *The New York Herald*! You made it, friend. Honestly, I never thought you would. I thought your dream was too far in the clouds. But me, I thought for sure I'd get my wish."

O'Hara continued to write as they talked.

"What was your wish, Tom?"

"I thought I'd come home and my girl would be waitin'. I believed Anne would be waitin' for me. I was foolish to expect that. She needed things I couldn't give her. I was too poor. The only thing I had to give the most beautiful woman in Elkville was me. Now, that's a laugh."

O'Hara studied Tom's face and was surprised to see that he was not hiding behind his usual bravado. In its place the reporter saw what he thought to be the real Tom Dooley, for perhaps the first time.

"I don't think that's funny at all. Laura Foster wanted just you."

Tom smiled at that remark. It was a surprisingly warm smile.

"Yeah, I think she did. It's hard to believe, ain't it?" She told me once that she'd been lookin' for me for a long time, said she knew that someday I'd come. It sounded like the daydream of some foolish little girl. But, what amazed me about Laura is that she didn't care if anybody thought she was foolish or not. She believed it, I could tell. And sometimes, not all the time, but sometimes, I believed it, too."

Touched by Tom's honesty, O'Hara nodded to him. "Sounds like she loved you, pure and simple. That must have been pretty different from Anne's love. What was it about Anne? Why couldn't you just leave her alone?"

Tom scooted to the corner of the wall and leaned up against it. He spoke so candidly that O'Hara felt like he was eavesdropping on someone's private thoughts.

"Anne Melton could walk into a room, and I'd know she was there before I ever saw her. The way she looks, the way she grins, those dark eyes. No, sir, there has never been anything pure and simple about Anne. But God help me, I would let them hang me tomorrow for one more night with that woman."

"Tom!"

"I'd say your life's been pretty easy, O'Hara. You lived in the city, right?"

"Well, yes . . . "

"I bet you lived with your family 'til you was grown . . . went to school . . . had nice clothes and good food . . . am I right?"

For some reason, O'Hara felt almost offended by the question.

"Well, yes, but . . . "

Tom put out his hand to quiet the reporter.

"There's no shame in that. You are one of the lucky ones. But what I am tryin' to describe to you, you probably won't ever understand completely. Anne and I have been together since we was pretty young. My mama saw to it that my family had something on the table every mornin' and every night to eat. It may have been only biscuits or cornbread, but we had somethin'. Anne couldn't count on that. Sometimes the only thing she saw on the table was a liquor bottle. I made sure she got somethin' to eat, when I could. There was always men around her mama's house when Anne was growin' up. Lots of men come to call on Lotty. That's how I first met Anne. I was just a kid and I heard some of the men talkin' about Lotty's house."

Tom stopped.

"It's probably best we don't go into that. Anyway, when my clothes were fallin' apart, Anne would take the things these men left behind and she'd bring 'em to me. Our mamas were too busy survivin' to do much motherin', so we were runnin' wild at an early age. My mama read the Bible to us when she had the time, but she was always tired. Lotty Foster wouldn't have read the Bible even if she could read." Tom looked directly at O'Hara. "We have been lookin' out for each other for as long as I can remember. We learned to be tough together. We learned to fight, and I tell you right now, it don't matter how delicate she looks, Anne fights just like a man when she's mad."

Tom shook his head and gave O'Hara a knowing look.

"She's a wild cat that one is."

Tom laughed as if he was remembering a time with Anne and then sobered himself and continued.

"To tame her would be to kill her, and I wouldn't want to tame her for the world. Once you know what lovin' somethin' that wild and free is like," Tom grinned and winked at his friend, "well, it makes everything else . . . pure and simple."

O'Hara closed his notebook and stood up. Tom stood up with him.

"You make me sound like I've missed out."

Tom shook O'Hara's hand. "You have."

"Goodnight, Tom. I guess I better get my boring self to bed."

"Night, then. I'll see you in the mornin'."

Michael O'Hara got to the door and smiled at the man who once led him through the smoke and the pines to safety.

"I'll be there, Tom. Don't you worry, I'll be there."

On his way out, he passed by Anne's cell. She was sleeping quietly on her cot. *How much was a woman like that really worth*, he thought. O'Hara was curious about the things Tom had said. But then, look where he was now. Tom was in jail and O'Hara was a free man with his whole life in front of him.

He'd take a pure and simple girl any day, he thought. *The complicated ones could kill you.*

CHAPTER FIFTY

The wee hours of a winter morning are dead silent. Most of the world is not only sleeping, but reluctant to wake. It's the closest to hibernation mankind can get. On this particular morning, however, Tom came out of his wintry sleep wide-awake.

It was just before sunrise. Tom's second trial was about to begin. The jail was silent and still. The last rays of moonlight were spilling through the bars of his window. He could see his breath in the light. Tom sat up and put his feet on the stone slab floor. It was ice cold. Quickly he put on his boots and walked to the corner of his cell, calling to Anne.

"I'm here," she whispered.

Relieved, Tom closed his eyes. He was grateful she was awake. He had much to talk about.

"I want you to know, Anne, that no matter what happens, I aim to protect you. I aim to protect you and get you home to Mary Beth."

There was a long silence before she spoke.

"That first time you came to Mama's and we talked, I knew right then and there you were gonna be a part of my life. It may sound silly to you, but it's the truth. I was right, too. You were a part of me, from that day on. No matter what happens in that courtroom, Tom, they can't take you away from me. Some people can live an entire lifetime and not have what I have with you. Whether we come through this or not, we'll always be together. No court of law or hangman is gonna change that."

Tom pressed against the bars and whispered, "Tell me about Mary Beth, Anne. I have to know the truth."

The two lovers whispered together as they watched the sun rise from their separate cells. They talked until the sheriff came for them and placed Tom once again, before his judge and jury.

CHAPTER FIFTY-ONE

Judge Shipp assessed the packed courtroom. He intended to get this trial over with as quickly as possible. Emotions were high and reelection time was around the corner. He had things to do. With an official rap of his gavel, Shipp called for order. Silence fell on the room. The judge instructed the jury while the witnesses were taken to a holding room. By the time all preliminaries were complete the morning was almost gone. Judge Shipp recessed the court until one o'clock at which time he would hear opening statements.

Tom ate the mid day meal in his cell with his family. Anne took her meal with James, Lotty and Mary Beth. No one talked much. There wasn't much to say. For the Dooleys and the Meltons, it had become a way of life over the past year and a half.

Governor Vance did not eat. His stomach was in knots, so he chose to work with his team instead. Richard Allison and David Furches were waiting for him as he walked into a small room off the main courtroom. From the first, Judge Shipp's attitude was a concern and continued to be. The men concentrated on tearing Solicitor Caldwell's case apart piece by piece. Vance rehearsed his opening statement, allowing Allison and Furches to point out any flaws or weaknesses.

Finally, everyone was called back to the courtroom and Judge Shipp reconvened with one swift rap of the gavel. He looked to the jury, then to the prosecution.

"This court is now in session. Solicitor Caldwell, have you prepared an opening statement?"

Caldwell stood up from his table. Will and James Foster sat beside him.

"I have, Your Honor."

"Then, you may proceed."

Solicitor Caldwell turned to the jury and began. "Laura Foster was only twenty years of age when she took her mare and left her family to meet the man of her dreams. She was in love. She had a proposal of marriage . . . and

217

she was carrying her lover's child. Tom Dooley was the man she loved. He proposed marriage to Laura Foster, and it was his child that she carried."

"Objection, Your Honor! There's no proof the child was his!" shouted Governor Vance.

"Sustained," Judge Shipp declared.

Will Foster's fingers gripped the side of his chair. Governor Vance had burned his bridges with the Foster family at the courthouse. Will knew Vance would try and tear his daughter's reputation apart again. He had been warned beforehand by the prosecution. But that did not make it any easier. Caldwell nodded to Will in support. James patted his father's shoulder.

Caldwell ignored Vance and continued, "Tom Dooley proposed marriage because he knew the child Laura Foster carried was his. They made their plans and the perfect ending to the perfect love story was about to unfold . . . or was it? At the same time he proposed marriage to Laura Foster, his married lover, waited for his return. And return he did! The defense will show that Tom Dooley was with Anne Melton the night before Laura Foster was murdered. The prosecution will show the night before Laura turned up missing, these two illicit lovers plotted her death. They had motive ladies and gentlemen and more than enough opportunity."

Caldwell turned and pointed a finger, walking over to the defense table.

He looked directly at Tom and challenged him, "What were Laura's last thoughts, I wonder? Who did she see in those woods on the morning of her murder? It is a question that haunts her family and an entire community."

Then, he turned back to the courtroom, "Tom Dooley killed Laura Foster and we all know it. This time, for the last time, I intend to prove to the good people of this courtroom, his guilt. It's time to hang Tom Dooley and be done with it so that Laura Foster's father and brother might have a chance to reclaim their lives — or at least what is left of them."

The courtroom exploded in an uproar of support. Tom turned to see his mother and sisters weeping in the row behind him. Looking back, Anne saw her mother holding Mary Beth's hand. Her husband, James, and her brother, Thomas, stared straight ahead.

When Judge Shipp and the bailiff finally succeeded in quieting the courtroom, Governor Vance stood to address the jury. Everyone waited to see what he could possibly say to make any difference.

Vance studied the room before he spoke. "Solicitor Caldwell has made a very bold statement and it appears that most of you agree with him. He just said, '*I believe it's time we hang Tom Dooley and be done with it.*' In some ways, I agree with him." Vance waited a moment allowing the shocked courtroom to digest his comment. "It's been a year and a half since Laura Foster was murdered. Everyone is tired and outraged that her killer has not been punished. I, too, want to see justice done—but you see, that's my problem with all of this. I do not believe that hanging Tom Dooley will accomplish that, because I do not believe Tom Dooley killed Laura Foster."

Angry reactions came from every corner of the room. Judge Shipp warned the spectators they would be removed if further outbursts occurred.

Vance continued, "An appeal was granted from the first trial because the evidence was all circumstantial. There was not one shred of hard evidence. Remember that. If we allow the courts to sentence Tom Dooley to hang based on *circumstantial evidence*, who's to say that tomorrow we all won't end up in jail because our neighbor, or girlfriend, or husband, wants us there? Don't you see? Without absolute proof, we cannot tell beyond the shadow of a doubt that Tom killed Laura. Without absolute proof, we may be allowing a murderer to walk free among us."

Vance walked over to the jury and leaned in as if he was confiding in one of his dearest friends.

"I am no different than any of you. I want to see Laura Foster's murderer hang and, like Solicitor Caldwell so aptly put it, *be done with it*. But, to not be sure and sentence this man to death would make me as guilty as the actual person that pierced her heart. I believe that hanging an innocent man would make *me* a murderer, too. Ladies and gentlemen, I do not want blood on my hands—or yours. Weigh all the evidence carefully and when you come up short, deliver a verdict of not guilty so that we can begin to look for the real killer."

Governor Vance took one last look around the room before he sat down. Eyes would not meet his as he glanced from corner to corner. *That was a good sign*, he thought. *Shame was a good sign*.

Judge Shipp turned to Caldwell, "Solicitor Caldwell, you may call your first witness."

Walter Caldwell nodded, and turning to the crowd announced, "The state calls J.W. Winkler to the stand."

The bailiff went to the witness room and collected J.W. Winkler. J.W. was led to the witness box, sworn in, and seated.

"Mr. Winkler, you were part of the search party that found Laura's body, were you not?"

"I was," J.W. replied.

"Tell us about your search and how the body was found, Mr. Winkler."

J.W. seemed to be concentrating with all of his might to remember any and every thing that might be of help. Slowly, he began.

"The search for Laura lasted a couple of months. I looked for her seven or eight of those days myself. One day, we followed Reedy Branch from the old Bates' place and formed a battle line . . . you know . . . all lined up 'side each other and just walkin' forward. Later in the day, Colonel Horton came down from the holler—where he'd been searchin'—and asked us to foller him. As I walked up, I looked over and seen a dogwood tree with a rope tied around it. The end of the rope looked like it'd been chewed on. There were branches broken on the other trees around the dogwood, like there'd been a struggle of some kind. It was there that I noticed a funny discolored spot on the ground. It stuck out even though some twigs'd been placed over it, as if someone had tried to hide it. When we got closer there was an awful odor. I've smelled death before, and there's no mistakin' it. We dug and hit somethin' right away 'cause the grave was so shallow. It was Laura Foster's body. I recognized her teeth . . . she had a small space between her two front teeth . . . and I recognized her cheekbones. They were high. My niece was a pretty little thing. I've seen Laura in the dress she was wearin' many times. It was homespun."

"Thank you, Mr. Winkler. I have nothing further at this time," Caldwell said.

Judge Shipp turned to Governor Vance. "Cross-examination, Mr. Vance?"

"I do have one question, Your Honor."

Vance walked over to J.W. "Sounds like you got a pretty good look around while you were up in that holler, Mr. Winkler."

J.W. nodded his head.

"Did you see any evidence that would lead you to believe that Tom Dooley was ever there at the burial site? Any clothing fragments—another set of hoof prints or mattock prints?"

"No sir, I did not," J.W. answered.

Governor Vance looked to Judge Shipp. "No further questions, Your Honor."

The bailiff led J.W. back to the witness room. Colonel James Horton was called to the stand. He was brief in his statement and visibly shaken as he tried to recount his discovery of Laura's body.

"I led the search party to the spot where my horse had reared. Following Reedy Branch, I realized it made perfect sense to carry the body down through the water and cross over to the holler to bury her. That's why our dogs couldn't pick up the scent, and it took us so long to find her. I'm still not sure why I left the search party and rode my horse up that holler, except that it was close to sunset, and I noticed a peculiar golden light streaming down from the trees there. Gentlemen, I have always been a practical man, but I know my horse reared out of fear. He was spooked at the spot where Laura Foster was buried. That's the only way I can explain it to you. He was spooked—and so was I."

After the colonel's testimony, the courtroom fell silent as he was taken back to the witness room. Everyone understood. Colonel Horton had spoken an unexplainable truth, and they all respected him for having the courage to tell it.

With no further questions, court was adjourned until the following day at 9:00 a.m.

CHAPTER FIFTY-TWO

The following morning, Walter Caldwell called his next witness. "The state calls Dr. George Carter to the stand."

Doc Carter was brought out and sworn in. He looked helplessly to the Fosters and then to Tom. He decided before coming to court, he would not volunteer anything. He would only answer what was asked of him and he intended to stick to the facts.

"Doc Carter, you examined the body of the victim, did you not?"

"I did."

"Please describe for the court what you saw at the shallow grave where the victim was found."

"The victim's name was Laura," he reminded Caldwell. "Her name was Laura," Doc Carter murmured loud enough for the room to hear it.

Caldwell nodded for him to continue. "I stand corrected, Doctor Carter. Tell us about the grave where Laura Foster was found."

"I examined the body at the spot where it was found . . . a ridge about a half mile from Lotty Foster's house in Wilkes County. It was the last of August. I noticed a place cut through her clothes. Upon further examination, I discovered a stab wound between the third and fourth ribs. The body was lying on its right side, face up. The hole it was laying in was two and a half feet deep and real narrow. It was not long enough for the body. The legs appeared to have been broken to fit the body into the grave."

Shocked reactions spread through the courtroom.

Judge Shipp rapped his gavel and reminded the crowd he would enforce order within the courtroom. If needed, he would close the trial to the public. This got everyone's attention. No one wanted to miss a single thing that took place.

Doc Carter continued, "A bundle of clothes was in the grave with the body, and the victim's apron had been folded neatly and placed across her face. The body was so decomposed I could not tell whether the sharp weapon used had cut the heart or not."

Caldwell turned to Doc Carter. "Why do you think someone would place an apron across the victim's face, Dr. Carter?" Was it perhaps a final act of respect or some misplaced feelings for the victim?"

Doc Carter stammered, "Well, I . . . "

"Objection, Your Honor! He's asking the witness to speculate," Vance interrupted.

"Sustained. Solicitor Caldwell, stick to the facts," Shipp warned.

Caldwell smiled. He had raised the question and that was the most important thing. "I'll withdraw the question, Your Honor."

Doc Carter was taken back to the waiting room. The morning was filled with several other witnesses, all testifying about the discovery of Laura's body. Each witness added their own personal touch to the story making it hard to gather the facts.

The court was recessed until one o'clock.

Shortly after the mid day meal the state called Anne's brother, Thomas Foster to the stand. Tom watched as they brought Thomas out to testify. He had known him since he was a small boy. Tom tried not to think about what Thomas might say. Blood was thicker than water, and he knew that. Tom also knew Thomas loved his sister. Anne had been a mother to the little ones, when Lotty was not. Thomas would do or say anything to protect her. No one could blame him for that.

Thomas took his seat in the witness box. He was careful to look only at Anne. His eyes would not meet Tom's as he spoke.

"On Thursday, the day before Laura Foster disappeared, Tom came to our house and asked my mama, Lotty Foster, if he could borrow a mattock. I saw him the next mornin', Friday mornin' sometime after breakfast. He was on the Gladys Fork Road."

"And where is the Gladys Fork Road in relation to the Bates' place," Caldwell asked.

Thomas was caught off guard. "Well sir, you turn directly off Gladys Fork to the path leading up to the Bates Place."

"So you mean to tell me you saw Mr. Dooley headed straight for the place where Laura Foster turned up missing, on the same day she disappeared, with a mattock?"

"Yes, sir," Thomas murmured to Caldwell.

"No further questions, Your Honor."

Judge Shipp turned to Governor Vance. "Do you care to question this witness, Counselor?"

"As a matter of fact, I do, Your Honor. Thomas, could a person passing your house go to either James Melton's house or the Bates' place?"

Thomas nodded. "I suppose they could."

"Did you stay around long enough to see which path Mr. Dooley chose?"

"No, sir, I didn't. I was in a hurry to . . . "

Governor Vance waved a hand to halt the boy from continuing. "No further questions, Your Honor."

Thomas was directed to step down from the witness stand. His mother, Lotty Foster, was called as the next witness. Vance and his team knew she was one to watch. Lotty and Vance had crossed paths many times in the long drawn out months of Anne's incarceration. This woman would be interested in protecting her daughter and nothing else and she would stop at nothing to accomplish it.

Anne was careful not to look at Tom as her mama walked by. She knew there was bad blood between the two. Lotty had hated Tom since the first time she had caught Anne in bed with him. They were thirteen years old at the time. Lotty had expected Anne to follow her own rules and use her body for money—not pleasure. She had always feared her daughter's relationship with him would get in the way of her ambitions. Lotty Foster wanted more for herself and her children. Sadly enough, Anne thought, these were the two people she loved the most. Lotty nodded to Anne as she walked past, holding her head high. Anne knew all too well that folks in Elkville criticized her mama for her temper and her wild ways, but it was that very determination that enabled her to raise her children. Though many in Elkville lost children during the war, none of Lotty's children starved to death. She was quick to remind her brood of that when they complained or fought. She was also quick to remind them as long as she had life in her body, she would do whatever she needed to protect them.

Lotty Foster took a deep breath and began, "I am the mother of Mrs. Anne Melton. The prisoner came to my house on the Thursday before Laura was killed. He asked to borrow my mattock. He got it and started off in the direction of his mama's house. I saw him again that Thursday with my daughter, Perline Foster and Jack Keaton. They came to my house to drink some shine and pop some corn. Said it was a goin' away party for Tom."

Solicitor Caldwell laughed and walked over to Lotty.

"Are you telling me, Miz Foster, that on the night before his intended marriage to Laura Foster, Tom Dooley was with your daughter?"

"Yes, he was."

"Please tell the court about the party at your house, Miz Foster."

"Tom Dooley came to the house with my daughter. Jack Keaton and Perline Foster were there, too. They'd all been drinkin' and Tom told us he was gonna go off the next mornin' and meet up with Laura Foster. Said he had some business to take care of."

"Did he mention marriage to you, Miz Foster?"

"No, he did not."

Bewildered, Tom looked to Vance, "That's a lie!" Vance motioned for him to be quiet.

Lotty continued, "He told Anne several times in front of the rest of us how much he loved her. Told us all over and over he was not the marryin' kind. By the time he left the house, we had all gone to bed. I heard footsteps and looked up to see him leavin'. It was just before daybreak. He looked tired and angry. When I asked him where he was goin', he said he was gonna go and take care of some things once and for all."

"What do you think he meant by that, Miz Foster?"

"Objection!" Vance interrupted. "This allows for speculation!"

"Overruled," Shipp shot back.

Lotty Foster looked at Caldwell and in a loud clear voice, she said, "Well, I didn't think much of it at the time. I just thought he was gonna tell her he was through with her, but then when she turned up missin' . . . "

"Thank you, Miz Foster. No further questions, Your Honor."

But Governor Vance did have a few questions for Lotty Foster.

"When I speak to you, do you prefer to be called Miz Foster or Miz Triplette?"

Caldwell jumped to his feet. He knew where Vance was going with this. He would try and discredit his witness with past suspicions that she murdered her husband, Mr. Triplette.

"Objection!" he shouted.

Judge Shipp surprisingly held up his hand. "Overruled. I'll allow it, Counselor, but I expect you to show me where you are going with this."

Vance turned to Lotty. He was on the attack now, and his question had taken her by surprise.

"Isn't it true that you've already been on trial under suspicion of murder, in the mysterious death of your husband, Mr. Triplette?"

He had it wrong, she thought. *It was the baby.*

Shaken, Lotty looked around the courtroom yelling, "Who told you somethin' like that? Was it Perline? Well, I was never on trial for my husband's death He died of natural causes."

Governor Vance ignored her words. "What about the baby?"

Lotty sat stunned, frozen in her chair. *He did know. He had been playing with her.* She had never hated anyone so much in all of her life.

"I was acquitted."

"My, my, Miz Foster! You are no stranger to accusations are you?" Vance asked in his most sarcastic tone. "And now here you are again trying to protect your girl. Like mother, like daughter, isn't that right? Tell me, what would you do, to protect Anne and keep your comfortable arrangement with James Melton?"

Murmurs filled the courtroom. Lotty knew she would have to ignore the whispers and remember why she was there.

"I am the mother of seven healthy children, and I am not on trial here! Tom Dooley is!" she screamed.

She clasped her hands tightly in her lap to keep control as she leaned in to Governor Vance. *He was no different from any other man*, she told herself. *Far from perfect!*

"Mr. Triplette, Mr. Dooley . . . Mr. Vance," Lotty paused for a second and then added with as much sarcasm as she could muster, "you all want what you want. Well, let me tell you right now, Mr. Fancy Lawyer . . . Tom Dooley killed that girl . . . "

Anne couldn't stand it anymore, "Mama, please," she cried out.

Lotty turned to her daughter, "Shut up, Anne!" she snapped. Almost hissing now, she added, " . . . and he buried her with my mattock."

It was easy for Anne to see what her mother was doing. She knew Lotty meant to cast guilt on Tom and away from her. Helplessly, Anne buried her face in her hands and wept.

Lotty turned to the spectators in the room. She held her head high and looked directly at as many of them as she could make eye contact with.

"I suppose you want the good people in this courtroom to think it was just a coincidence. That Tom Dooley needed to do a little diggin' on that day." Lotty Foster turned to Governor Vance and declared, "Well, it's no coincidence, and I am not afraid of you . . . so you do your worst! I'm ready for ya!"

Governor Vance stared at her for a moment. They were at a standoff in their little war and Vance was out of ammunition. Zeb turned to Judge Shipp.

"No further questions, Your Honor."

Court was adjourned.

CHAPTER FIFTY-THREE

The next morning was spent with various witnesses for the state. Martha Gilbert and Betsy Scott testified as they had done in the first trial.

Martha was short and to the point. "I saw Tom Dooley on the Friday mornin' Laura was killed, on the road between the Bates' place and his mama's house. He was diggin' with a mattock. When I asked him what he was doin', he said there was a place in the road that needed to be widened."

Betsy Scott recounted her meeting with Laura on the morning she turned up missing. She tried to be as accurate as she knew how, not knowing what to believe about Tom anymore. Betsy just stuck to the facts.

"I met Laura on the road. She was ridin' her mare bareback and carrying a bundle of clothes in her lap. It was Friday mornin', the day she turned up missin'. I asked Laura where she was goin'. She said she was goin' to meet up with Tom Dooley at the Bates' place."

Jack Keaton seemed pleased to testify. He had managed to stay out of trouble since his release from jail. He kept mostly to himself and ended his on-again off-again relationship with Perline — much to her dismay — shortly after he was released from jail. Tom watched his cousin closely as he took his seat on the witness stand. He'd known Jack all his life — yet today, he seemed a complete stranger. Jack avoided looking at Tom when he gave his testimony.

"My buddy Carson and me saw Mary Dooley on that Friday evening near Lotty Foster's house. We asked her where Tom was. She said she hadn't seen him all day."

That was a lie, Tom thought. It was clear to Tom his cousin Jack and Perline Foster had conspired before their relationship ended. When Ben Ferguson took the stand later on, he made a point of telling the jury Jack Keaton was bad for stealing and lying. Ben's words made Tom smile. Good old Ben! He just wanted the truth.

Calvin Cowles was the next to take the stand.

"After Laura turned up missing, there was an awful lot of accusin' goin' on. I heard plenty at the store. Several fellas run off and left. There were five of 'em altogether. That boy up Buffalo Cove, Jack Keaton, another boy over on Stony Fork . . . and Perline Foster left for awhile, too. Tom Dooley was the last to leave . . . after things started heatin' up and everybody started accusing everybody . . . that boy was the very last to leave."

Caldwell left Calvin's testimony alone, but Governor Vance was quick to have Calvin discuss the relationships between the other boys and Laura. Calvin revealed that Laura had courted and jilted them all. Vance's last question backfired on him, though.

"Would you say Laura Foster was a morally loose young woman, Mr. Cowles?"

Tom turned to see the look of disapproval on Calvin's face as his friend asked him that question.

"I can't say, Zeb. I was never intimate with her myself and certainly not invited to witness any heated moments."

Vance shot an agitated look at his old friend.

"No further questions, Your Honor."

After a long break for the mid day meal, Celia Scott testified. Celia kept to herself after she and her husband reported the fight at her house to the sheriff. On the stand, she was nervous and emotional as she told the courtroom what she had witnessed.

"I am the wife of Mr. James Scott," she said, looking to her husband for support. "I hired Perline Foster to come to my house and help me with my chores one day. Anne Melton came to the house carrying a stick and grabbed Perline by the hair of the head and started yellin' and usin' foul language. She told Perline to go home. Then, Anne threw Perline to the ground and started chokin' her. She was mad because Perline had bragged to Ben Ferguson that she and Tom had killed and then done away with Laura Foster. I heard Perline say to Anne, and I'll never forget this as long as I live, she said, 'It is the truth and you know it. You are as deep in the mud as I am in the mire.' Then, Anne called Perline a liar. Perline slapped Anne and ran into the woods. I thought she would follow her but instead, Anne . . . well . . . she turned on me and told me to let what I saw that day be my dying secret. She . . . she said she would follow me straight to hell if I told."

By the time Celia finished the rest of her testimony, she was in such a state she had to be helped to her feet and supported on the way out of the courtroom. She accidentally caught sight of Anne on her way and started screaming and wailing so loud her husband was barely able to get her out of the courtroom. Doc Carter quickly got up and followed the Scott's to the holding room. He ended up having to give her something to calm her down.

After everyone was settled again, the state called its last witness of the day. Caldwell patted Will Foster on the back and motioned him to the witness stand.

"Mr. Foster, tell us about the mornin' your daughter, Laura, turned up missin'."

Will Foster took a drink from the glass of water the bailiff had been requested to bring him. His mouth was dry, and his voice shook slightly as he spoke.

"Laura Foster was my daughter. She lived with me and her brother, James. Her mama's dead. Tom Dooley courted my daughter for several months, and then he stopped. I didn't see him again for a long while. The Sunday before Laura was kilt, he showed back up, and they talked. He came back the following Wednesday. I saw 'em whisperin' with their heads together. On Friday mornin', I woke up and found that Laura was gone. Some of her clothes was missin' from her room. When I went outside, I realized her mare was missin', too. I saw the mare tracks and followed 'em. They led me to the ole Bates' place . . . but after that I lost 'em. I stopped at James Scott's place for breakfast and then went on to James Melton's. By the time I got to James Melton's place it was about eight o'clock. Anne Melton was in bed. Her clothes were off and layin' in the floor. They looked wet and muddy. I visited several houses, but no one knew where Laura was. I ended up at Francis Melton's. He invited me to spend the night there."

When Will finished his testimony, he surprised the packed courtroom. They had expected him to just go quietly and sit with his family to wait. He did not.

Instead, he looked deliberately around the room at the sea of faces —neighbors, family, friends and enemies. His face was pale and his eyes had dark circles under them. Will's voice shook as he spoke, but his message was loud and clear.

"There's been some talk that on the day Laura turned up missin' I said I didn't care about Laura just so's I found my mare . . . and that I said I'd kill Laura myself if I found her. Those are lies and I wish my neighbors would let me alone to grieve in peace!"

Overcome with emotion, Will slammed his fist on the witness box. No one in the shocked courtroom moved a muscle or uttered a word.

Shocked at this gentle man's sudden outburst, it was Caldwell that finally turned to Judge Shipp. "No further questions, Your Honor."

Judge Shipp turned to Vance, "Would you like to cross examine, Counselor?"

"I would, Your Honor."

Vance paused for a moment giving Will time to collect himself. Slowly, he approached him speaking softly and respectfully.

"Was Tom Dooley the only man your daughter had a relationship with in the last year of her life?"

"No, sir, she courted Jack Keaton, too."

"Did Laura's relationship with Jack Keaton end well, Mr. Foster?"

"No, it didn't."

Will knew where Vance was going with this. He wanted to show Jack Keaton was a strong suspect. Will decided to be truthful with him. Jack Keaton could just as easily have killed Laura as Tom. All Will wanted was the truth.

"Tell us about that," Vance asked respectfully.

"Well, sir, Laura lost interest in Jack. She started seein' another fella up the road from us near Buffalo Cove. Jack got mad and kept tryin' to come around. Laura was upset about it. One evening me and James had to ask Jack to leave. He came by to try and get Laura to go back out with him. He left mad. We made a point of not bein' around him anymore."

"And, why is that, Mr. Foster?" Vance asked.

"Because he'd been makin' threats to folks about me and James. Said we needed to mind our own business. Said what was between him and Laura was nothing to us."

"What kind of threats did he make, Mr. Foster?"

"Objection," yelled Caldwell.

"Overruled," Judge Shipp allowed. "You may continue, Mr. Vance."

"What kind of threats did he make?" Vance repeated.

"He threatened to do away with our whole family. He said we better keep one eye open while we was sleepin' if we knew what was good for us."

Vance looked over at Caldwell and grinned. Jack Keaton had threatened Laura's family. This was just what Vance needed the audience to hear. "No further questions, Your Honor."

231

Court was adjourned. Tomorrow would be the tough one, Vance thought. Tomorrow the state would bring their star witness to the stand. Perline had turned on Tom and Anne with a vengeance and the prosecution had lapped it up. They clearly wanted a murderer and Perline gave them two—Tom Dooley and Anne Melton. He imagined she was looking forward to her moment of glory. Although he had heard her testimony in the first trial, Vance had no doubt there would be new twists and turns from Perline Foster. *This time, he would be ready for her* he promised himself.

CHAPTER FIFTY-FOUR

The state called Perline Foster to the stand. Vance watched her as she marched across the courtroom and took her seat. This woman was very different from the one he met when he first arrived in Wilkes. Well dressed and neat in her appearance, Perline exuded a confidence Vance had not seen before. Smiling, she took her oath and sat down. She looked at Tom and Anne and grinned. Anne felt a white hot anger wash over her. Perline was dressed in one of Anne's favorite dresses. It was burgundy. Lotty made it for Anne as a gift after Mary Beth was born. Perline's dirty blonde hair was pulled back in a bow in the same fashion that Anne often wore.

Perline wants to be me, she thought. *She wants to do away with me and take my place!*

Vance noticed the reaction from Anne and looked at her, puzzled.

"She's wearin' my dress. Perline Foster is paradin' around in one of my dresses," Anne fumed under her breath.

Vance started to answer Anne, but the prosecutor began.

"Miz Foster, tell us about your relationship with the defendant and how you came to work for the Meltons."

In her sweetest voice, Perline began her story.

"I went to work for the Meltons shortly after they was married. After Tom Dooley came back from the war, he was at the house most every day while I was there. He stayed there sometimes at night. I have seen him in bed with Anne Melton. James Melton did not sleep with his wife. I was used many times as a blind for Tom and Anne. Anne left the house on the Thursday night before Laura was murdered, with a canteen of liquor. She left in the direction of her mama's house. She was supposed to meet up with Tom. She didn't come back until Friday mornin' about an hour before day. She came and got in bed with me. Her dress and shoes was wet and muddy. Later that mornin', Tom came to see her. He stood over her in bed and they talked. When he left they was both cryin'. I went out and worked in the fields with Jonathan Gilbert and James Melton 'til three o'clock. Anne stayed in the bed for most of the day."

Perline leaned over to Solicitor Caldwell and grinned at him flirtatiously. She acted like she was taking him into her confidence, and he was the only one in the room. Caldwell seemed captivated.

"A couple of days later, Anne took me to the place where the body was buried. I could see the body through the dirt. I was so scared; I wouldn't go all the way over to it. Anne threw more dirt over the body and took leaves and twigs to cover it up. The next day when Tom came over, I said to him, 'I thought you run off with Laura Foster'; and he said, 'I ain't got no use for Laura Foster.'"

The packed courtroom began to whisper and murmur amongst themselves. "Thank you, Miz Foster."

Caldwell smiled and nodded to Governor Vance as he took his seat.

Vance moved slowly and deliberately to the witness stand.

"Did you have any use for Laura Foster, Perline?"

Perline bristled, "She was all right, I reckon."

Vance laughed at the remark.

"Is that why you told Ben Ferguson and Jack Adkins that you and Tom Dooley killed Laura Foster? Because she was just . . . alright?"

Perline was on the hot seat now.

"I was jokin' . . . that's all . . . I had gone to Watauga for a few days," she stammered. "I just forgot to mention to anybody that I was goin'; and when I come back, people was acting all funny and suspicious of me . . . so I made a little joke! I told Ben, I said, 'Sure! Me and Tom killed Laura Foster and run off to Tennessee,' but, it was just a joke!"

Vance turned to the courtroom and gave them a knowing look. Then he turned back to Perline.

"Isn't it true, Miz Foster, that you hate Anne Melton because she's a beautiful woman? That you are jealous of the relationship between her and Tom Dooley?"

Perline felt her newfound confidence faltering, "Why would I be jealous of Anne Melton? She's married to an old man! Besides, she's jealous of ME . . . "

Members of the courtroom snickered.

Perline tried to continue, "It's true! Tom told me so one day . . . he . . . "

"Look at you, Perline," Vance interrupted, "sitting there in one of Anne Melton's dresses. By the way, did she give you permission to go through her personal belongings, or did you just help yourself now that you have her locked up? Come on now, Perline! Do you really expect this court to believe that Anne Melton is jealous of you?"

Perline put her hands on her shoulders as if to hide the dress.

"It's true, she . . . "

"She what?" Vance yelled.

"She has threatened me over Tom before!"

"And, why would she do that?"

"Because she caught Tom and me in bed together once!"

Tom and Anne sprang to their feet.

"Liar!" Anne screamed, springing to her feet. A deputy put his hands on Anne's shoulders and shoved her back into her chair. The heavy sound of her shackles clanked against the defense table.

"That's a lie, and you know it!" Tom yelled. Vance shot Tom a warning look, and he fell silent.

Perline looked at Tom. She watched him as he denied what had passed between them. To Perline, it was as if he was denying she even existed.

Judge Shipp pounded his gavel.

"Order in the court! Order in the court!"

He stopped to point a finger at Tom and Anne.

"If there are any further outbursts in this courtroom, the two of you will be removed."

Vance turned and motioned for them to sit down. He was angry now. Perline Foster was a bold faced liar, and he intended to prove it.

"Isn't it true that your little *joke* with Ben Ferguson was intended to send Tom to his grave because he rejected your affections?"

The hateful words hurt Perline's ears, and she wanted him to stop.

"No!" she declared.

"Isn't it true you wanted Laura Foster dead and Anne Melton in jail?"

Again, she denied his question. "No!"

"The grave you described is the one you dug, isn't it?"

Vance turned to his audience and laughed. He leaned towards them as if he was including them in a private joke.

"Anne Melton's never done that kind of work in her life! And, we all know it. But, you have, haven't you, Perline? Digging a shallow grave like that would be nothing for you!"

Tears began to stream down Perline's face.

"I'm not the guilty one here and you know it! All I've ever been is a lookout or a blind . . . nothin' more! Nothin' more!"

Vance's mood changed. His voice became quiet and deliberate.

"Until this time . . . until now. You got tired of always watching, didn't you, Perline?"

Perline struggled to find the words. Choking on her own anger, she tried to speak. "I ain't nothin' more than a blind . . . I . . ."

With all eyes upon her, Vance did the unspeakable to Perline Foster. He dismissed her. Turning around, he walked away from her as if she was no longer there. His actions were more than she could bear. *She was nobody's mistake*, she thought. Before she could regain her composure Governor Vance spoke to Judge Shipp.

"No further questions, Your Honor."

Vance was finished with Perline Foster.

Out of control now, Perline sprang from her chair. With all the venom she could muster, she screamed at Governor Vance, "Anne Melton killed that girl, and you know it! Open your eyes and see the truth!"

Vance had waited for this. She was right where he wanted her. Whirling around to face her, he fired each word at Perline as if he were firing a pistol. "My eyes are wide open, Miz Foster—and I'm looking right at the truth!"

Completely out of control, Perline Foster charged at Governor Vance. Two deputies and the bailiff rushed over and with great effort managed to pry her off of him.

Kicking and screaming, Perline Foster was not led from the courtroom that day; she was removed.

The state rested.

The afternoon was spent listening to character witnesses for the defense. Washington Anderson, a neighbor of Tom's, testified he was in the same regiment with him in the Army. He knew Tom to be a good soldier and an honest man. When cross-examined by Solicitor Caldwell, Anderson did state he was with Tom one night when he met Caroline Barnes near Reedy Branch. He said the two spent the night together in the woods, and he was with them.

Caroline was sitting in the back when Washington gave his testimony. She broke into tears and ran from the courtroom. Jack Adkins followed her. This time, however, he did not appear to be quite as smitten with Miss Barnes.

J.W. Winkler was recalled to testify as to what he overheard Perline say on the day Will came to the store looking for Laura. She had looked at Jack

Keaton and kissed him on the lips and said, "I'd swear a lie for Tom Dooley, any day, wouldn't you, Jack?" J.W. said the two laughed about Perline's remark and left together.

Vance's last attempt at discrediting Perline Foster's testimony was questioning Anne's brother, Thomas. Thomas told the court he had seen Perline and Tom sitting in each other's laps several times at the Melton cabin. The boy's testimony cast Perline in a jealous light, and Vance was pleased.

The afternoon dragged on until almost five o'clock. Judge Shipp instructed the jurors and witnesses to return the next morning at nine.

The next morning Mary Dooley was called to the stand. The tiny woman sat down in the witness box and looked at her boy. She was fighting for his life and she knew it. Mary touched the carved wooden cross around her neck. Tom made it for her when he was a young boy. Mary spent the morning before her testimony praying that God would help her find the right words to say.

"I am Tom Dooley's mother. He turned twenty-two on the twentieth of June. His home is with me. Tom was not at the house on that Friday mornin'. I was out early that day lookin' for him. I got back around noon. I found Tom lying on the bed. He got up around suppertime, but wouldn't eat and he went off to the barn for awhile. When he come back in, he ate; and then went on to bed about the usual time. That night, I heard him makin' a little moan. He had been complainin' of chills during supper, so I went in his room and bent over him to see if he was all right."

She addressed the packed courtroom full of spectators, pleading, "He is my sole remainin' son. Both of his brothers were killed in the war."

Tears streamed down her worn face. "I bent over him and gave him a little kiss." Mary Dooley made one last plea to the jurors, "Please," she begged, "he is my last remainin' boy!"

Judge Shipp recessed the court. "We will take an hour recess; and when we return, we will hear closing arguments."

An hour later, Solicitor Caldwell addressed the crowd in closing.

"The evidence is clear. It was Tom Dooley that Laura Foster left her home to meet on the Friday she turned up missing. On the Thursday before, Tom borrowed a mattock from Lotty Foster, his girlfriend's mother. Martha Gilbert has testified she saw the defendant later that day, digging within a few hundred yards of the shallow grave where Laura's body was later found. We've also learned that Tom Dooley was so in love with Laura Foster that he spent the night before his wedding day with another man's wife. His own

237

mother has testified that she woke to find her son missing from the house that Friday morning and went off looking for him. All parties have testified that Anne and Tom were together all night, the night before the murder. I believe Laura's grave was waiting for her in that holler before she ever reached the Bates' place. Will Foster and Perline Foster have both testified that when Anne Melton returned to the Melton cabin the next morning, her clothes and shoes were wet and muddy. Laura Foster's fate was sealed the night before at Lotty Foster's cabin. It was clearly premeditated cold-blooded murder. A young girl's life was taken to satisfy the selfishness of a man who was not willing to be responsible for his child and to pacify his jealous lover. Laura Foster deserves nothing less than a verdict of guilty and the harshest punishment this court has to offer. It is up to you to see that her life and the life of her unborn child are avenged."

Governor Vance looked at Tom. The young man was deathly pale. Governor Vance patted his shoulder and heard just the slightest sigh escape from Tom's lips. Vance stood and addressed the courtroom.

"I find it interesting that, in all of this, no one has produced a murder weapon. Nor has anyone, in over two hundred witnesses in the last year and a half, been able to say they saw Tom Dooley with Laura Foster on that fateful Friday morning. We have heard over and over that Tom borrowed a mattock from Lotty Foster the day before the murder. Yet, no one found any mattock prints at the scene and mattock prints, as we all know, are unmistakable!"

Vance laughed and turned around. He scanned the crowd, making eye contact with every spectator and jury member that would return his gaze.

"*You* have based an entire case on a witness as unreliable as Perline Foster! It is common knowledge that she desired Tom Dooley and that her affections were not returned. It is common knowledge that she was jealous of Anne Melton. She sat before you yesterday in one of Anne's own dresses! Perline Foster wanted to *be* Anne Melton, and it is common knowledge in the community of Elkville that she was jealous of both Anne *and* her cousin, Laura Foster. Perline Foster had motive, and she had opportunity. What difference would marriage have really made to Anne and Tom? Please tell me — what difference would one more spouse have made to those two? But, it made a big difference to someone like Perline Foster, who had never been married and had designs on Tom. She was privy to Tom's marriage plans because she was with Anne and Tom and Jack Keaton the night before the murder at Lotty Foster's house. If Anne Melton had really taken her to the grave where

Laura was buried, why then did she not come forward? It would have been to her advantage to do so. Anne would have been locked away, and Perline could have finally had Tom all to herself. Finally, I ask you, why did Tom, of his own free will, allow the posse to bring him back to Wilkes County? He had already made it safely into Tennessee. The unanswered questions in this case are endless, and the testimony is hearsay and circumstantial. Hanging Tom Dooley will not bring Laura Foster back, and it will not relieve your consciences or see justice done. Hanging Tom Dooley will not bring an end to this sordid tale of murder and deceit. You have a responsibility to continue the search for evidence. It is only with evidence and fact that you will find Laura's killer. For me ladies and gentlemen, one murder is enough. I beg this court to bring back a sentence of *not guilty* and allow this young man to go back to his mother and sisters where he belongs."

No one moved. Vance looked around studying the faces of the jury and onlookers. He could not read their reaction to his words. Judge Shipp instructed the jury. He asked them to consider all the evidence carefully. Governor Vance smiled a sarcastic smile. *As far as he was concerned, there was no evidence.* The judge wished the jury Godspeed and bid them farewell as the bailiff led them to a guarded room. The jury was officially out.

Tom and Anne were taken back to their cells. Vance talked with them both before leaving to review his notes. It was around three o'clock. Around five o'clock the sheriff came to collect the prisoners and bring them back to the courtroom. The jury had reached its verdict in less than two hours. Vance feared the worst. A quick decision was usually not good for the defendant. It usually meant minds were already made up before the trial began.

Tom and Anne sat with Governor Vance and his team. Will and James Foster sat down beside Solicitor Caldwell and the rest of the prosecution. The jury entered the room and filed into the jury box.

Judge Shipp spoke to the entire courtroom before they began.

"This trial has been lengthy and emotions high. Before the verdict is read, I want to caution each and every one of you. Should any of you create a disturbance in my courtroom, regardless of the outcome of this trial, you will be held in contempt and escorted to jail."

Everyone sat quietly and waited.

Judge Shipp turned to the jury, "Gentlemen, have you reached a verdict?"

The foreman answered, "Yes, we have, Your Honor."

Judge Shipp asked, "What say you?"

The foreman handed a piece of paper to the clerk, who walked over and delivered it to Judge Shipp. Judge Shipp read the verdict. Tom tried to read his face, but it was the face of a man that had read many such verdicts. It told him nothing.

Shipp looked at Tom. "Will the defendant please rise?"

Tom willed himself to stand. Vance stood alongside him.

The foreman read the verdict. His voice was loud and clear.

"We, the jury, find the defendant, Thomas C. Dooley . . . guilty of the murder of Laura Foster."

Mary Dooley's tiny body slumped in the seat behind her son. Tom could hear her muffled sobs. This time he turned to his mother, but there was no comfort for either of them in doing so.

Anne blocked out all of the commotion around her and looked only at Tom.

Lotty Foster sat behind Anne watching her daughter's heart break. Tears filled Lotty's eyes. No matter what happened, it was clear that her daughter loved him. *There were things much worse than death*, she thought.

The judge set sentencing for that evening at seven o'clock. The prisoners were removed, and the courtroom was cleared. As far as Judge Shipp was concerned, justice was served.

Young James Foster was not so sure. He took a hard look around the courtroom before he left that day. His eyes roamed the crowd. Jack Keaton and Perline Foster were huddled in a corner whispering. Lotty Foster looked deathly pale and Anne Melton . . . the look on her face . . . James shuddered. So many people testified, and so many of the stories told conflicted with one another. How were any of them ever really going to know what happened?

Sharply at seven, Tom was brought back before Judge Shipp to be sentenced. Tom Dooley and Anne Melton were brought before the court in shackles. Anne was seated directly behind Tom and Vance. Tom was asked to stand before the judge.

It felt to Anne as it had two years before when she and Tom stood together at their arraignment. She watched Judge Shipp, sitting behind the judge's bench. He held his Bible in his left hand, preparing a statement before him. *This was no trial*, she thought, *it was a condemnation to Hell*. She shuddered, knowing she would be next.

"Thomas C. Dooley, this court hereby sentences you to be taken this 25th day of January, 1868, to the jail of Iredell County from whence you came, there to remain until the 14th day of February AD 1868, and on that date you will be taken by the sheriff of said county to the place of public execution of said county and there between the hours of noon and four p.m. be hanged by the neck until dead . . . may God have mercy on your soul."

Tom stood stock still. After he took a moment to allow the words to sink in, he simply hung down his head.

CHAPTER FIFTY-FIVE

Governor Vance set to work immediately on an appeal. This time, Tom did not allow himself to be hopeful.

Anne slept much of the time during the day and paced the floors and whispered to Tom at night. Nightime was the only time they had any privacy.

Tom played his fiddle mostly. There was a tune in his head that wouldn't go away. It came out of nowhere, sad and forlorn and he found himself playing it over and over.

One of the deputies befriended Tom during his long stay in Statesville. Tom's friend listened one evening as he played the melancholy tune. He told Tom about a fiddler friend of his and later brought the man by to hear Tom play. The deputy allowed the two to play together in Tom's cell. It was one of the most peaceful times Tom experienced since his move to Statesville. Once the man memorized the melody, he left, promising Tom he would write words to the song. The fiddler told Tom he would come back and play it for him when it was finished. Tom encouraged him to come back soon. He had become more and more convinced that his time was short.

"I'm bound to die," he told him.

Weeks passed. His execution date was postponed, awaiting a response to Vance's appeal. Finally, Governor Vance came to see him on April 17 to give him the news. The Supreme Court found no error and Judge Anderson Mitchell set a new date of execution — May 1, 1868.

"I'm sorry, Tom," Vance told him. "I tried everything I could but their minds have been made up since the day you were captured in Tennessee. You should've never surrendered."

"Well, you might'a thought different if you'd a seen that noose, Governor," Tom answered. "I didn't have much choice."

"I'm goin' home to Buncombe County for a few days, but don't you worry, I'll be back before . . . " Vance's voice faltered, full of emotion.

Tom reached out and patted Vance on the shoulder. "You've been right with me through it all. I ain't worried. I know you'll be here for me when the time comes."

With that, Tom and Vance said their goodbyes and Vance left the jail.

Tom knew it was finally over. *After the sun sets, I will have thirteen days left to live,* Tom thought. *Thirteen unlucky days.* Up to that point, he always believed he would eventually be set free, but with the finality of Vance's departure, desperation overtook him. That night, using a nail from his cot, Tom managed to tap out a small corner of glass at the bottom of the jail cell window. It was directly behind one of the bars and not noticeable unless someone was looking for it. He sat up all night listening to Anne pace and talk. As she did, he used the tiny shard of glass to begin the slow process of sawing away a link in the chains between his ankles. Tom intended to escape.

Each day, he slowly chiseled the chain's link with time passing much faster than Tom had hoped.

On April 29, the deputy brought his friend back to see Tom.

"We have something we want you to hear," he said.

Tom closed his eyes and listened to the ballad that announced his death.

Hang down your head, Tom Dooley, hang down your head and cry.
Hang down your head, Tom Dooley, poor boy you're bound to die.

Anne listened to the sweet, sad song in her cell and wept. Little did she know she would hear that haunting ballad being sung by folks in Elkville for the rest of her life.

The next morning Tom awoke to the sounds of the men in the sheriff's office talking and laughing. Normal conversation, and a normal day was unfolding around him. Life was going on as usual for everyone but him. He knew if he didn't do something quick this would be the last full day of his life. Tom had always thought he had an extra dose of life in him. Surviving the deaths of his father and brothers, and coming back from the war, made him feel like nothing could touch him. He held on to that same feeling for two long years and continued to believe it—until now. His hands shook as he tried to finish sawing the link on the chain at his feet. He was almost there. He planned to have the chain chiseled in two by nightfall.

The next morning, the deputy came to bring Tom's breakfast. Maybe it was because it was the day of his hanging, but he delivered it earlier than expected. The deputy noticed he was acting funny the minute he reached his cell. He had jumped when his friend slid the tray of food through the bars. When Tom bent down to take the food, the deputy saw that his hands were shaking. Still, the deputy brushed off his behavior as understandable given the circumstances.

"Tom, you all right?" he asked. "I can have someone fetch the doctor if you want me to. He can give you somethin' to calm you down."

"No, I'm doing fine," he answered.

"Alright then, I'll be back to get your tray in a little while—but if you change your mind, let me know."

Relieved, he relaxed just long enough to drop his arm slightly. The piece of glass fell from his sleeve and splintered on the hard floor of the cell. The deputy heard the glass break and quickly looked down and called for help. In seconds, Tom found himself face down on the floor, being searched from head to toe. The old shackles were replaced with new ones. It was then that Tom finally accepted that he was going to die.

Tom spent the rest of the afternoon pacing and praying. His family would be there soon. His mama wanted the family to gather at the jail for supper. She was cooking all of his favorite foods at one of the deputy's homes. He smiled at the thought of her. Although his family had always been poor, while growing up, the Dooley children never really thought about it. The love his mama gave her children had been enough. Cooking for her family had been one of the many ways she showed them.

The Methodist minister was invited to come, too. Tom had asked his mama to bring him. He wanted to be baptized.

CHAPTER FIFTY-SIX

Are you washed,
In the blood,
Are you washed in the blood of the lamb?
Are your garments spotless, are they white as snow,
Are you washed in the blood of the lamb?

The minister's wife sang the old hymn with no music. Her voice sounded like the women at church back home. Tom was grateful for that. The high pitched nasal voices he heard up north during the war always made the little hairs on the back of his neck stand up, and not in a good way. This woman's voice was full and earthy. She sang from her heart and it touched his soul in a way he could not explain.

The preacher placed his hand on Tom's head; the blessed water dripping from his fingers.

"Thomas Dooley, I baptize you in the name of the Father, the Son, and the Holy Ghost."

There were amens all around the tiny cell. Tom took the preacher's hand and stood to his feet.

The preacher shook his hand.

"Congratulations, son, you are now a child of God. Go in peace tomorrow and meet your Maker."

"Thank you, Reverend. I will."

Tom wiped a tear from his eye. *He couldn't start this now. His mama was in enough pain,* he thought.

The minister looked around the room at the small gathering.

"I'll leave you now to talk with your family and friends. God Bless you, Tom."

Everyone shook hands and said their good-byes.

The preacher's wife kissed Tom on the cheek.

"We'll meet again, son."

The little cell was full. Tom's mama and sisters were there. Calvin and Martha Cowles stood at the cell door, and Governor Vance was sitting near the window with Michael O'Hara.

Tom's mama came over to him and put her arms around him.

"I love you so much," she whispered between the tears, "so much."

Tom hurt more for her than he did for himself. He held her to him.

"I know you do, and I love you too, Mama. That was the finest meal I ever ate, and I thank ya for it. For a minute, your cookin' made me forget where I was. I felt like I was home in your kitchen. You must'a worked yourself to death. My fresh pressed shirt and pants look real nice. You've always took real good care of me, and I'm gonna look like a real gentleman tomorrow."

He tried to laugh but it was a hollow attempt. There was no joy in Tom's eyes — only tears.

"You need to go on and get some rest, Mama. You've done all you can do."

It was true. Mary Dooley had done her best. Her children were always fed and clothed no matter what she had to sacrifice. Tom had seen her in the same dress every day for months at a time. The house was always spotless and the Bible lay by her bed. She taught her children to pray, and she taught them to be kind. Tom had been a challenge for Mary, and he felt ashamed of that now. Without the support of her husband after he died, she had not always known how to handle him. Sometimes Mary wondered how things might have turned out if Tom's daddy had lived. Still, his mama knew deep down that Tom had made his choices all by himself. The path he chose had not been because of anything he learned in the Dooley home.

Eliza knew her mama did not want to leave. She took Mary by the hand and tried to guide her out of the cell.

"Come on, Mama, do what Tom says. You've got to be strong for him. Otherwise, he'll go to heaven frettin' over you. You don't want him to do that, now do you?"

Mary Dooley reluctantly agreed not wanting to add to Tom's suffering. Eliza ran to her brother and hugged him tight. With everyone's encouragement, Eliza was able to lead her mama from the room.

Tom put his hand on his sister Anna's shoulder as she turned to go. She would be the eldest sibling now, and the responsibility of their mama would fall on her.

"Anna, I want you to thank Cajah for me. I know he did a nice job on my coffin. I appreciate you and him bringin' the wagon to take me back home."

Anna studied her brother's face, trying to memorize every line and curve.

"Cajah was glad to do it, Tom. Colonel Horton's wife gave us her red satin dancin' dress, and Mama and Eliza and me lined the inside of it for you. It's fit for a king."

A sob rose in her throat as she struggled to speak.

"I love you, brother," she managed to say.

Tom nodded, "You are the oldest now; you need to be brave for Mama and Eliza, ya hear?"

"I will," she nodded.

Anna turned to leave. She was weak and her stomach was queasy. She had not told her brother about the baby, believing it would make things even more difficult for him. She needed some air.

"Anna," she heard him say, "I love you, too."

The two ran to each other and held on tight.

Martha Cowles saw the sheriff standing outside the door and realized time was running out. She needed to say her good-byes quickly or she would miss her chance. Resolutely, she approached the handsome young man she had watched grow up and hugged him.

"Bon soir and God bless. You were always the prettiest of Mary's babies," she said, looking at his handsome face. "I wonder if that's what's done this. Sometimes I wonder if you were just too good lookin' for your own good."

Calvin stepped over to his wife, chiding her

"Now, Martha! What kind of thing is that to say to Tom?"

Martha looked back at her husband with eyes filled with anger and hurt. "The truthful thing," she said, shaking her head. "Jealousy has much power!"

Calvin shook his head. *She was right*, he thought, *half the men in Elkville were happy to see Tom hang.* He'd heard them laugh and make jokes at the store. Some thought with Tom gone, their wives would no longer stray from the marriage bed. *The truth was*, Calvin laughed to himself, *no one strayed from home unless they wanted to.* Some of those people should take a hard look at themselves instead of blaming other folks. He doubted if Tom's death would make any marriages in Elkville better or worse. The kindly storekeeper walked over to the condemned man. *At twenty-two*, Calvin thought, *he should be getting married and having a family—not this.*

Calvin's voice shook as he spoke. "For the first time in my life, I'm at a loss for words . . . so I'll just wish you a good journey, son."

"I'll see you on the other side," Tom whispered in the old man's ear.

Calvin put his arm around Tom, and the two men embraced. Martha took her husband's hand and the couple quietly exited the cell.

Governor Vance sat on Tom's cot watching the goodbyes. O'Hara sat on a stool in the corner writing furiously. Tom turned to them.

"Would you stay for just a minute, Governor? I want to give you something. I think you'll be able to use it later."

"What is it, Tom?" Vance asked.

Tom handed Vance a piece of paper. Vance moved to the lantern on the table beside Tom's cot to read it.

"Statement of Thomas C. Dooley," he read. "I declare that I am the only person that had any hand in the murder of Laura Foster, April 30, 1868."

Vance turned to his client in disbelief holding out the crudely written piece of paper to him.

"Don't do this, Tom," he begged. "It's not right! If it's Anne you're tryin' to protect, I can promise you she'll never hang. A jury of men would have to send her to the gallows, and I've heard them laugh and talk. I've listened to public opinion. They say she's too pretty to hang! I swear to you she will never set foot on a gallows!"

But Tom only stiffened. He was resolute.

"It's time for you to go, Governor. I'll see you tomorrow."

Vance tried to protest but Tom continued.

"You'll walk with me and my family, won't ya?"

"I'll be there, don't you worry," he answered, shaking his head.

Tom walked over to his friend. His tone was earnest and sincere. "Zeb, you gotta promise me you'll take care of Anne. I can't go in peace tomorrow unless I know she's gonna be all right."

Vance shook the note at Tom in frustration.

"I think you just took care of that."

Tom ignored him.

"Give me your word you'll defend her."

There was clearly nothing Vance could do. Tom was going to die and his final torment was over Anne.

"I give you my word."

Vance shook Tom's hand, holding it tight.

"It has been an honor to know you, son."

The two men looked at each other and nodded. Vance could see that Tom found great relief in knowing that he would defend her.

O'Hara was the last to leave. The two young men stared at each other for a moment.

"I can't stop this, friend. I wish I could. But, I give you my word that I will make sure you are not forgotten. I won't let these people forget you."

O'Hara nodded and abruptly left the room, knowing nothing else to say or do.

CHAPTER FIFTY-SEVEN

The day of the hanging was cool and sunny as most days are in early May. It was much the same as it was two years before when Laura Foster left her home to meet up with Tom Dooley at the old Bates' place. On this day the spring air was cool enough to prompt the women to pull their shawls and day coats from their cedar chests and put them on .

The train yard was as crowded as anyone had ever seen it. Carpetbaggers charged through the crowd selling little locks of what they professed to be Laura Foster's hair. Popped corn, fried apple pies, and cider were being sold up near the depot. One enterprising young boy was selling tiny nooses he'd made as mementos. Men gathered around the small depot as the last train until late afternoon screamed its way into the station. They drank and spouted out their versions of Laura Foster's murder while they waited for noon to come.

Construction was being completed on the gallows down by the railroad tracks. In the middle of all the commotion, the pounding of hammers could be heard as the men drove the last nails into it. After the hanging, they would take the tall structure apart and reuse the lumber to add on to the local school house. It was customary to donate the materials used in a hanging for a good cause. After a life had been taken in this way, people believed it was important that they turn a bad thing into something good. The gesture eased their own guilt a bit.

Nothing would be wasted—except a young man's life.

James Foster looked up, gazing at that gallows for a long time. "I don't think until just now I've ever really believed Laura was dead," he told his papa. "It's been like a dream to me. One that I just can't wake up from. We've been so busy tryin' to piece everything together . . . and busy with the trial . . . I felt more like I was fightin' for her life, than fightin' to convict her killer."

James turned to his father with a look of disbelief. "Papa, Laura's really gone."

He repeated the words over and over until the hard truth sank in. "She's really gone."

Will placed his hand on his son's shoulder.

"I don't know what I feel, James. Everybody in this town has accused everyone else. They even told lies on me! It's turned into a travelin' show. Look around you — people are eatin' and laughin' and sellin' little trinkets. My girl's dead, and these people are havin' the time of their lives!"

James looked around. What he saw disgusted him.

"Do you really think Tom killed her, Papa?"

Will didn't answer right away. When he did, he spoke like a man that had come to the end of his rope.

"I think so . . . I think . . . James, to tell you the truth, I don't know what I think. The only thing I do know is that a court of law found him guilty and has seen fit to sentence him to death by hangin'. That's all I really know."

The uncertainty in Will's voice washed over the young man like ice water. James had pondered that question many times since the day he watched Tom Dooley taken from the courtroom after he was sentenced to die. Sometimes, late at night, he became so haunted by the question he believed he saw Tom sitting on the edge of his bed. Tom would always turn to him and start to say something — but James always woke before Tom could speak. James shuddered to himself remembering his dreams.

"If that's how you really feel . . . how are you gonna be able to sleep at night when this is over?"

Will Foster looked at his son and began to laugh — not a laugh of pleasure — but of pain — high pitched, like a sob. James watched as his papa's shoulders shook and knew that even though there was a smile on his face, he was weeping.

"I ain't been able to sleep a full night in the last two years, James. What difference does it make?" Will asked. "What difference does it really make?"

Sadly, James knew his papa was right. His sister was gone and they were no closer to finding out what really happened than they were the day Laura turned up missing. With no confession and lots of speculation their simple lives had been filled with suspicions, accusations, searches, arrests, trials and — finally this. James wondered if his family would ever be normal again. He doubted it. The young man didn't even know what normal meant anymore.

James Foster had learned much in the two years after his sister's death. He'd learned the danger of bad choices, vicious gossip, and of people who

251

thought more of themselves than they should. He'd seen the danger of people who sat in judgement—and the pain they caused. They seemed to leave no one out—judging not only the accused—but judging the victim as well. A few times since Laura was murdered, he accidentally walked up on people questioning his sister's character and gossiping about her. Some even went as far as to say that Laura had "asked for it." Sickened by their ignorance and cruelty, James felt anger, hurt, and embarrassment for his family. No matter what anyone tried to say, he knew that nothing, short of self-defense, gave anyone the right to take another person's life. No one deserved to be murdered.

James thought back to the funeral. Many family members and friends came, but there were others attending that he barely knew. One curiosity seeker had even tried to open the coffin *"to see the wound."* This kind of morbid curiosity surrounded James and his father for a long time.

On the witness stand, many testified with little to tell. It was clear to James they had come to be a part of the excitement and nothing more. Looking around the train yard, he could see those same thrill seekers had come out in full force to see Tom Dooley hang.

As people continued to pour into the train yard, James and Will faded into the crowd to wait. They both felt committed to see things through, but wanted to avoid conversation. *Maybe one day, they would feel different,* James thought. *Maybe one day soon his father would be able to sleep—and maybe with time, Tom would no longer sit on the edge of his bed in the middle of the night.*

At the jail, the sheriff and one of his deputies entered the corridor. Tom had just finished his last meal and dressed in the clean freshly pressed clothes his mother brought to him the night before. He sat listening to their footsteps. They were coming for him.

"It's time to go, Tom," the sheriff said when they reached his cell.

Tom nodded. He stood and walked without a word to the cell door as the sheriff unlocked it. One of the deputies bent down and checked the chains on his ankles. It was clear that they would be taking no more chances with him. Tom understood. Finally, when the deputies were satisfied that he was secure, he stepped out into the long hallway and began his final journey to the gallows. The sound of his own footsteps echoed in his ears.

As he passed Anne's cell, Tom was allowed to stop for a moment

"I guess this is it," Tom whispered. "I won't be comin' back, Anne. For the first time, I won't be comin' back to you."

Anne searched his face.

"Then, I'll have to come to you," she said. "I won't be long."

A curious smile crossed her lips.

"You told me once to wait for you. Well, now it's your turn. You wait for me. You hear me, Tom Dooley? I swear to you, I won't be long."

Tom put his face to the bars of her cell and kissed Anne goodbye. He smiled and gave her a wink. Then he quickly turned and walked away.

The sheriff guided him from the corridor. Tom heard Anne for the last time as the door opened to the outside world.

"You wait for me!" she yelled to him.

Tom shielded his eyes as the door slammed behind him. The bright light was blinding. When his eyes adjusted, he looked around. The crisp spring air filled his lungs, and he marveled at the sweet taste and smell of it. Warm sun danced on his skin. Standing perfectly still, he could feel its warmth despite the cool air. Its rays touched and rejuvenated every nerve in his body.

Tom turned to find his family waiting with Governor Vance. He noticed O'Hara was not there with them. *Probably already down by the gallows*, Tom thought. He laughed to himself. *A reporter to the very end!*

Cajah stood by Anna's side, and Tom was grateful. His mother and sisters would need the help of Anna's husband now more than ever. The sheriff turned Tom towards the wagon. It was waiting by the door. His coffin was already loaded in the back.

"Here let me give you a hand, Tom," the deputy said.

With the deputy's help, Tom climbed on and made his way to the polished pine box that his brother in law had made for him. He sat down on it and the wagon headed for the gallows. Tom's family and Governor Vance followed behind the wagon.

Along with the family Tom realized the deputy's friend was there, too. He began to play his fiddle and sing his mournful ballad to Tom's tune.

> *Hang down your head, Tom Dooley,*
> *Hang down your head and cry.*
> *Hang down your head, Tom Dooley,*
> *Poor boy, you're bound to die.*

It's melody was sad, Tom thought, *like his life*. In the last two years, he'd been given a lot of time to think. It was the one positive thing he could find in all that had transpired. He knew now that every person comes to a point in his life that drastically changes his course. It could be a little thing or monumental, but everybody reaches that point. It's a moment when they could have — or should have — said or done something different. Tom had made many wrong choices in his short years, and he knew that. He deeply regretted many of those choices.

Tom closed his eyes and listened to the fiddler, brushing away the warm tears from his face. *He would not be remembered this way*, he thought. *The people who had condemned him to die would not see him shed one single tear.* Governor Vance saw Tom's emotion and ordered the fiddler to stop.

Calvin and Martha Cowles waited in the crowd down by the train tracks. Martha was nervous. She kept looking around for Mary Dooley.

"Do you see Mary anywhere in the crowd?" she asked her husband.

The old storekeeper took his wife's hands in his and gently kissed them. He knew how upset she was; how upset they both were.

"I'd say she's with her boy. Are you all right?"

"I've thought about her all night. I just can't get her out of my mind. This is her only remaining son. You heard her at the trial. She worships him. What's she going to do, Calvin? What is Mary going to do?" Then, desperately, she turned to him, "I wish there was something that you could do. I wish there was something you could do to stop this!"

Martha did love Calvin, and he knew it. She always put so much faith in his ability to do anything. He was touched by that faith now.

"Now Martha, I'll not be able to stop Tom from hangin'. This has gone too far and you know that. Mary Dooley will be all right. She's a strong woman . . . and about as determined as anybody you'd ever want to meet. How many women do you know that would walk from Elkville to Statesville once a week for over a year with fresh clothes for her son? Besides, don't forget, she's still got Eliza and Anna and Anna's husband, Cajah. She has family, Martha. That's what's gonna get her through this."

"There are so many broken hearts, Calvin, and so many sides to this story . . . "

"I know, Darlin'," Calvin answered, "I know."

As Martha and Calvin moved closer to the gallows, she saw Lotty Foster walking towards the train tracks. She was with her sons, Thomas, Sam and Pinkney, and several of the girls. Beside her stood Mary Beth holding her grandma's hand. Martha had not seen the little girl in a while. The Meltons had been very protective of her since Anne was arrested, not wanting idle gossipers to say mean things that she might hear. Looking at her now, Martha marveled at how beautiful Mary Beth was and how much she looked like her mother. When Lotty saw the Cowles, she walked over to them. Martha noticed her eyes were red and swollen. It was easy to tell she'd been crying. Anne's mother looked more frail than Martha had ever seen her.

Martha made her way through the crowd to speak to Lotty; but before she could greet her, Lotty spoke in a surprisingly gentle almost timid tone.

"Good mornin' to ya, Miz Cowles. I'm pleased to see a friendly face. You've always been so kind to me and my girl and I've always appreciated it—but today your smilin' face means more to me than you'll ever know."

Martha Cowles smiled. *Sometimes in the worst of situations, good things could come,* she thought. Maybe this would be one of those times for Lotty Foster. Martha reached out and took her hand. Lotty started to say something else, but Gwendolyn Smith interrupted her. Gwen had been watching and listening from nearby.

As abrupt and cruel as ever, she pushed herself between the two women and began her tirade, "This is what happens when you let the devil choose your path, Lotty Foster."

Gwen's loud and cruel remarks got the attention of everyone in earshot. She was so loud she scared Mary Beth. The child started to whimper and hid behind her grandma's skirts. She was frightened by all the commotion.

Gwendolyn continued, "I thank God every day that I had the strength to choose the path of righteousness."

Martha Cowles had reached her limit with Gwendolyn Smith.

"Gwen, when I speak to God, I look up to him. But you!" she accused, "You have lifted yourself so high up in self righteousness . . . I imagine that you have to look down pretty far to even see God!"

Onlookers began to laugh. To Gwendolyn's horror she realized they were laughing at her.

Martha ignored the crowd and continued, "The path you speak of is not a path I'll be taking!"

Humiliated, Gwendolyn managed to find her voice. "I'll be buying my goods at the store up on German Hill from now on, Martha!"

"I don't expect you'll be doin' Calvin and me any harm," Martha retorted.

With that, Gwendolyn Smith turned and left. She didn't even stay for the hanging. She was too afraid someone would say something to her or laugh at her again. Martha turned back to Anne's mama. Lotty Foster was laughing and crying at the same time.

"I'm not used to people bein' nice to me, Miz Cowles." Lotty said, wiping her eyes.

There was such a look of surprise on Lotty's face, it was clear she didn't know what to do.

"Kindness hurts more I believe," she told Martha.

Martha Cowles took Lotty's hand and squeezed it.

"Let it hurt, Lotty, that's the only way to get the poison out . . . let it hurt . . . and . . . one day, when it's all gone, your heart will be light again. God bless you and Anne . . . and this beautiful baby girl."

Lotty could not find the words to answer. Timidly, she nodded to Martha. "Good day, Miz Cowles." she said.

Lotty looked up to see Perline Foster making her way through the crowd.

Perline came waltzing in like she was the Queen of Statesville. People were watching her every move and whispering. It was clear to Lotty and Martha Cowles that she was loving every minute of it.

Not noticing Lotty or Martha, Perline marched up to a cider table a few yards from them and declared in a loud voice, "I'll have some cider, please!"

The woman at the table stepped back, not wanting to serve the likes of Perline Foster. Perline laughed at the woman and picked up a mug, dipping some cider from the bowl. All eyes were on her, and she knew it. Spitefully, she took a big deliberate drink from the mug, and with much relish, poured what was left back into the bowl. Slamming the mug down on the table she turned and left the woman at the cider table speechless and headed in the direction of the gallows.

Before she reached the train tracks, Michael O'Hara stopped her.

"Miz Foster!" he asked. May I have a word with you? Would you say that it was your testimony that brought Tom Dooley here today?"

Perline wanted to be done with Michael O'Hara. She had no time for him today. There was a hanging to witness, and she was anxious to witness it.

"Two women brought Tom Dooley here today," she snapped; "one's dead; and one's in jail."

She turned to leave but O'Hara stepped in front of her.

"Are you sure there wasn't a third woman, Perline? Someone that felt left out? Someone who wanted revenge?"

Just as Perline started to answer, she saw Lotty coming towards her. She had not seen Perline since the trial, but had been looking forward to their next meeting.

"I can't think right now, I just can't think!" Perline blurted out. "Leave me alone!"

Perline ran as fast as she could towards the deputies. They were standing near the gallows. She did not intend to face her Aunt Lotty ever again.

Lotty started to follow Perline, but the sound of horses and wagon wheels made her pause. The wagon passed by her on its way down the hill to the train tracks. It was time. She ran to her family. Mary Beth was holding Thomas's hand. Michael O'Hara was left standing alone. Clutching his journal, he ran to his camera. He set it up earlier on the station dock.

The wagon was driven directly under the gallows. The sheriff helped Tom to his feet and down to the ground. Tom's family crowded around, surrounding him with hugs and tears and final goodbyes. Finally, Tom turned his attention to his mama. Gently he kissed her forehead.

"It's alright, Mama. You've been watchin' out for me and holdin' on to me my whole life. It's all right now," he whispered to her; "you can let go."

Mary Dooley drew her son to her and held him tight.

"I can't let you go, Tom! God, help me, I can't!."

She turned to the crowd and begged. "Please don't take him from me, please!"

Vance looked out into the sea of people. They would not look directly at Mary. Many cast their eyes to the ground. He stared into the faces of Tom's accusers with contempt.

Anna and Eliza pulled their mama away as the sheriff stepped in to take their brother. He and the deputies helped him back onto the wagon.

Tom stared up at the wooden beam above him and held onto a raw wooden support post. It was the first time he had allowed himself to look at the deadly structure. Feeling sick to his stomach from the sight of it, he looked down only to see the shadow of the noose that hung above, waiting for him.

Tom was cornered with no way out and found himself slipping into his old well-known bravado.

"That's an awful clean rope you got there, Sheriff. It's a good thing I washed my neck this mornin'!"

It was the wrong thing to say, and he immediately regretted it.

There was nervous laughter all around.

"Tom, please," his mama pleaded.

"I'm sorry, Mama."

The sheriff looked at him and asked, "Do you have any last words, son?" Tom answered, "I do."

From the corner of his eye, Tom could see the wooden shed where he knew the hangman waited. The deputies told him when the signal came from the sheriff, the man would put on his hood and come to the gallows. Tom knew the man was ready. He could see his eyes peering through a slat in the door. *You'll have to wait*, he thought, *I have a few things to say first.*

"I don't rightly know where to start. Governor Vance, I want to thank you for all you done for me. You did the best you could, and I'm much obliged. Mama, I'm sorry to see you hurtin' because of me. I never meant to cause you no pain. I wish I could take the hurt I've caused you with me. Eliza, Anna, you take good care of her for me, you hear me? I want everyone here to know that this woman is a godly woman and the finest mother a man could have. Nothin' that I have ever done wrong in my life is her fault! Mary Dooley put her children above all else . . . even herself. You all know I have not been a God fearin' man. My temper at times has been bad, and I have been known for fightin'. Temper, put with women and whiskey, has been my undoin'. If I could change that now . . . I would . . . but I can't. To those of you who condemn me, my memory will not go lightly. I'll be watchin' you, and I defy you to prove that I killed that girl. The truth is, my only crime is that I loved two women too much."

Tom stared out at the sea of onlookers and took a step forward. A hush fell on the crowd. The sound of his chains echoed in the silence as Tom Dooley held up his right hand.

"Gentlemen, do you see this hand? Does it tremble?" With absolute conviction, Tom Dooley proclaimed his innocence just seconds before his death. His voice was loud and clear. "I never harmed a hair on Laura Foster's head!"

No one moved. Tom looked once more at his mother and sisters. He scanned the crowd until he found Lotty Foster standing beside the the prettiest little girl in the whole world. Tom fixed his eyes on his daughter.

He turned to the sheriff.

"I'm ready."

Time slowed down. The sheriff patted Tom on the shoulder and walked away. One of the deputies nodded to the man in the shed. The hangman came out, his face covered with a black hood. All Tom could see was his eyes. Icy blue eyes stared at him from the black cloth. The hooded man placed the noose around his neck and Tom braced himself for death. He concentrated on his hands and feet determined to keep them still. He had control over nothing left in his life, so he would make every effort to die with dignity. Tom took one last look at the sky and one last breath of fresh spring air. The hangman placed the hood over Tom's head and tightened the noose around it.

"Lift your legs as best you can when the wagon moves," the hangman whispered. "You want to fall hard and fast. Snapping your neck would be a blessing, you understand?"

Tom nodded.

The hangman stepped to the ground and raised one hand. The driver of the wagon waited for his signal.

The hangman's signal was swift. The man driving the wagon grabbed the reins and charged off. Tom was jerked from the wagon boards before he realized the signal had been given. Caught off guard, he failed to lift his legs as the hangman instructed him to do; and as a result, death was not sudden for him. For a full five minutes, the curious spectators stood frozen, watching. In the last seconds of Tom's life some of the faint at heart turned away, but most watched with morbid curiosity waiting for death to take him.

Back at the jail, Anne Melton paced the floor of her tiny cell. Her heart was beating so fast she thought it would explode.

What happened next caught her completely off guard. Anne felt a sharp tug to her neck and fell to her knees. Gasping for air, she clutched her throat. The deputy standing in the corridor saw her fall and ran to her cell and opened it. She fell to the floor, arms flailing, trying to grab the air with her fingers. Sharp, dry rasps rose from her throat, and she began to turn blue. Frantically, he lifted her up to a sitting position and shook her, but could not get her to respond. Anne remained motionless on the cold stone floor. Try as he might, the deputy could not detect a single breath coming from her lips.

"Somebody come quick!" he yelled. "Somebody help us!"

But no one came. No one heard his cries. They were all down at the railroad tracks watching Tom Dooley hang.

Pieces of Tom's life came to him as he swung to his death. The pain faded in his neck and a flood of images poured over him. Anne was there standing by the creek in the moonlight, her dark hair glistening in its glow. Lightning bugs sparkled in and out of the pines. He could hear the sound of water and wind, and the smell of honeysuckle wafted into his lungs. From a distance Tom's brothers waved to him. William and John were young again and wrestling in the yard at home. Tom walked past his brothers and into the house he had longed to see for the last two years. The room was filled with the smell of biscuits and ham, and his mama stood at the cook stove working. The room seemed to fade, and Tom's attention turned to the sound of laughter. It was coming from somewhere behind him. Whirling around he saw her. She was far off in the distance, but Tom knew who she was. He watched Laura Foster as she waved to him in her pretty blue dress — the one she wore when they danced together in the barn at Colonel Horton's. She was whispering something to him, but he couldn't make out the words. Her voice sounded like music and the trickling sounds of old Elk Creek.

Suddenly, Tom felt weary and found that he no longer had the strength to move. His hands and feet felt like lead shot. Slowly, he began to sink to the ground. He lay there listening to the slowed rhythm of his heart. Just as his eyes began to close familiar arms wrapped around him — strong, muscular arms. Tom knew who was there even before he looked up. Tom Dooley wept for joy as he looked into the face of his father.

"Tom, I've come to take you home."

Cradled in his father's arms, Tom found the strength to get back to his feet. Magnificent streams of amber and gold poured down from the sky. In its beams, his brothers and grandparents stood, beckoning for him to follow them. Tom's father let go of his son and nodded for him to go there, and he found himself happy to do it. There was a peacefulness in the light that he had never felt before. More than anything in the world he wanted to be a part of it. As he turned to go, something made him hesitate . . . an uneasiness stopped him. His daddy put his hand on Tom's shoulder.

"Don't worry," his daddy told him, "she'll be along."

Tom nodded. Gently his father released him and Tom felt strong again. Clarity washed over him and he knew it was time to go. The two men joined hands and walked together into the light.

Tom did not look back again.

As Tom Dooley took his last breath, Anne Melton gasped her first. She had not been able to breathe since Tom dropped from the gallows. It had been a full five minutes. The deputy thought she was dead for sure.

Anne Melton screamed a gasping scream as the air flooded back into her lungs. She turned her face to the floor and wept, begging and pleading for Tom to come back and take her with him.

The deputy stood by and helplessly watched.

CHAPTER FIFTY-EIGHT

The hangman cut the body down and the noose was quickly removed from Tom's neck. He was placed in the coffin that waited for him in the back of the wagon. Anna put camphor in the coffin to mask the smell of death during the trip home. Several friends in Statesville offered to let the Dooleys spend the night, but Mary would have none of it.

"I want to take my boy home," was all she said.

No one argued with her.

Cajah drove the wagon carrying Tom's body, back to Elkville with Anna riding on the buckboard beside him. Calvin and Martha provided a buggy for Mary and Eliza.

The next evening friends of the family came to the Dooley home with food and drink. Tom was laid out in the great room of the cabin. He'd been cleaned up by his mama and sisters and dressed in his grandfather's old suit coat. His grandfather's suit coat was the only one left in the house. Mary Dooley had been saving it for a wedding, not a funeral. Copper pennies were placed on Tom's eyes to keep them closed, and a scarf was placed under his chin and tied at the top of his head to keep his mouth closed.

The next morning Tom Dooley was buried on the family farm. The preacher prayed; and the choir sang; but Mary Dooley heard not one single word. She stood quietly and prayed for her son, noticing no one. She no longer felt the same about her neighbors.

Mary kept to herself long after the visitors were gone. Anna spent the night with her Mama after the funeral. In the middle of the night, Anna got up to check on her and found her sitting up in bed, wide-awake.

"Are you all right?" she asked.

Mary Dooley turned to her daughter. Her eyes were swollen from crying. Her face looked ashen in the lamplit room.

"No, Anna, I'm not all right. I have been in a living hell for the past two years, and I do not believe for one second that my boy killed Laura Foster. But I know in my heart who did.

Anna nodded. "She never fooled me, Mama."

Mary shrugged. "Why is it that a man can know a woman for ten years and never really know her? But a woman can know another woman for ten minutes and know exactly who she is. Girl, it didn't even take me ten minutes with Anne Melton! And through it all, I've watched my own neighbors turn against my son. I've listened to their lies grow bigger with time, and I saw their excitement on the day your brother was hanged. Many of those same people came to see him buried this morning. I want to move from here, Anna. I can't live beside these people anymore."

Anna walked over and sat on the edge of her mama's bed. She took her mother's hand and held it tight.

"We'll find a new place for you, Mama, I promise."

As Anna walked out of the room she heard her mama say again in a voice that was barely audible, "No, I'm not all right, Anna. I'm not all right."

CHAPTER FIFTY-NINE

Lotty stood on Anne and James' porch and leaned up against the rail, letting the cool air revive her. When Anne took her last breath, she almost stopped breathing with her. All that she'd ever wanted for her daughter was a better life than her own. For a long time, she convinced herself that she'd succeeded, but looking back now she knew the pain her plans had caused far outweighed the benefits.

Lotty always blamed her dangerous man for the way her own life turned out. Truth was, she was the one that made the choice to leave with him. In one quick minute, she changed her whole life. *Joseph*, she thought with a smile, they called him Joe, and Anne was his child. Lotty loved all of her children, but there was something about a firstborn daughter. Anne was the spitting image of her Daddy, and Lotty had loved them both.

Tom Dooley was a handsome boy. When he first started coming around, she was shocked at how much he looked like Joe. For that reason, Lotty marked him to be the same right off. Turned out—he was. The only difference had been, that no matter what good or bad transpired between the two, Tom never stopped loving Anne; and Anne never stopped loving him. Maybe it was because the bond was formed between them at such an early age. Whatever it was—it was real; and it was powerful; and she had been wrong to keep them apart. She knew that now.

When James Melton came along he seemed like the answer to Lotty's prayers. Anne possessed such beauty that Lotty always hoped it would be a ticket out of poverty for her daughter. When James came to Lotty and asked her to talk to Anne, she felt like she was on top of the world. Lotty saw a chance not only for Anne but for the whole family. James proved true to his word. He took good care of Anne and saw to it that Lotty and Anne's brothers and sisters had what they needed, too. Even after Anne was arrested, he took responsibility for her family. Anne's husband loved Mary Beth as his own. James Melton was a rare man; and although Lotty did not understand him, she respected him.

After Tom Dooley was hanged, Anne was put on trial and acquitted. Tom's note cleared Anne, and she was released after a short trial. James Melton was there waiting when it was all over. He took Anne home, and she seemed genuinely grateful to him.

Anne came back to Elkville, and with Tom and Perline gone, became a wife to James and a mother to Mary Beth. Everyone commented on the change in her. Lotty knew the truth, though. She saw it in her eyes. They were empty. In her mind, Anne was in another time and place where she roamed the woods and climbed the rocks in the creek with *him*. Lotty knew her girl was just going through the motions. Only with Mary Beth did she ever see a spark of life in Anne after she returned home. Mary Beth was the only person that seemed to ground her to the earth.

Perline vanished as soon as Anne was free. She left the Melton cabin after she turned state's evidence and went back to Granville Dooley's down on the creek. She knew there would be no turning back the day she slapped Anne at Celia Scott's house. Although James was a kind man, and she had worked hard for him, she knew where his allegiance lay and feared he would harm her for the trouble she'd caused. Perline Foster left the Melton's with what little she came with and a dress she stole from Anne's closet. It was the red one with black lace that she'd made for the molassy boiling. Lotty hadn't spoken to Perline since Anne's arrest. She made up her mind that what happened to Perline Foster was of no importance to her. Perline would have to answer for her own sins someday, just like everybody else. Lotty heard that Perline actually found a man to marry her. Rumor was that she and her man were both sick with the pocks. She heard about it at the store. Ben Ferguson told Lotty that Perline had a baby, too. He heard the child was mulatto. Perline's husband was white.

Anne stayed quiet and kept to herself. Lotty tried to help in the cabin; but surprisingly, Anne did most of the chores. James still did his best to see to it that she was well cared for. About a year after she came home, Anne gave birth to another baby girl. They named her Liza. Liza was blonde and blue eyed like James. Anne cared for the baby as best she could, but after another year had passed, Anne's demeanor took a drastic turn. She ranted and raved over the silliest things. Sometimes she would run off into the woods and it would take James and Lotty more than a day to find her. Anne's eyesight was going, too. In the last year she found she needed glasses. It was getting harder and harder for her to see. On those "bad days" when she ran off, she would be confused and always agitated. Her family would spend hours searching for her; and when they finally found her, it would take at least two people to get her home — most times she was violent. Some said it was the pocks working on her. People feared the pocks because there was no cure. Everyone knew it would eventually eat away at a person's mind; and over time, the disease would kill its victim. Anne never talked about her illness with her mama. She never complained. Whatever it was, Lotty just knew that her girl was sick.

Lotty stood on the porch and let her mind take her where it wanted to go. She thought back to just three days before, when Anne jumped out of bed, during one of her crazy spells, dressed herself and hitched the horse to the wagon. She had taken off in the direction of the old Bates' place. James was out in the fields working on the morning it happened. He was coming in for something to drink when he happened to look up and see the wagon rounding the bend. He ran to the barn, bridled his mare and took off after Anne, riding bareback.

What he found when he caught up with her was an overturned wagon with Anne pinned underneath. She wasn't moving, and her breathing was shallow. He saw that her eyes were glassy and fixed. James wasted no time in running for help.

Neighbors heard his cries and ran to his aid. Several men helped him get the wagon off of Anne while others made a stretcher from sapling trunks and burlap to carry her home. One man ran to fetch the doctor.

She was carried home on the burlap stretcher and placed in her bed. Doc Carter arrived and examined her. He gave Anne something for the pain and told Lotty and James to prepare for the worst. In and out of consciousness, Anne kept murmuring something about the horse — something about the horse being spooked. In and out of consciousness, she kept trying to tell folks what she had seen when the horse reared; but no one could make sense of it. The kindly old doctor gave her laudanum to help her rest.

On the third day, Doc Carter sat down with Lotty and James and told them time was short. He told them he was sorry, but there was nothing else that he could do for her. Anne's breathing changed to short rasps. The sound was familiar to the old doctor. When he heard the death rattle, Doc Carter knew Anne wouldn't make it through the day. James and Lotty stayed by her side the whole time. By late afternoon, she refused the laudanum and asked to speak to her mama and her husband alone. James went outside with his neighbors and friends to wait while Anne talked to Lotty.

"I'm goin' to be with him now, Mama," she whispered, "it's time. It's finally time."

Lotty reached over and smoothed Anne's hair away from her forehead and wiped the sweat with a cool cloth. She had done this through fevers and headaches many times when Anne was a little girl. Lotty noticed that Anne didn't seem to be in pain. Her mind seemed clear, and there was a peaceful look in her eyes. She gave Anne a sip of water and patiently waited for her to speak again.

Anne talked of many things that day, and her mama hung on her daughter's every word.

When Anne was ready to talk to James, she reached out and took Lotty's hand.

"Today, he's comin' back for me again . . . and when he does, this time, you have to let me go."

Lotty knew she was speaking of Tom. She nodded and gently kissed her daughter's forehead.

"I swear to you. I won't stop you this time."

Anne and her mama made their peace.

Lotty stood up and started off to get James. When she reached the door, she turned back.

"I'll be back in as soon as you two finish talkin'. You wait for me, Anne. Please don't go 'til I get back."

Anne smiled a weak smile.

"I won't, Mama."

James brought the girls in with him. Lotty stood at the door and waited. Anne kissed each one and hugged them tight. Mary Beth was eleven now and the spitting image of her mama.

Mary Beth looked at her mama for a long while before she spoke. "Please don't go, Mama."

"Life is not about the leavin', Mary Beth. It's about the precious time you have together — no matter how short that time may be. It's taken me my whole lifetime to figure that out, so you remember it. I've been with you as long as time would allow, and I'll love you and be with you long after today. You hear me talkin'?"

Mary Beth looked at her again, hard and serious.

"I hate you!" she screamed.

She turned and tried to run from the room, but her grandma stopped her at the door. The child buried her head in her grandma's skirts and sobbed.

Anne spoke softly to her, "I love you, Mary Beth. I love you and I know you love me, too."

Mary Beth pulled away from her grandma and ran from the room. Lotty walked back in and took the baby, leaving James alone to talk to his wife.

James looked at Anne. Her dark hair lay in soft curls against the pillow. She was so beautiful—even now. He'd never believed for one second that he had any kind of hold on this woman; and yet, to know any part of her, had been a privilege to him.

"James, when I'm gone, I hope you'll find somebody else to love. I want you to be happy more than anything in the world. You deserve better than me."

Tears sprang to James' eyes. He smiled and touched her cheek.

"Don't you see, Anne, that's what has held me to you for all of these years. I never thought anyone could really love me. I didn't think I deserved it, somehow. I know I'm nothin' much to look at. Women don't find me excitin', and I can never think of the right things to say. After I came home from the war, with a bum leg and using a cane, I was a broken man. I just never thought anyone could ever really love me."

Anne tried to speak, but James stopped her. She let him go on. It was important to him, she could tell.

"Then one day I saw you at the store. You were runnin' an errand for your mama. I thought you were the most beautiful thing I'd ever seen. When you came down off the porch, I heard some of the women laughin' over by the shed. It didn't take a smart man to figure out that they were talkin' about you. You heard 'em, too. I could tell by the look on your face. When you walked away, you dropped your poke. I helped you pick it up, and our eyes met. It was just for a second, but I knew that look. You were broken too—broken just like me. You thanked me and went on your way. I watched you until you were clean outta sight, wonderin' to myself how anything that beautiful could be broken. That's when I decided to talk to your mama. I really believed, if I could fix you, I could fix me, too."

Anne reached out her arms and James knelt down by her bed. She cradled his head in her lap and stroked his hair as she spoke.

"There's all kinds of love, James. You did fix me as best you could, and I love you for that. But, there are things about me that can't be fixed. Now, you go out and find the kind of love you deserve." She kissed him gently on the forehead. "You have been a foolish man, and I have used you somethin' awful."

For the first time since she had known him, James Melton sobbed. He buried his head in her gown and sobbed.

It's funny how you can know someone for most of your life and never really know them. That's the way it was for James and Anne that day. A wall had been broken down, and the two talked for most of an hour. They said things to each other that they had always wanted to say, but somehow never could.

As the daylight started to fade, so did Anne. The last things they shared were secrets—secrets best kept that way. James vowed to his wife that he would take the things they talked about that late afternoon with him to his grave, and James Melton again proved to be a man of his word.

Anne took her last breath with her mama, James and the little girls by her side. She was peaceful, almost hopeful as she waited for death to take her. When the moment came, she turned her eyes to the hill towards Laura's Ridge and let out a final gasp of air.

Gently, as only a mother could, Lotty went to Anne and closed her eyes and wiped away the spittle from her mouth with her apron.

Suddenly, a wail came from under Anne's bed as Shadow ran out with her litter of kittens. It startled everyone in the room as the little black balls of fur scampered across the floor and out. Lotty turned and ran out on the porch for air. There was Shadow crouched under a rocker, guarding her litter. Once out in the open, Lotty breathed in the cool spring air. In a few minutes, James joined her with the girls.

Gwendolyn Smith stood in the yard with the others. Since the accident, the women in the community took turns standing vigil outside the cabin and bringing food. It was customary for the neighbors to provide a deathwatch; and because of Anne's notoriety, there was a crowd.

When Gwen saw James and Lotty on the porch, she came running up and asked them, "What did she say? Did she confess? Did she purge?"

Lotty was offended by the question. Purging was an old wives tale in the community. Many believed that when a person died, if they did not confess their sins, their soul could still be saved if they foamed from the mouth. The foam was the release of their sins. It was considered a second chance for the righteous, if they died a sudden death. For others it was a pardon only God could give.

When Gwendolyn died, Lotty thought, *she wouldn't be able to muster enough foam from her entire body to let out the amount of purging she would need to do.*

No sir, foaming at the mouth wouldn't save old Gwendolyn Smith from burning. Lotty wanted to smack her right there, but did not have the strength.

Instead, she looked at Gwendolyn long and hard. She took a good look at the woman who had made it her life's work to attack Lotty at every turn. Gwen stood there in her dark dress and white preacher's collar all starched to perfection. Her face was stern and pinched. There was not the tiniest hint of a laugh line on it, only deep folds from a lifetime of frowns. Lotty may have lost at love with Joe, but Gwendolyn had even refused herself the chance to lose. She almost pitied Gwen for the things she would never know. Joe broke Lotty's heart, but she'd rather have the life she chose with all its ups and downs any day, than live with the likes of Mr. Smith.

Lotty leaned over the porch and managed a smile, "Anne said *you* did it, Gwen."

James Melton started to laugh. Some of the neighbors standing in the yard joined in with him. Gwendolyn Smith heard laughter all around her. In a huff, she marched off through the crowd towards the path back to her house. As James watched her stomp off, he laughed even harder. Lotty had never seen him like that before. She laughed with him not knowing what else to do. She laughed with him until he started to cry. He cried until the pain deepened into sobs and Lotty put her arms around him and held on. When James calmed down she spoke gently to him.

"I'll be back in a little while to help with Anne," she said.

He was a plain and simple man, Lotty thought. *But in all her life, he was the kindest man she'd ever known.* She left him standing on the porch talking to Louisa Gilbert. Later, she would remember that, because James ended up marrying Louisa. James' sister, Sarah, had brought Louisa with her that day to help out. Sarah had come to cook for her brother and the girls. Lotty could smell and hear meat frying as she walked away. Oddly enough, it made her think of Hell.

Lotty walked across the trail and up the hill to the Melton family cemetery. *Anne would rest there soon*, she thought. Standing at the top of the hill, she looked all around her. The old Bates' place on the ridge where Laura Foster had been murdered was just in sight. When she looked behind her and down the hill, she could see James Melton's cabin. Reedy Branch ran right along beside it. Barely in view was the holler where Laura's body was found. If Lotty looked over far enough to the right, she could just make out the top of her own roof. It had been where she had moved so many years before . . .

where she had raised her children. Her parents' cabin was just up the road; gone except for an old stone chimney.

So many people had come and gone . . . so many years. When Martha Cowles passed, Lotty had gone to the funeral to pay her respects. Calvin, like most men, couldn't stand to be alone. After a short time, he remarried, sold the store and moved to Wilkesboro. His new wife, Ida, was Governor Holden's daughter. Lotty wondered how Zeb Vance liked that. His old buddy, Calvin, was sleeping with the enemy. Like everything else, things changed and people passed; but life just kept on going.

Lotty walked from the cemetery down the road to the creek. Her feet moved with effortless familiarity across the rocks. She reached the biggest one and stopped. The large boulder was Anne's rock. It had been her favorite. Lotty sat down and closed her eyes, listening to the sounds of old Elk Creek. Lotty let her mind take her to another time—a time when Tom and Anne were still small. Smiling she remembered them running to the edge of the woods to catch lightning bugs in the evening after supper. In her mind she heard their laughter flowing in and out like water. She remembered her niece, Laura, joining in—chestnut hair and always smiling. She had almost forgotten how beautiful they were!

It was so real to her that she didn't want to open her eyes. She followed them in her mind through the fields and the woods, stepping over rocks . . .

The whispers of the creek interrupted her thoughts. "Lotty! Lotty! Come home. It's time to come home," it gurgled.

Hesitantly, she opened her eyes and listened to the invitations gurgling in the water until they fell silent. When the whispers were gone, she stood up to leave. Behind her, in the dusk, a mist was forming on the water.

The three of them stood there watching her. The mist of the creek and the golden light of dusk held them for her to see. Feeling them behind her, she turned and gazed upon them.

"I'm coming soon," Carlotta Foster said aloud, "but I'll be raisin' my granddaughters first."

Without another thought, she stepped off the rock where she stood, into the swift water of old Elk Creek. She did not fight it—allowing herself to sink to the bottom like a stone. It was quiet there under the water, and peaceful. Slowly she decended until her feet found its murky bottom. Once there, she made no effort to float up. Instead, Lotty let the creek cradle her in its watery womb. She felt safe on the creek's floor separated from the pain lying above the water's surface. It was the thought of her two grandaughters that made her push off the bottom of the creek with her feet and begin her climb to its surface. The cool, late evening air slapped her hard in the face as her head broke through the water. Lotty grabbed hold of the nearest rock and pulled herself to safety. Air rushed into her lungs, making her gasp. It was as if she was taking her first breath. The air smelled and tasted clean and fresh. She stood up on Anne's rock and made her way over the moss boulders to the creek bank. Standing once again on solid ground, Lotty Foster started the long climb up the hill to the Melton cabin.

This time she would get it right, she thought.

SOME OF THE PLAYERS AND THEIR TESTIMONY

J.W. Winkler (Laura's uncle)
We dug and hit something right away because the grave was so shallow. It was Laura Foster's body. I recognized her dress and her cheekbones. I've seen Laura in that dress many times. It was homespun.

Colonel James Horton (Member of the search party)
I led the search party to the spot where my horse had reared. Following Reedy Branch, I realized it made perfect sense to carry the body down through the water and cross over to the holler to bury her. That's why our dogs couldn't pick up the scent, and it took us so long to find her. I'm still not sure why I left the search party and rode my horse up that holler, except that it was close to sunset; and I noticed a peculiar golden light streaming down from the trees there. Gentlemen, I have always been a practical man, but I know my horse reared out of fear. He was spooked at the spot where Laura Foster was buried. That's the only way I can explain it to you. He was spooked . . . and so was I.

Doctor Carter
I noticed a place cut through her dress. Upon further examination, I discovered a stab wound between the third and fourth ribs. The body was lying on its right side, face up. The hole it was laying in was two and a half feet deep and real narrow. It was not long enough for the body. The legs appeared to have been broken to fit the body into the grave. A bundle of clothes was in the grave with the body, and the victim's apron had been folded neatly and placed across her face. The body was so decomposed I could not tell whether the sharp weapon used had cut through the heart or not.

Thomas Foster (Anne Melton's brother)

On the Thursday before the Friday when Laura disappeared, Tom came out to our house and asked my mama, Lotty Foster, if he could borrow a mattock. I saw him the next morning, Friday morning sometime after breakfast. He was on the Gladys Fork Road before you turn off to the Bates place.

Lotty Foster (Anne's mother)

I am the mother of Mrs. Anne Melton. The prisoner came to my house on the Thursday before Laura was killed. He asked to borrow my mattock. He got it and started off in the direction of his mother's house. I saw him again that same day with my daughter Anne, Perline Foster and Jack Keaton. They came to my house to drink some shine and pop some corn—said it was a going away party for Tom.

Martha Gilbert (Neighbor)

I saw Tom Dooley on the Friday morning Laura was killed, on the road between the Bates place and his mama's house. He was digging with a mattock. When I asked him what he was doing, he said there was a place in the road that needed to be widened.

Betsy Scott (Neighbor)

I saw Laura coming from her father's place past the Scott's house. She was riding her mare bareback and carrying a bundle of clothes in her lap. It was Friday morning—the day she turned up missing. I asked Laura where she was going. She said she was going to meet up with Tom Dooley at the Bates place.

Jack Keaton (Tom's cousin and a suspect in the murder)

My buddy Carson and me saw Mary Dooley on that Friday evening near Lotty Foster's house. We asked her where Tom was. She said she hadn't seen him all day.

Celia Scott (Neighbor)

I hired Perline Foster to come to my house and help me with my chores one day. Anne Melton came to the house carrying a stick and grabbed Perline by the hair of the head and started yelling and using foul language. She told Perline to go home. Then Anne threw Perline to the ground and started choking her. She was mad because Perline had bragged to Ben Ferguson that she and Tom had killed and then done away with Laura Foster. I heard Perline say to Anne . . . and I'll never forget this as long as I live . . . : "*It is the truth and you know it. You are as deep in the mud as I am in the mire.*" Then Anne called Perline a liar. They fought some more and Perline ran into the woods. But Anne—well she turned on me and told me to let what I saw be my dying secret. She said she would follow me straight to hell if I told!

Will Foster (Laura's father)

Laura Foster was my daughter. She lived with me and her brother, James. Her mama's dead. Tom Dooley courted my daughter for several months; and then he stopped; and I didn't see him again for a long while. The Sunday before Laura was killed, he showed back up and they talked. Then he came back the following Wednesday. I saw them whisperin' with their heads together. On Friday mornin' I woke up and found that Laura was gone. Some of her clothes was missin' too. I saw the mare tracks and followed 'em. They led me to the ol' Bates place . . . but after that I lost 'em. I stopped at James Scott's place for breakfast and then went on to James Melton's. By the time I got to James Melton's place, it was about eight o'clock. Anne Melton was in bed. Her clothes were off and layin' in the floor. They looked wet and muddy. I visited several houses, but no one knew where Laura was. I ended up at Francis Melton's. He invited me to spend the night there. There has been some talk that on the day Laura turned up missing, I said I didn't care about Laura just so I found my mare, and that I would kill Laura myself if I found her. Those are lies, and I wish my neighbors would let me alone to grieve in peace.

Perline Foster (State's key witness and cousin and serving girl to Anne Melton)

I went to work for the Meltons shortly after they was married. After Tom Dooley came back from the war, he was at the house most every day while I was there. He stayed there sometimes at night. I have seen him in bed with Anne Melton.

James Melton did not sleep with his wife. I was used many times as a blind for Tom and Anne. Anne left the house on the Thursday night before Laura was murdered, with a canteen of liquor, and went in the direction of her mama's house. She was supposed to meet up with Tom. She didn't come back until Friday morning about an hour before day. She came and got in bed with me. Her dress and shoes was wet and muddy. Later that morning Tom came to see her. He stood over her in the bed and they talked. When he left they was both crying. I went out and worked in the fields with Jonathan Gilbert and James Melton 'til three o'clock. Anne stayed in the bed for most of the day. A couple of days later, Anne took me to the place where the body was buried. I could see the body through the dirt. I was so scared I wouldn't go all the way over to it. Anne threw more dirt over the body and took leaves and twigs to cover it up. The next day when Tom came over I said to him, *'I thought you run off with Laura Foster,'* and he said, *'I ain't got no use for Laura Foster.'*

Mary Dooley (Tom's mother)
I am Tom Dooley's mother. He turned twenty-two on the twentieth of June. His home is with me. Tom was not at the house on that Friday morning. I was out early that day and got back around noon. I found Tom lying on the bed. He got up around suppertime but wouldn't eat. He went off to the barn for awhile and then came back and ate. He went to bed about the usual time. That night, I heard him making a little moan. He had been complaining of chills during supper so I went in his room and bent over him to see if he was all right. He is my sole remaining son. Both of his brothers were killed in the war. I bent over and kissed him. He is my last remaining boy.

Governor Zebulon B. Vance (Tom's Defense Attorney)
The life of this Confederate is worth a thousand wenches the likes of Laura Foster!

ABOUT THE AUTHOR

Karen Wheeling Reynolds grew up in Elkville, North Carolina (now Ferguson). Her father and mother, Maurice and Joyce Wheeling ran a grocery store on Elk Creek beside the Wilkes-Caldwell County line, as did her grandfather Henry Wheeling and her great great great grandfather Calvin Cowles.

As a child she had the luxury of hearing the many stories of Tom Dula (pronounced Dooley), Laura Foster and Anne Melton at her father's store. Her first grade teacher Docia Greene was Anne Melton's granddaughter; and Grade Allen, one of Anne's grandsons was a regular customer at her father's store. Edith Marie Carter of Whippoorwill Academy was Karen's art teacher and created a series of paintings depicting the story of Tom Dooley. As a student, she watched Edith's story unfold on the canvases. The series of paintings now hang in the Dooley museum at Whippoorwill Academy in Ferguson, NC off Hwy 268 West. Roaming the hills and creeks of Ferguson on horseback with her friend Lynn, she enjoyed a charmed childhood—one with lightning bugs, honeysuckle, bright stars, molassy boilings, hayrides, and always the sounds of Elk Creek close by—running through the heart of the community.

Tragedy ended this way of life for her at sixteen when her father was robbed and murdered in his store on December 13, 1973. She and her mother moved to Wilkesboro, North Carolina shortly after the murder. Karen rarely went back to Ferguson in the years that followed. It was not until she was approached by Steve Critz and the Wilkes Playmakers in North Wilkesboro, to write a script for a stage version of the legend of Tom, Laura and Anne, that she returned to the community where she grew up. A flood of memories and stories came back to her as well as a wonderful group of people from the area offering support.

Karen lives in Wilkesboro with her husband David and has two children, Ben and Maggie Sloop and two grandchildren, Roslin and Ethan. She is employed by Wilkes Playmakers, Inc. in North Wilkesboro as their Executive Director and is a SAG actress. Both she, and her husband David, are represented by Talent One in Raleigh, North Carolina (actor's resume @ talentone.net).

Her play, *Tom Dooley: A Wilkes County Legend,* is now in its eleventh season and directed by her husband David, who is the instructor of theatre at Wilkes Community College in Wilkesboro, NC. The cast of *"Dooley"* was invited to perform the courtroom scene in Greensboro, NC at the North Carolina Governor's Conference on Tourism in 2003. The group was also invited to perform for the NC Supreme Court Society of Historians at their Annual Meeting in Raleigh, NC in 2004. The show won a Paul Green Multi Media Award from The North Carolina Society of Historians in 2002 and the first publication of this novel under the name *Tom Dooley: A Wilkes County Legend* won a Cox Fiction Award in 2003 from the Society. The entire project, encompassing the play, book, and soundtrack by local artists also won their highest honor, The President's Award in 2004. The outdoor drama is a proud member of The Institute of Outdoor Drama at East Carolina University in Greenville, NC. (www.outdoordrama.unc.edu).

Reynolds has written five plays *Tom Dooley: A Wilkes County Legend, The Scarlett O'Hara Complex, Shadow Dancing*, an adaptation of Charles Dickens' *A Christmas Carol* and a second outdoor drama, *Moonshine & Thunder: The Junior Johnson Story*.

For more information about the outdoor drama performed annually in July at The Forest's Edge Amphitheatre in Wilkesboro, North Carolina, visit www.wilkesplaymakers.com.

ABOUT THE COVER DESIGNER

Jessica Barlow is a portrait and commercial photographer, specializing in children's photography. A professional photographer since 2008, she owns and operates Jessica Barlow Photography, located in Wilkesboro, North Carolina. Jessica has won several national print awards and was named NC Children's Photographer of the Year in 2010. As a lifelong resident of the area in which the Dooley story takes place, Jessica is honored to have worked with Mrs. Reynolds on the cover art for the book.

http://www.jessicabarlowphotography.com/

Special Thanks to:

Local Historians:

Attorney, Greg Luck

Ike Forester

Joan Baity

R. G. Absher

Gary Coffey

Storytellers, Descendants & Consultants:

Steve Critz

John Hawkins

Gary Corley

Dr. Steve Duncan

Christine Horton Clonch

Amelia Shepherd

Connie Scott Call

Donna Call Watts

Randy Greene

Novella Scott Baker

Tom Scott

Mary Triplette

Bruce Bowers

Charles Shedd

Laura Ferguson

Ken Welborn

Jerry Lankford and
The Elkville String Band

Sandra Watts

Linda Bumgarner

Ethel Burke Shumate

Jerry, Rita and Jessica Marie Smith

Joan Wheeling Dean and Carolyn
Wheeling Young

Joyce Wheeling

Edith Marie Carter

Misty Bass

Julie Mullis

Joe Connelly

Melissa, Chad, and Caitlin Walker

Doug Cotton

Jacob Reeves

William Davidson

Lucas Matney

Susan Ringo

William, Meret & Caitlin Burke

Jessica & Colin Barlow

Maggie & Roslin Sloop

Travis and Nicole Collins

David Johnson, Dave's World of
Music, www.davesworldofmusic.com

David Reynolds, Editing

Lori Byington, Editing

Alice Osborn *Write from the Inside Out*

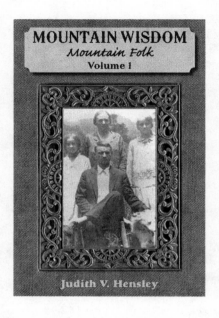

MOUNTAIN WISDOM: *Mountain Folk, Volume 1* is a collection of Home
Remedies, Superstitions, Beauty Tips, Dream Interpretations, Rhymes, Riddles,
and Weather Predictions. It comes from notes and such recorded by author Judith
Victoria Hensley over the last thirty plus years while listening to people talk from
Kentucky, Tennessee, Virginia, North and South Carolina, and Georgia. A native
Appalachian, Hensley wrote down the "mountain wisdom" as she heard it and
has also compiled an enormous collection of vintage photos in this one amazing
volume. MOUNTAIN WISDOM: *Mountain Folk, Volume 1,* is chock full of
interesting and downright outrageous authentic Appalachian knowledge; and let's
face it, some of it is pretty doggoned funny, too. Readers everywhere will benefit
from Hensley's work.

Available at fine retailers or may be ordered at www.littlecreekbooks.com

ISBN: 978-0-9843192-7-5

To order Mountain Girl Press titles, please go to
www.mountaingirlpress.com

Take a step back in time to the Civil War Era and enjoy a rich and compelling tale woven by Suzanne Mays in *The Man Inside the Mountain.*

Essie Bell, is a woman alone on her farm in rural West Virginia during the last months of the Civil War. Mourning the death of her husband, and yearning for the son presumed dead by the Union Army, life could not be any harder. While everyone else urges her to sell her farm and move to town, Essie finds it a place a solace. When new people begin to enter Essie's life she finds she is still needed. If only she could answer the burning question, "Who is the man inside the mountain?"

Join author Tammy Robinson Smith for a literary treat for all ages, *Emmybeth Speaks.*

Emmybeth Johnson is a nine year old girl who lives in Little Creek, Tennessee in the foothills of the Appalachian Mountains. Her story begins late in the summer of 1971. Emmybeth likes to know what is happening with the adults in her life and in the community in general. She has a favorite "hidey hole" where she can listen as her mother, grandmother and the ladies from her church's sewing circle discuss the latest news and gossip from Little Creek. Emmybeth treats the reader to the "goings on" of the community from her naïve perspective, which is sometimes closer to the truth than she knows!

Visit the hills and hollers of Kentucky as Susan Noe Harmon explores the lives of three generations of Appalachian women in her first novel, *Under the Weeping Willow.*

Step into the lives of one Kentucky family who will capture your heart and leave you wanting more. Belle, Pearl and Sara, three generations of Appalachian women, will teach you about life in a 1950s family and how it touched the future. *Under the Weeping Willow* is a story about the closeness of family and how they enjoy the good times and pull together through the bad. Come into their world and live and learn from it along with them. You will feel like you've found a home and a family of Kentucky kin.

Enter the world of Appalachian women and see what happens when struggles are faced and overcome.

The stories depicted in **_The Zinnia Tales_**, **_Self-Rising Flowers_**, and **_Christmas Blooms_**, will take you to a place where strong women survive. Each short story collection is filled with stories that celebrate what it means to be an "Appalachian woman," Each collection will strike a note with anyone who has ever called the mountains home, or just wishes she lives there. Readers will delight in the warmth of these tales which demonstrate the richness of the place where these women live their lives, and tell their stories. Fiction about women, written by women, these rich works exemplify the Mountain Girl Press mission statement: Stories that celebrate the wit, humor and strength of Appalachian women.

To read more about *Little Creek Books' other titles*
please go to
www.littlecreekbooks.com

Nonfiction Titles

TO HIDE THE TRUTH, Susan Noe Harmon

SINKING CREEK JOURNAL: An environmental book of days, Fred Waage

EATING LOCAL IN VIRGINIA, Phyllis Wilson

IN THE GARDEN WITH BILLY: Lessons About Life, Love & Tomatoes, Renea Winchester

MOUNTAIN WISDOM: Mountain Folk, Judith V. Hensley

CHICKEN IN THE CAR AND THE CAR WON'T GO: Nearly 200 Ways to enjoy Chicagoland with Tweens and Teens, Melisa Wells

Young Adult Fiction Titles

MARTY MATTERS & MARTY MAYHEM, Jessica Hayworth

SARA JANE IS A PAIN, Rebecca Williams Spindler & Madelyn Spindler

Fiction

DEATHOSCOPE, John Clark, MD

THE TRAVELING TEA LADIES, Death in Dallas, Melanie O'Hara Salyers

Children's Books

WILLY THE SILLY-HAIRED SNOWMAN, Connie Clyburn

Poetry

HEART BALLADS: A potpourri of poetry, Betty Kossick

Tom Dooley
A Wilkes County Legend

Presented yearly by the Wilkes Playmakers, Inc. of North Wilkesboro, NC.

Written and directed by Karen Wheeling Reynolds, author of TOM DOOLEY: *The Man Behind the Ballad.*

For information about tickets, please go to www.wilkesplaymakers.com, or you may call the box office at (336) 838-PLAY. The mailing address for the Wilkes Playmakers, Inc. is P.O. Box 397, North Wilkesboro, NC 28659.

Tom Dooley: A Wilkes County Legend is the dramatization of the well-known 1868 Wilkes County love triangle that resulted in the murder of Laura Foster and the subsequent hanging of Tom Dula (pronounced Dooley). Folklore and legend say that he confessed to the murder to protect his true love, Anne Melton. The soundtrack for the show is by musical artist, David Johnson and Appalachian dancing is also featured.

People nationwide have been fascinated and intrigued with the Tom Dooley story for over a century. The murder of Laura Foster in the Elkville community, now known as Ferguson, in North Carolina was one of the nation's first highly publicized crimes of passion. Tom Dooley hanged for the crime but many questions were left unanswered. The Kingston Trio catapulted Tom Dooley to fame again in the 1960s with the song "Hang Down Your Head Tom Dooley." Visitors still travel from far and wide to visit the graves and tour the countryside where the story took place.

Wilkes Playmakers has been a part of Wilkes County Theatre and North Carolina Community Theatre since 1990. The organization is committed to expanding both the availability of and interest in the arts and drama in the Wilkes region of Northwestern North Carolina. The Wilkes Playmakers home is Benton Hall, which is the old North Wilkesboro elementary school located at 300 D Street, North Wilkesboro, North Carolina.

Wilkes Playmakers is an independent, non-profit community theater company dedicated to the cultural enhancement of the children, adults and senior citizens of Wilkes County through theater.

To learn more about the performances or to purchase tickets please visit **www.wilkesplaymakers.com**

CPSIA information can be obtained at www.ICGtesting.com
Printed in the USA
LVOW040240041111

253476LV00002B/119/P